MW00860911

GIVENCHY

CATWALK

GIVENCHY

CATWALK

The Complete Collections

Texts by Alexandre Samson and Anders Christian Madsen
With over 1,200 photographs

Yale University Press

CONTENTS

THE COLLECTIONS

CLARE WAIGHT KELLER

MATTHEW M. WILLIAMS

INTRODUCTION

'The shortest path to elegance is simplicity'

Hubert de Givenchy

When Hubert de Givenchy founded his fashion house at 8 rue Alfred de Vigny on 18 December 1951, haute couture was enjoying a new golden age, which had been ushered in by Christian Dior's first collection in 1947. Called the 'New Look', this collection brought the discipline, which had struggled during the Second World War, back into centre stage, attracting a new international – especially American – clientele. Throughout the following decade, Dior shaped the fashion world with his designs, which were synonymous with a rediscovered sense of luxury. At the age of 24, Hubert de Givenchy was well aware of the societal changes that were taking place around him. While the established couturiers sought to restrict the female body, confining it within creations that were as impractical as they were luxurious, he recognized that women's lifestyles were changing as they became more independent. First appearing in the United States, ready-to-wear fashions, with clothes that were immediately available, offered one possible response. But after the Second World War, couturiers looked down on this industrial approach to production, and it was still limited to boutiques that were relegated to the ground floor of fashion houses. Givenchy was well placed to understand the phenomenon. After training under Jacques Fath, Robert Piguet and Lucien Lelong, he had made his name as the director of Elsa Schiaparelli's boutique, reusing fabric from the haute couture line to create comfortable, flexible designs – thereby anticipating the 'separates' that would make him famous a few years later.

Hubert de Givenchy embraced the modern feel of ready-to-wear fashion. His first haute couture collection, presented on 1 February 1952, adopted an innovative approach that incorporated the industrial production model alongside haute couture designs created by hand. He made comfort one of the main criteria in his early work. His separates were designed to meet the needs of modern women, offering adaptable pieces that each woman could combine in her own way. The lightweight ruffled sleeves of the Bettina blouse emphasized the wearer's movements, while the skirt and the novel use of shirting fabric – which until then had only been used for men's shirts – prioritized ease. The collection brought Givenchy immediate recognition and wide acclaim. On 9 April 1952, he was one of six couturiers present at the 'April in Paris' ball hosted at the Waldorf Astoria Hotel in New York. Barely two months after launching his first collection, Givenchy was already appearing alongside established couturiers such as Christian Dior and Pierre Balmain. The press referred to him as 'the youngest of the couturiers', a title he would hold until the appointment of Yves Saint Laurent as the head of Christian Dior in 1958.

However, Hubert de Givenchy was aware of contemporary criticisms about designs that looked too 'boutique', too much like ready-to-wear fashions. Building on his exceptional success, with each new collection he gradually moved away from separates and placed himself firmly within the tradition of luxury haute couture. His collection 'On the Theme of Freedom' (Autumn/Winter 1955–1956) marked a turning point in his career. Three years on from his debut, the young couturier joined forces with a figure he regarded as a mentor, Cristóbal Balenciaga, whom he had met in New York in 1953. The two designers exchanged ideas, brainstormed together, and attended rehearsals of each other's shows. This close association between two couturiers and their fashion houses – a rarity in the history of fashion – is comparable to pairings of artists such as Georges Braque and Pablo Picasso, or Maurice de Vlaminck and André Derain. An established couturier before the Second World War, revered by the press and by his peers, Cristóbal Balenciaga became Givenchy's mentor.

This turning point was first and foremost a creative one. Hubert de Givenchy's designs moved away from the inventiveness of his early offerings, the comfortable, lightweight feel of pieces that were easy to wear, in favour of more complex silhouettes. The press described his looks as 'avant-garde', saying they echoed the spirit of Balenciaga's designs. Givenchy did not embrace the typical silhouette of the 1950s, with its narrow waist and generous skirt, notably presenting a 'shirt' dress that de-emphasized the waist and left the body uninhibited – a sign of the new styles to come in the 1960s. These bold offerings featured lighter touches, a sense of humour that was missing from the Spanish couturier's radical, often austere, though always sublime creations. Givenchy's youthful approach set him apart from his mentor.

This new aesthetic was accompanied by a significant change to the timing of Givenchy's shows. In January 1956, in an effort to combat the damage caused by copies of their designs being made after their haute couture collections were presented to the press – with spies hidden among the audience – and the sometimes negative influence that journalists had on the selections of international buyers, Givenchy and Balenciaga made the unprecedented decision to remove themselves from the official calendar of runway shows. Their collections would be shown first to buyers during fashion week, then, one month later, to journalists, who met the announcement with anger. While the press felt snubbed by the pair, whom they dubbed 'Givenchiaga', and did not understand the radical decision, a number of other couturiers envied the designers' courage, although they did not dare take the same step themselves. While a large swathe of the media decided to no longer cover the pair's shows, the most influential magazines, such as *Vogue* and *Harper's Bazaar*, remained loyal to them. In time, the strength of their designs won through and the press soon began to refer to the pair as 'leading lights' in the fashion world, as their ideas were taken up by other designers.

The two men also became geographically closer in 1959 when Givenchy moved his atelier to 3 avenue George V, opposite Balenciaga's. While Balenciaga's creations remained the symbol of refined modernity, Givenchy's designs offered a fresh look aimed directly at the younger generations. Balenciaga's rarefied creations were reserved for a more mature clientele. Younger clients who wanted to wear the Spanish couturier's designs were redirected towards Givenchy, who later took on Balenciaga's clients when his mentor's fashion house closed down in 1968.

In 1967, Givenchy decided to return to the traditional calendar for his shows. At the same time, the couturier was one of the first to recognize the growing importance of logos in the fashion world. As fashion was becoming more popular on the international stage and competition was hotting up between the brands, the fashion houses sought to set themselves apart by having a symbol that would be instantly recognizable. Hubert de Givenchy approached the designer Pierre Dinand, whom he had met while working for Schiaparelli. Dinand looked to their shared memories for inspiration in designing the '4G' logo. The pair remembered Elsa Schiaparelli's uncle, Ernesto Schiaparelli, a respected Egyptologist who in 1904 had discovered one of the most beautiful tombs in the Valley of the Kings, that of Queen Nefertari, wife of Pharaoh Ramses II. While studying the simplified transcriptions of hieroglyphs, Dinand noticed that the H of Hubert took the shape of a meander motif that was reminiscent of the G of Givenchy. He set four of the letters together, mirroring each other, in a square, a symbol of stability, and thereby created one of the most recognizable logos in the world, which has appeared on all of Givenchy's most successful fragrances, including L'Interdit (1957) and Givenchy Gentleman (1975).

As the 1960s drew to a close, the couturier returned to his first love, embracing sporty, lightweight clothing, when he launched his ready-to-wear line 'Givenchy nouvelle boutique' in 1968, and then again when launching his 'Givenchy Gentlemen' menswear collections in 1969. The couturier added a touch of humour, playing around with inventive details and dynamic prints, all while exploring the new trend for sexy designs that revealed the body through cut-outs and transparent fabrics.

In the 1970s, Hubert de Givenchy was one of the eminent figures in the fashion world who, like Yves Saint Laurent, sought to keep the fire of haute couture burning. One symbol of the changing times was the fashion show on the evening of 28 November 1973 that is now known as the 'Battle of Versailles'. The gala was put on to raise funds for the château's restoration, and it pitted five American designers against five French couturiers – including Givenchy – whose beautiful, classic designs clashed with the dynamism of the Americans. The event highlighted the paradigm shift that was taking place during the 1970s, challenging the hegemony of Paris as the international capital of the fashion world, with New York, London and Milan becoming more prominent.

Hubert de Givenchy remained faithful to his clientele. Relationships with key clients were built on trust, anticipating their needs and exceeding their expectations, so much so that friendships often developed. Like a number of other designers, he was financially supported by licensing deals and the success of his fragrances, so he decided to present distinguished, classic haute couture shows, offering clothes that appealed to his most loyal clients. While haute couture was considered outdated by some, it ensured the survival of traditional skills. Givenchy became a symbol of classic good taste, although his shows still retained a certain boldness, such as in the Autumn/Winter 1979–1980 collection, which was dedicated to celebrating the beauty of Black women and featured almost exclusively models of African heritage. Throughout the 1980s, Givenchy's haute couture shows typically included summer collections that embraced the light feel of 'flower women', and more theatrical, extravagant winter collections that celebrated great figures of the 20th century, such as Mariano Fortuny, Christian Bérard and Madame Grès.

In 1995, after a career spanning 43 years, Hubert de Givenchy retired to pursue his passion for art. In his lifetime, he saw the fashion house he created live on under the artistic direction of six different designers. LVMH, which has owned the label since 1988, announced John Galliano as Hubert de Givenchy's immediate successor. He only stayed for a year, with his time at Givenchy now seen as laying the groundwork for his announcement as the head of Christian Dior. The British designer presented four collections which captured the media's attention and ushered in a new era of spectacular shows at Givenchy. He was followed by Alexander McQueen, who maintained the theatrical feel of the runway shows. His sometimes brutal creative vision created a certain tension between the brand's traditional image and his bold, transgressive designs. In 1997, McQueen decided to move away from the founding designer's vision and use the Givenchy ateliers as a laboratory for developing his own ideas. With hindsight, his five years as artistic director allowed him to perfect his technical expertise and also benefitted communications around the house, with collections that demonstrated bold creativity as well as the preserved savoir-faire of its ateliers. Givenchy was now endowed with an aura of subversiveness that McQueen's successors would be able to build upon.

Givenchy's move into the 21st century was gradual, as Anders Christian Madsen explores here in his rigorous texts. In 2001, Julien Macdonald's appointment as artistic director eased tensions, and he brought his sexy, glamorous approach to the label's designs.

Riccardo Tisci took over in 2004. In collection after collection, the Italian designer embraced a dark romanticism, combining the technical expertise of sportswear design with the virtuosic refinement of haute couture. He was also the first artistic director at Givenchy to present influential menswear collections that made a lasting impression. Tisci drew on and reinterpreted Hubert de Givenchy's passion for comfort, sensuality, transparent fabrics and prints, as well as Alexander McQueen's transgressive, animal-themed creations, transforming Givenchy into a must-have brand in the late 2000s. The *maison* became an integral part of pop culture around the world. Givenchy was everywhere, from the costumes worn by Madonna for her Super Bowl performance (2012) to the lyrics of Beyoncé songs such as 'Formation' (2016).

The arrival of Clare Waight Keller in 2017, as the first female artistic director at Givenchy, heralded a return to the spontaneous sophistication of the creations of Hubert de Givenchy. Her balanced tailoring, floaty dresses and refined embroidery came together to create highly elegant haute couture collections.

In 2020, despite the pandemic, Matthew M. Williams brought Givenchy right up to date. He embraced the house's historical values and played around with ideas inspired by social media culture, presenting graphic tailoring, impeccably modelled statement accessories, and designs that were clearly influenced by streetwear.

The history of the 20th century has painted Hubert de Givenchy as a guardian of elegance and French good taste in haute couture, a status that implies a certain haughtiness, rather than emphasizing the dynamism, sense of humour and modern feel of his earliest designs. One could point to the photographic prints of fruits and vegetables, the 18th-century chandelier motifs, the trompe-l'œil flames and animal-fur prints developed in collaboration with the textile designer Andrée Brossin de Méré. In the late 1950s, Givenchy experimented with transparent fabrics, layering translucent printed voiles over a base fabric printed with the same pattern, or creating dresses in transparent embroidered tulle that revealed an opaque base layer. In the 1970s, he returned to his inventive prints: colourful lettering, inked paper, stylized scrolls and checked patterns. He was one of the first couturiers to draw inspiration from contemporary art, with his 1971 tribute to the paintings of Mark Rothko (1903–1970). Matthew M. Williams echoed this approach when he collaborated with the American artist Josh Smith for the Spring/Summer 2022 collection.

Today, Givenchy is surrounded by a community of artists and the brand is associated with famous figures such as Ariana Grande, Kendall Jenner, Rosalía, Gigi Hadid, Bella Hadid and the musician Alkaline. This continues the tradition established by the founder of the *maison*. Hubert de Givenchy was ahead of his time in his understanding of the importance of publicity and marketing, using the recognizable faces of iconic women of their time. The work of the influential Bettina Graziani, who was both press secretary and model for the fashion house, set the tone for the first Givenchy collection long before the show took place. In 1953, the couturier met Audrey Hepburn and became friends with the young actress, whose star was rising in Hollywood. Now legendary, their unique friendship helped them both to thrive professionally, Hubert de Givenchy regularly dressing Hepburn for events and on screen. The actress also agreed for her image to be used for the perfume L'Interdit, which was inspired by her. In his shows, at the same time, Givenchy featured Jacky, a model who looked very similar to the actress, drawing on a long-established tradition in haute couture of using models who resembled famous clients.

Since its early days, the house of Givenchy has often managed to find a place for its designs not only in the history of fashion but in history overall. In 1961, Blake Edwards's film *Breakfast at Tiffany's* showcased the couturier's talent for designing black dresses, whether short or long, which were memorably worn by the film's protagonist Holly Golightly, played by Audrey Hepburn. This feat was repeated on 19 May 2018, when Givenchy became the first French fashion house to have designed a wedding dress for a member of the British royal family. Clare Waight Keller designed the dress worn by Meghan Markle for her wedding to Prince Harry. This exceptional creation, completed in the utmost secrecy at the Givenchy ateliers in Paris, was admired by almost 1.9 billion viewers across the world. Furthermore, few couture houses can claim to have had such a big influence on streetwear. In 1952, the Bettina blouse, as well as the separates, was widely copied; so too the black sweater printed with a snarling Rottweiler head that appeared in 2011, which can still be seen on streets right across the globe.

This book is an opportunity to trace the creative development of the fashion house's founder and his successors, to explore their early days, their triumphs, their doubts, their innovations. It is also an opportunity to examine the reactions they provoked at the time, and how these are echoed in our own. A total of almost 180 collections testifies to a level of inventiveness and luxury that may well surprise the general public. The heart of Givenchy beats with the pulse of the times, while maintaining a rare balance between commercial propositions and spectacular presentations.

This book has allowed us to cast new light on that history in unexpected ways. Among these surprises, the reader will discover that Hubert de Givenchy was the first couturier whose work was celebrated by a major museum in his lifetime. The exhibition 'Givenchy: Thirty Years', which ran from 11 May to 2 October 1982 at the Fashion Institute of Technology in New York, took place a year before the retrospective dedicated to Yves Saint Laurent at the Costume Institute at the Metropolitan Museum of Art in New York. This little-known fact serves as a reminder that the history of the Givenchy brand is not as well-known as it deserves to be among both the general public and fashion historians. Hubert de Givenchy's reluctance to enter the media spotlight was most likely a contributing factor to the relative lack of recognition for his work, which the label's heritage project, launched in 2016, and this book are seeking to redress. The reader will discover a rich and diverse creative legacy spanning seven decades, begun by Hubert de Givenchy and further enriched, since 1995, by the creative visions of six successive designers, including Matthew M. Williams today.

Alexandre Samson

THE COLLECTIONS

HUBERT DE GIVENCHY

A SHORT BIOGRAPHY

Hubert Taffin de Givenchy (20 February 1927 – 10 March 2018) was born in Beauvais into a family of factory owners and showed an interest in fashion from childhood. At the age of 17, he began working as an assistant to Jacques Fath and became friends with the artist, set designer and costume designer Christian Bérard, who recommended him to fashion designer Robert Piguet in 1946. After a short subsequent period working for Lucien Lelong, Givenchy moved to Elsa Schiaparelli's fashion house, where he worked between 1948 and 1951, and began to truly make his name. Schiaparelli gave him responsibility for creating certain designs and for running the boutique on the ground floor, where he made clothes from offcuts of fabric used in earlier collections. His comfortable, flexible sportswear, which was among the first emerging ready-to-wear designs, was a success. Schiaparelli said she wanted to name Givenchy her successor, but he grew tired of her broken promises and decided to launch his own fashion house instead. Despite the difficult economic climate of the post-war era, he set up his studio in a grand house at 8 rue Alfred de Vigny, with the help of Louis Fontaine, president of the fabled chain-store Prisunic.

With support from Bettina Graziani, who was both his press secretary and the key model for his collections, and from his *directrice* Hélène Bouilloux-Laffont, on 1 February 1952 Givenchy launched what *The New York Times* described as 'one of the most phenomenal debuts in the Paris couture'. Within a year, Hubert de Givenchy had established himself as one of the great names of Parisian haute couture. The enthusiastic reception for his separates, his cotton blouses and his trompe-l'œil prints was a factor in bringing down the average age of haute couture clients by about 40 years, to 20. His fresh vision – bursting with zest for life and a sense of humour – was epitomized by Audrey Hepburn, whose championing of the designer contributed to his success on the international stage.

In 1955, Givenchy gained his independence by buying back the shares in his company and embarked on a radical new creative direction, influenced by Cristóbal Balenciaga, who had been both a friend and mentor since 1953. In an attempt to combat the damage caused by illegal copies, the pair decided to present their designs to the press one month after they showed them to buyers, a practice they continued until 1967.

That same year, Givenchy designed the 4G logo, with Pierre Dinand. The two men had met when they worked for Elsa Schiaparelli and remembered that her great-uncle had been an Egyptologist, which gave Dinand the idea of writing Givenchy in hieroglyphs. He discovered that the hieroglyph for the letter H was a rectangular spiral similar to the capital letter G in the Roman alphabet. Placing four H hieroglyphs in a square created a pattern that also evoked ancient Greek meanders.

In 1957, Givenchy launched the perfume L'Interdit, dedicated to Audrey Hepburn. It was followed by further successful perfumes, such as Givenchy III (1970), Ysatis (1984) and Amarige (1991).

Alongside his haute couture designs, Hubert de Givenchy early in his career also created ready-to-wear collections. His 'Grande Boutique', launched in 1953, was followed by 'Givenchy Université', a ready-to-wear diffusion line that ran from 1954 to 1957, then 'Givenchy Nouvelle Boutique' from 1968.

With support from famous clients such as Lauren Bacall, Jacqueline Kennedy, Greta Garbo, Marlene Dietrich and Wallis Simpson, women whose expectations he understood, his success grew throughout the 1970s, culminating in recognition from institutions in the fashion world. The first retrospective of his work was organized by the luxury department-store chain B. Altman & Company in New York in 1977. This was followed by a major exhibition at the Fashion Institute of Technology in 1982. Givenchy was the first couturier to be celebrated in this way while he was still active. More exhibitions followed, first in Tokyo, then in Paris, to celebrate the fortieth anniversary of his fashion house in 1991.

In 1988, Givenchy was acquired by the LVMH group. After presenting his final collection in July 1995, Hubert de Givenchy dedicated himself to charity work, exhibitions and his passion for art, notably becoming president of Christie's France in 1997.

Alexandre Samson

SEPARATES, BLOUSES AND SHIRTING

After three months of work, culminating in a show that lasted one and a half hours and saw 75 outfits modelled on the runway, Hubert de Givenchy became 'the *enfant terrible* of fashion', according to *L'Album du Figaro*. '[S]ince Spring 1947 (when Dior launched the New Look)', noted the press, including *Elle*, 'we have not witnessed … such a momentous event.'

Having already made a name for himself as director of the Schiaparelli boutique, Givenchy showed designs for his first collection that embraced familiar aspects of his signature style: 'One distinctive feature is that all the dresses are made of two separate pieces,' wrote *Elle*. This was true of both day dresses and evening gowns, and was a response to the needs of modern women. It caused shockwaves in an era when one-piece dresses were the norm.

The blouses were the star of the show. One design, called Bettina (named after Bettina Graziani, seen here modelling the blouse: right and opposite, bottom right), was such a success that four months later *Elle* found there were almost 100,000 illegal copies in Paris alone. Their success was partly down to Givenchy's innovative use of a previously unloved material – shirting, a catch-all term for a range of cotton fabrics such as organdie and poplin. Givenchy elevated the fabric, embellishing it with broderie anglaise in black thread, paying close attention to every detail of the cut and adding sophisticated pockets.

The couturier's designs also responded to the contemporary taste for sumptuously embellished evening gowns. He presented a long dress with a train (see p. 33) and a short navy bolero made of Chantilly lace, entirely covered in crystals, opening onto a bustier in ivory-coloured taffeta.

The press also commented on Givenchy's penchant for surprising accessories, some of which hinted at Schiaparelli's influence, such as straw ballet pumps embellished with silk, asymmetrical hats and woven straw summer bags.

The entire collection evoked a sense of comfort and freedom reminiscent of the sportswear trend. Although his designs were haute couture, Givenchy's approach was unprecedented in the way it borrowed from the techniques of ready-to-wear fashion. He used different production methods and, as noted in *Vogue*, 'many [of his clothes] are ready made, one requiring one fitting and just a few strictly made to order'.

A.S.

ANIMAL-FUR PRINTS AND JEWELRY-INSPIRED EMBROIDERY

The young couturier worked closely with textile designer Andrée Brossin de Méré, using photographs to create a series of highly realistic animal-fur prints. As was his custom, Hubert de Givenchy gave each of his designs a name. The dress Les Chats (see opposite, bottom left), which was a hit with the press, was made from silk printed to look like grey fur, with little cats' heads peeking out.

These surrealist prints were used to create surprising linings that contrasted sharply with a piece's more sober exterior: fur, huge flames or bright blue silk faille with diamond-shaped pleats, as in the design L'Écrin (see right). Givenchy's home town of Beauvais was famous for tapestry manufacturing, and the designer drew on this technique to create large naturalistic-looking roses.

Alongside the floaty, voluminous blouses that had been the stars of his first collection (see p. 26), Givenchy presented La Rose (see p. 39, right), a black velvet sheath dress worn under a bolero embellished with large bright pink petals.

For his ballgowns, the couturier drew inspiration from a jewelry box in his personal collection, as well as jewellers' display cases, and embroidered large motifs inspired by necklaces onto the skirts of Les Grenats (see p. 40, left) and Les Saphirs (see p. 40, right), while Versailles (see p. 41) featured an oversized pattern based on the luxurious necklace created in 1778 and offered to Marie Antoinette.

This collection also included surprising accessories, such as a handbag with a flap that was secured with a huge pin buckle and a leopard-print satchel with a gold handle (see p. 36 left).

On 7 November 1952, Hubert de Givenchy presented a mid-season winter collection, which built on the success of his main collection. The lantern-shaped pleats in the black satin skirt of the Gibraltar evening gown (see p. 39, top left) were reflected in the top half of the outfit, in stretch jersey outlining a plunging back.

The *Herald Tribune* wrote that 'the collection … may silence those critics who refused to consider [Givenchy] more than a boutique designer'.

A.S.

'A TRIBUTE TO FEMALE BEAUTY'

This collection of 180 designs was dedicated to female beauty, inspired by legendary women such as Cleopatra, Diana and Salome. Hubert de Givenchy's designs featured what *L'Écho d'Oran* called 'the most beautiful prints in Paris'. He continued his partnership with Andrée Brossin de Méré (see p. 34), creating trompe-l'œil prints, which, according to *Paris-Presse*, appeared on 75% of the designs and could be divided into three categories.

The first group was inspired by gardens: the designs featured colourful prints of fruits and vegetables, including citrus peel. The Nassau dress (see p. 46, right) was decorated with pineapple motifs and the Écossé ensemble (see p. 44, top right) with green pea pods. The second group featured marine designs: shellfish, seafood, turtle shells and, seen from above, huge waves in various shades of blue crashing onto a beach. Finally, the third group consisted of reproductions of draped fabrics, as if these had been photographed and then colourized in shades ranging from blue to bright pink. The Leonardo da Vinci design seemed to give away its references to the Renaissance painter's studies of draped fabric.

These surprising patterns were reflected in the embroidery on white organdie dresses such as Les Citrons (see opposite, top) and Les Tomates (see p. 45, left), both of which were embroidered with patches of fruit, and Nacre (see opposite, bottom), which was embroidered with oysters. The dress Les Muguets (see p. 48, right), which was covered with lily of the valley seed pods on a black background, even earned praise from Cristóbal Balenciaga when he first met Hubert de Givenchy in New York in the summer of 1953.

At around the same time, Audrey Hepburn chose to wear Inès de Castro (see p. 49), a white organdie evening gown embroidered with large black floral motifs, in the film *Sabrina*, directed by Billy Wilder, which was released in the United States on 22 September 1954.

La Dépêche Tunisienne described Givenchy's highly anticipated accessories as 'a firework display of new ideas, humorous touches, unusual accessories': a Panama hat that doubled as a bag with a gilded metal clasp, a bag that looked like a shopping basket, a bucket-shaped bag made from woven straw or canework with a leather border. Two large triangular scarves made from white surah fabric were printed to look like they were made of hair (see right), while the collection also featured earrings in the form of gilded peanuts.

A.S.

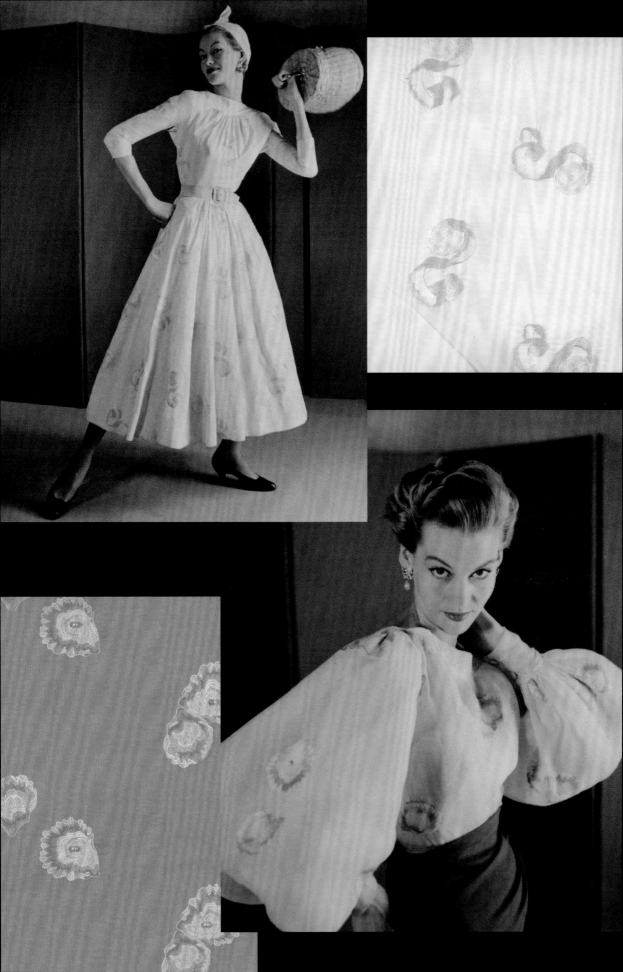

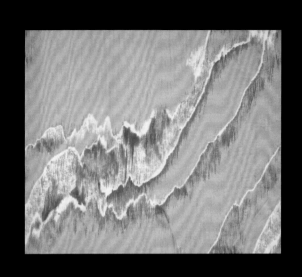

'LIGNE MYSTÈRE'

Hubert de Givenchy's 'Ligne Mystère' ('Mystery
Line') show was held after sundown, the designs
heavily inspired by his collection of 18th-century
artworks from China and Japan.

While coats with impressive pleated sleeves clearly
displayed an Asian influence, Givenchy also created
new silhouettes, with suit jackets that drew on
rounded shapes. The collection featured many black
satin coats with horizontal lines created by quilting,
while the Marengo suit (see opposite, top left)
boasted a huge pyramid-shaped collar made
of grey flannel with a band of light grey velvet.

Givenchy continued to embellish the backs of his
designs with pleats, rows of buttons or enormous
bows inspired by Japanese clothing, such as
Pois Noir (see p. 54, top left), a dress with a huge
obi-style bow, or Ombre (see opposite, bottom
right), which featured a sash tied in a large bow
with long trailing ends.

The outfit Les Ivoires (see p. 53) was characteristic
of the collection's dominant silhouette: a loose,
wide, dark-coloured coat that opened to reveal
a dress with a lining printed with thousands of
golden Buddha statues by Andrée Brossin de Méré.
Whether embroidered or printed, these Chinese
figures were a common feature on eveningwear
in this collection, in the blue and white shades
commonly found in Chinese porcelain.

The highly anticipated accessories were also
inspired by Asian cultures, such as a cone-shaped
hat in light beige felt with a chinstrap (see opposite,
top right) or a pair of satin heels with upturned toes.

While the collection divided critics, many journalists,
such as Nadeane Walker in the *News Dispatch*,
commented that Givenchy was 'abandoning the
prettiness and charm of his first creations in favor
of chicness and sophistication'.

A.S.

'ON THE THEME OF LUCK'

Hubert de Givenchy was highly superstitious and this collection, organized around the theme of luck, featured designs embellished with protective symbols. Lily of the valley bloomed on the short Parfumée evening cape, and clovers and turtles were embroidered on summer dresses, while there were also silvery fish motifs based on the enamel good-luck charm that the couturier always carried with him.

Givenchy returned to designing separates and cotton blouses, which he embellished with flowers.

According to the press, the return of Gabrielle Chanel, who launched her first collection in 14 years the day after Givenchy's show, inspired her fellow designers to focus on simplicity and pliability. Givenchy's increased use of jersey to make highly supple suits and bright red striped jerseys testified to this influence.

The designs also featured many trompe-l'œil buttons. In the same vein, Givenchy created a number of 'purposeless' belt buckles, which served solely as embellishments or were used to fasten the Zoé dress, while giving the impression of being too big, the two belt ties knotted and the buckles left hanging.

Once again, Andrée Brossin de Méré created most of the motifs, with pieces embroidered with letters, weeping willow branches or bamboo.

The embellishments revealed how deeply Givenchy was influenced by the 18th century. He was inspired by grand Venetian crystal chandeliers, which he used in large printed motifs on colourful dresses. He drew on the traditional toile de Jouy pattern, featuring bucolic scenes, while the Singerie dress, embroidered with dancing monkeys interspersed with scroll motifs, was inspired by the monkey designs on the rococo panels that Christophe Huet created for the Hôtel de Rohan in Paris, which he completed in 1750.

France-Soir wrote that Hubert de Givenchy was 'at a crossroads. He could keep moving straight ahead and present only pure ideas. Or he could choose to interpret his ideas to the fullest and use them to create dresses to be worn in real life. That is what he has chosen to do.'

A.S.

A PASSION FOR
THE 18TH CENTURY

This collection did not feature classic suits;
instead Hubert de Givenchy presented a number
of two-piece outfits with jackets that were playfully
adorned with wide pilgrim collars and dangling
woollen ties that ended in two huge pompoms.

As Carmel Snow, editor-in-chief of *Harper's Bazaar*,
wrote in the *New York Journal*, 'De Givenchy has
some unconscious love for the 18th century which
crops up constantly in his collection'. The influence
of the domino, a large hooded overcoat traditionally
worn to masquerade balls, was clear for all to see
in the suits and dresses with large collars that
could be draped over the head and worn as hoods.

Inspired by the 18th century, the 1.218 design
(see p.65, right) was so popular that *Dernière
Heure* in Algiers reported it had been ordered
almost 50 times. This short dress made of black
faille blossomed out into a wide crinoline-like skirt
gathered at the waist, and featured a plunging
V-neck bordered by two wide panels of black faille,
the point of the V touching the front of the skirt.

Once again, Givenchy worked with Andrée Brossin
de Méré, this time to create evening gowns with
prints inspired by elaborate wooden panelling, such
as that in Louis XV's private chambers in Versailles.
Its influence can clearly be seen in the large baskets
of flowers embroidered in multicoloured thread.

The white lace Versailles evening dress (see p.67),
which the *Midi Libre* praised as 'one of the highlights
of the collection', resembled a peacock's tail, with
a short skirt at the front and a long train at the back.
It remained one of Givenchy's favourite silhouettes
well into the 1960s.

Certain models, such as Jacky (see right and
opposite, bottom right), bore a striking resemblance
to Audrey Hepburn, whose Hollywood career was
going from strength to strength. They carried large
round bags in leopard print or leather, and wore
huge crystal earrings that matched their dresses.

A.S.

'A TRIBUTE TO THE BEAUTY OF AUDREY HEPBURN'

In a tribute to the beauty of Audrey Hepburn, Hubert de Givenchy created slender, tapering silhouettes. He even christened one of his designs Sabrina, in a knowing reference to the title role played by the famous actress in Billy Wilder's 1954 film.

Supple fabrics and simple cuts were elevated by unexpected details: diagonal rows of buttons, jacket pocket flaps repeated on the hem of a skirt. The vivid colours of a number of designs – yellow, blue and raspberry pink – were inspired by Givenchy's recent trip to Spain. One surprising feature of the collection was its use of a new synthetic material, Orlon, an acrylic fibre created by DuPont de Nemours.

While long sheath dresses, some worn under satin frock coats, served to highlight the models' figures, the influence of the 18th century was noticeable once again in the skirts, inspired by the pannier hoops worn by ladies at that time, on either side of the elongated diamond-shaped bodices. These were embroidered with garlands of flowers, while the collection also featured large lockets in the shape of vases overflowing with flowers.

Andrée Brossin de Méré created prints inspired by classic jewelry: pearl necklaces, cameo carvings and even Renaissance pendants, such as the Canning Jewel (see p. 73, left), a merman figure mounted in enamelled gold set with diamonds, attributed to the goldsmith Benvenuto Cellini, in the collection of the Victoria and Albert Museum in London. The evening gown La Cascade (see p. 72, right), its bodice and skirt embroidered all over with waves, was the star of the show.

While some critics bemoaned the couturier's more subdued style, the boldness of his early years still shone through in the collection's accessories, such as an oversized boater (the largest seen in the Paris fashion world that season), innovative hair clips that Givenchy had launched the previous season, and a long gold cigarette-holder embellished with fringing along its entire length. 'I am not looking to strike a killer blow,' the designer told L'Aurore. 'Instead, each season, I am trying to perfect the style that I want to embody.'

A.S.

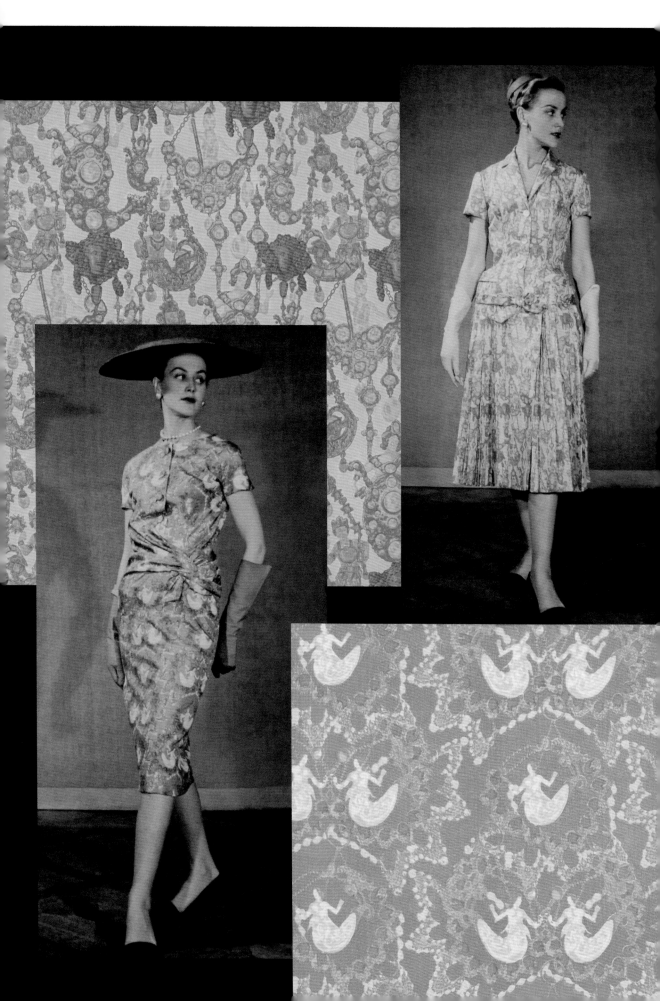

'ON THE THEME OF FREEDOM'

Le Journal du Dimanche described the models as 'boneless', while *Le Monde* saw Givenchy's designs as a 'denial of the female body'. That season, 'Givenchy caused a stir'. The response was so virulent that the designer left the show before it had finished. His collection 'on the theme of freedom' marked a creative turning point, both in Hubert de Givenchy's career and in the fashion world of the 1950s.

The floaty early pieces gave way to brave experiments: the day dresses and suits no longer inhibited the body's movement in any way; instead they 'hung from the shoulders and skimmed the body without ever hugging it', meaning there was no need for a corset.

The press wrote that 'these dresses are surprising but they may be the starting point for a new aesthetic'. The design that grabbed the headlines, a daytime shirt dress (see p. 76, right), was made from four tiered bands of jersey cashmere and weighed only 350 grams, making it one of the lightest dresses ever created.

This sense of weightlessness permeated the entire collection. The coats were masterpieces with unexpected cuts and shapes created by oversized storm flaps and cape-like effects. Black was the dominant colour, for both daywear and eveningwear, accentuated by Givenchy's juxtaposition of different fabrics and heavy use of shimmering moiré silk.

Women's Wear Daily wrote that Givenchy's models looked like 'strange creatures from another planet, of indeterminate shape and sex', while the hats in the collection were variously mocked or admired. They moved with every step the models took, and their geometric and graphic designs provided the finishing touches to the silhouettes.

The influence of Balenciaga was clear to see in this collection. The sense of freedom also reflected the independence that Hubert de Givenchy had recently gained through buying back the shares in his business from Louis Fontaine, the president of Prisunic.

A.S.

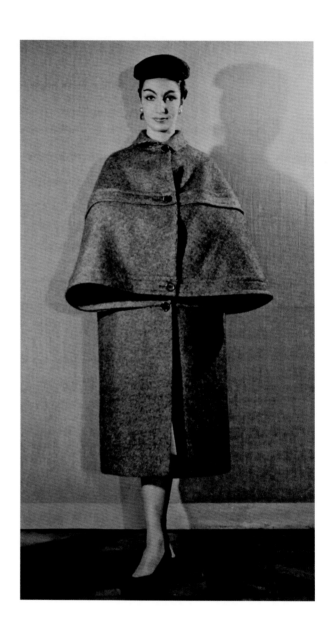

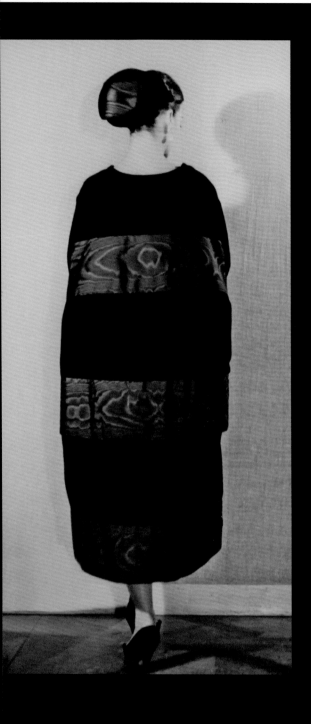

DISSIDENCE

In an effort to combat the illegal copies of their
designs that they suspected certain journalists
were enabling, Hubert de Givenchy and Cristóbal
Balenciaga decided not to present their collections
to the press until almost a month after they
showed them to buyers.

This collection confirmed Hubert de Givenchy's
radical new direction. The pared-down day dresses
wrapped around the body's natural curves without
seeking to contain them. They had no collars or
belts, so did not accentuate the waist. Playful
patterns of buttons were a common feature of
the collection. Givenchy paid great attention to
the backs of his clothes, embellishing them with
surprising features such as 'tailcoats' – rectangular
panels of fabric that hung from the backs of
the jackets. Loose-fitting and draped fabric
was everywhere, adding volume to the backs of
garments; likewise, shell-like swirls of taffeta were
rolled up on the fronts of skirts. Large flared capes,
made from point d'esprit tulle, were tied with
a satin ribbon, leaving the shoulders bare.

In March 1956, the press reported that the house of
Givenchy would design Audrey Hepburn's costumes
for Stanley Donen's film *Funny Face*. Givenchy drew
on this collection for the costumes that Hepburn
wore in the scenes shot in Paris.

Givenchy turned away from pastel tones in favour
of bolder colours evoking works by Van Gogh or
Gauguin.

Once again, the large hats surprised and divided
critics. Some were cylindrical, inspired by the
headdress worn by Nefertiti, Queen of Egypt, while
others were embellished with scallops or covered
in flowers, such as a pillbox hat made entirely from
a heap of white chrysanthemum petals.

A.S.

TIGHT HEMS

Once again, Hubert de Givenchy's decision to present his collection a month after the other couturiers' shows sparked opposition from some parts of the press. However, his gamble paid off, in the form of impressive sales to American buyers. His new creative direction continued to surprise some journalists, although they recognized that he was ahead of his time.

Black was again the dominant colour for both daywear and eveningwear. The clothes skimmed the body or floated free of it entirely. Capes and cape-like effects were everywhere: wound into asymmetrical loops in daywear designs, or fitted, such as in a short suede cape with buttons (see opposite, bottom right). Some looked like ponchos, folded and fastened at the back.

Another common thread in the collection was the high-waisted dresses and coats. The coats were embellished with fringing on the front and back, or fastened with very large buttons.

Billowing backs and skirts continued to dominate Givenchy's eveningwear designs, and he created a stunning bubble skirt for a cocktail dress (see p.90, left). The designs also featured swathes of fabric draped diagonally across the body and secured on one side of the skirt. These were shown alongside tunics worn over sheath-like evening dresses, hinting at Balenciaga's continued influence.

Skirts that were nipped in by a tight hem around the knees caught the attention of the press, while the collection also featured a draped blouse that seemed to make it impossible for the model to move her arms.

Audrey Hepburn chose some of the outfits to wear in Billy Wilder's film *Love in the Afternoon*, which was released in May 1957, including an embroidered organdie dress known as no.1722 and a high-waisted coat with two large buttons, christened no.1710 (see opposite, top left).

A.S.

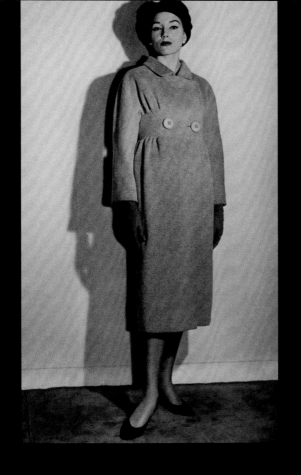

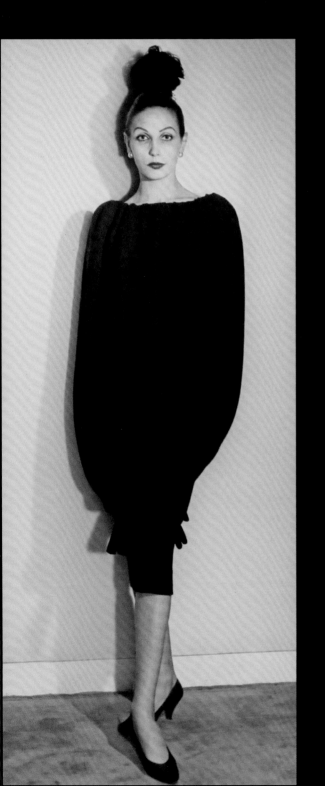

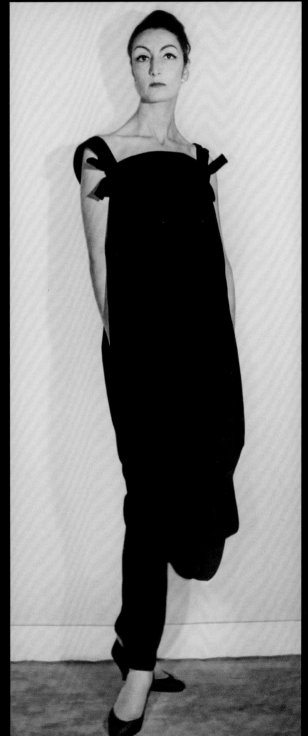

GEOMETRIC PATTERNS AND A TRIBUTE TO CHINA MACHADO

'My clothes are not designed for any particular type of woman,' Hubert de Givenchy told Faith Shipway in an interview for the *Evening Standard*. 'They are very high fashion, created to maintain the prestige of French couture.' This collection of 170 looks was the most important in the couturier's career to date and was partly inspired by the Asian and Portuguese heritage of his new model China Machado (see right and opposite).

Embellishments in the form of horizontal yokes or decorative belts created tiers in the much-praised skirts and sack dresses, while the hems of the coats had curves cut into them. The daywear designs included a number of puffy skirts with the material gathered into a tight hem, as well as tunic-like garments worn over a longer skirt. The evening gowns featured floaty swathes of material and collars that draped down over the chest like necklaces, alongside scarves with loops that cascaded down the back. Givenchy continued to experiment with bubble skirts, this time embellished with gathered fabric and embroidery.

Warp-printed flower motifs were interspersed with grid-like patterns that appeared on both daywear and eveningwear. These created an unusual graphic effect, like the polka dots that covered a long draped muslin dress, with one section of fabric turned up and worn as a cape (see p. 97, right). Although the shapes of the hats were more subdued, there were still some surprising designs, such as rounded hats reminiscent of mushrooms.

Acknowledging that some parts of the press were confused by his avant-garde ideas, Hubert de Givenchy told the *Evening Standard* that his work was 'like an abstract painting, not easy to decipher'.

A.S.

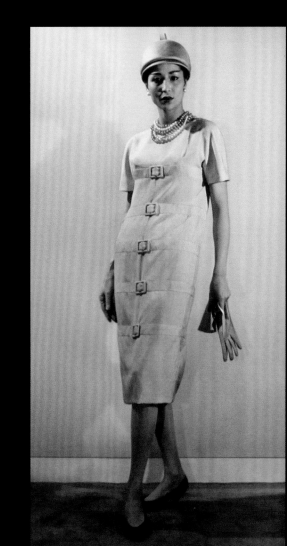

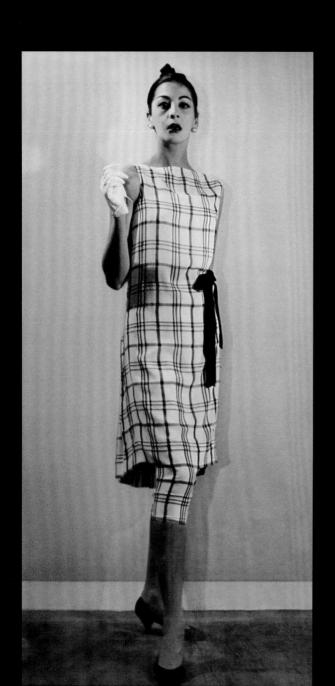

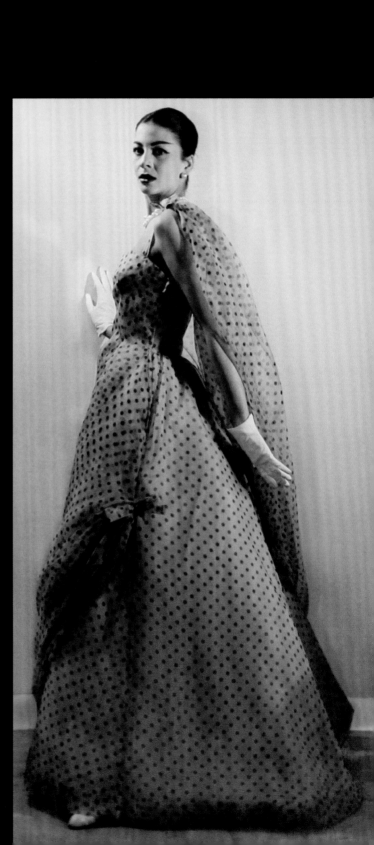

A NEW MATURITY

Building on a silhouette that Balenciaga and Givenchy had been exploring since 1955, the loose dress that floated away from the body, called a 'shirt dress' or 'sack dress', was instantly recognizable. It was made of wool jersey and featured large pockets and a turtleneck (see opposite, bottom right). The comfortable style was reminiscent of a loose pea jacket made of chestnut-brown wool or an 'egg-shaped' cape jacket. The round shape had echoes of the bubble skirts in earlier eveningwear collections. This season's evening skirts featured swathes of fabric fastened at the back with a single tail hanging down as a train (see p. 102, left).

Another design that built on the previous season's collection was a mink-edged dress with a swathe of fabric draped diagonally across the body and secured on one side of the skirt. Cocktail dresses boasted cape-like backs made of black lace or wool crepe, a fabric that Givenchy used more than any other designer.

Dramatic, sweeping hoods made of black point d'esprit tulle hung down over satin sheath dresses in light colours. The peacock-tail silhouette, with dresses that were short at the front and long at the back, was still a common sight, while contrasting with a number of longer petticoats made of faille with elaborate ruffles and flounces.

While the press commented that Hubert de Givenchy was displaying a certain restraint, a new maturity, his ingenuity still shone through, especially in the headwear, which was even more fantastical than before. The hats were abstract sculptures, ethereal structures swathed in tulle. Lace cloche hats, wreaths or towers of flounces that reached towards the sky: all served to highlight and amplify the strong silhouettes.

A.S.

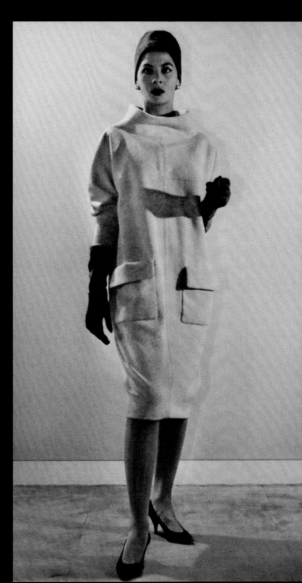

BABYDOLL DRESSES AND THE WIG TREND

'I always design with last season's collection in mind,' Hubert de Givenchy told *L'Aurore*. The shirt dress still reigned supreme, alongside cocktail dresses with 'puffy' or 'cape' backs, generous, ballooning coats and suits with short jackets. The high waistline of some of the day dresses was emphasized by wide belts made of supple leather that matched the dresses.

While some of the press pointed out that it was impractical, the 'babydoll' silhouette dominated the 'smart' day dresses and evening gowns. All of the dresses flared out from the shoulders or from a low-cut bustier, leaving the body free and uninhibited.

Givenchy used muslin, guipure lace, plumetis fabric and embroidered tulle to experiment with transparency and layering, techniques that would come to mark his career as a whole. Peacock-tail dresses, their hems plunging at the back, were entirely covered with petals made of taffeta and organza, or richly embroidered. The high waistline also featured on evening gowns with short, heavily embroidered bodices.

Working with the sisters Rosie and Maria Carita, Hubert de Givenchy created a trend for extravagant, wavy wigs – blonde, brunette and red – which were meant to be worn like hats with evening gowns.

Flouting the press ban, the famous *New York Herald Tribune* journalist Eugenia Sheppard donned a disguise so that she could slip unrecognized into the buyers' show, which took place a month before the press show.

A.S.

REVERSIBLE WOOL AND OBSCURED FACES

Hubert de Givenchy was dubbed an *'enfant terrible'*, a 'radical' and a 'rebel' by the press, but he presented what Eugenia Sheppard of the *New York Herald Tribune* enthusiastically described as 'definitely the most entertaining show of the season'.

The sober aesthetic of the Givenchy salons – with their walls painted grey, boasting no chandeliers or glasses of champagne for guests on arrival – allowed the designs to shine through. This collection picked up where the previous one had left off, with high waists, short skirts and dresses that followed the line of the body without clinging to it. For the first time in his career, Givenchy used double-faced wool to create reversible coats with contrasting inner and outer sides – chalky white and black, black and sky blue, or olive green and black. While some featured hoods, all had patch pockets.

In the eveningwear, the generous skirts flared out from the high waist, creating a silhouette like that of a pregnant woman. They were very short, some not even reaching the knee, hinting at the fashions to come in the 1960s. They were made of floaty crepe or faille, often longer at the back, and the hem was always tucked under, echoing the shape of the perfume bottle for the fragrance L'Interdit, which was released in the summer of 1957. Shimmering moiré fabric was once again used for a number of designs in the collection.

Givenchy played with obscuring part of his models' faces, adding high woollen collars, small hats that covered the eyes with a large flower, or, in one bold design, rectangles of black velvet that looked like blinkers (see opposite, bottom right).

Other hats looked like hanging mobiles, frozen in position, with even more ambitious asymmetrical arrangements of feathers and tulle. The press were used to Givenchy's creations by now, and Eugenia Sheppard wryly commented in the *New York Herald Tribune*, 'You'd think he is the Mad Hatter in person.'

A.S.

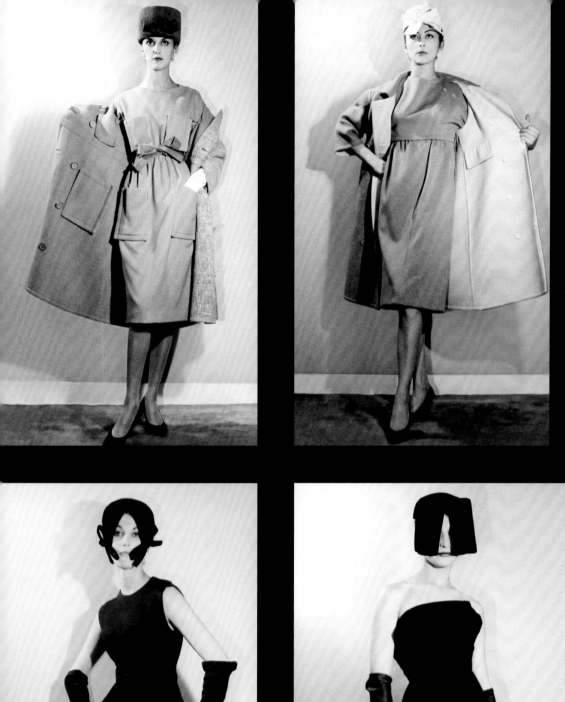

THE FIRST
COLLECTION AT
3 AVENUE GEORGE V

This was the first show that Hubert de Givenchy
held at the new premises he had acquired, in the
building formerly owned by the couturier Raphaël,
opposite the house of Balenciaga. The walls were
painted white and pearl grey, and the rooms were
lit by chandeliers, lending them a classic purity that
contrasted sharply with the more modest rooms
on the rue Alfred de Vigny. The show lasted 1 hour
and 50 minutes, and the collection was one of
effortless simplicity.

Unlike most of his contemporaries, Givenchy did not
accentuate the waist in his designs. He abandoned
the high waist of his earlier collections, lowering
it to the level of the upper hips and emphasizing it
with wide, supple kid belts. He built on the success
of his reversible wool coats from the previous
season (see p.110), presenting new designs
with light exteriors and dark interiors.

Aside from a few instances of embroidery and
warp-printed floral motifs, the collection did not
feature many patterns. The evening dresses were
generous – sack dresses, babydolls or trapeze
dresses – with some subtly highlighting the bust
before flaring out. A number of them featured long
trains, while the hems were sometimes cut out
into a central point at the front.

After five years of surprising and innovative hats,
the press noted that Givenchy's designs had been
significantly pared back, embracing simple, classic
shapes. However, the simplicity of this eveningwear
collection, which was at once 'eclectic' and 'difficult
to wear', proved a little disappointing for some of the
guests, as the *Manchester Guardian* commented.

A.S.

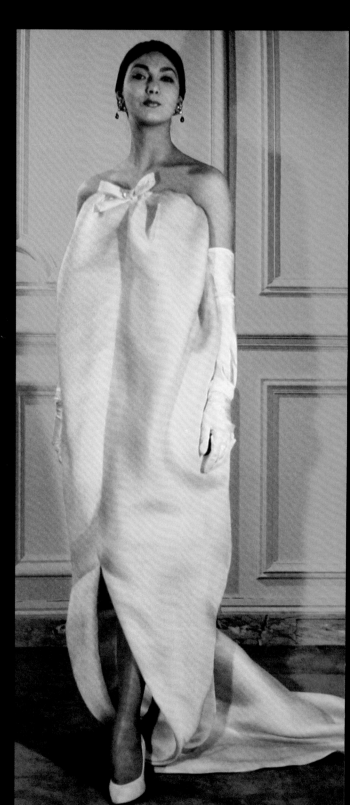

THE FIRST 'HOSTESS DRESSES'

While Hubert de Givenchy continued to present reversible coats and supple leather belts, this season's collection also featured coats with a fitted front and generous back. Like the suit jackets, they were fastened with decorative buttons that were suggestive of the grand brooches worn with evening gowns. Fur was also a common feature in the collection – in the lining of the large black leather coat that opened the show, but also on hats.

Princess-line evening dresses dominated, with a bust made of fitted panels that flared out beneath the breasts to form a domed skirt. A large black cape with a generous turtleneck and two lengths of fabric falling over the arms (see p.122) provided a touch of drama. An ingenious system of pleats behind the shoulder created a cape-like effect on the backs of coats and dresses.

A group of around ten dresses in the show 'caused a commotion', according to Canadian newspaper *The Daily Gleaner*. These were Givenchy's first 'hostess dresses', which would prove incredibly popular in the 1960s. Also known as negligees or 'television dresses', they were sumptuous loungewear made of silk taffeta in bright pink or lime green. While their generous trains built on the couturier's favourite silhouette, they were short and fitted at the front, and the skirts split into short trousers that came down to the knee. They marked the first appearance of trousers in Givenchy's haute couture collections.

At the end of the show, the round of applause – led by Audrey Hepburn and her husband, the actor, director and producer Mel Ferrer – lasted 25 minutes. The press response was rapturous. *The New York Times* wrote that Givenchy had presented 'the best collection of his career'. Some journalists compared him to Balenciaga, with the *Los Angeles Times* commenting that 'the pupil surpassed the master'.

A.S.

ELEGANCE AND FREEDOM

Hubert de Givenchy's collection, which brought the week of haute couture shows to a close, was described as more 'mature' by both buyers and the press. It embraced freedom and elegance, building on earlier collections.

Once again, the clothes highlighted the body without clinging to it. Flowing jersey dresses featured belts of fringed suede or brown or black satin ciré. The sheath dresses were fitted at the front, with looser material at the back that hung straight down, ending above the dress's hemline.

The coats were the standout designs of the collection, true masterpieces of construction. They featured rounded shoulders, kimono sleeves and pilgrim-style yokes. The collars and sleeves were barely perceptible. Some of the coats were made of reversible wool, with contrasting colours on the inner and outer sides or cross-hatched with large black and white checks. Others, like the suit jackets, were embellished with oversized buttons made of braid, horn or knotted thread.

Givenchy was fond of using fabrics with textured patterns. Ribbed fabric, ottoman fabric, honeycomb cotton, figured silk, textured silk, lace and guipure lace embroidered with flowers all featured prominently on both daywear and eveningwear.

The designer moved away from princess-line dresses in favour of a short, fitted bust and long skirt that was gathered at the waist and fell to the floor in the shape of an upside-down tulip. This silhouette would be a common sight in his work throughout most of the 1960s. Audrey Hepburn was thought to be a particular fan of it, just as she was of the generous, floaty loungewear that the press reported had been created especially for her to wear during her pregnancy.

A.S.

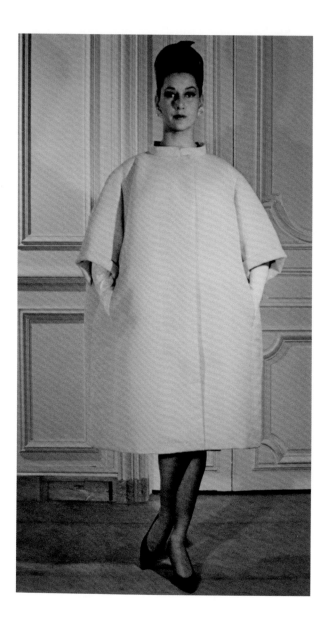

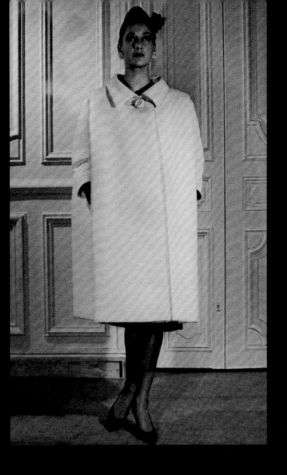

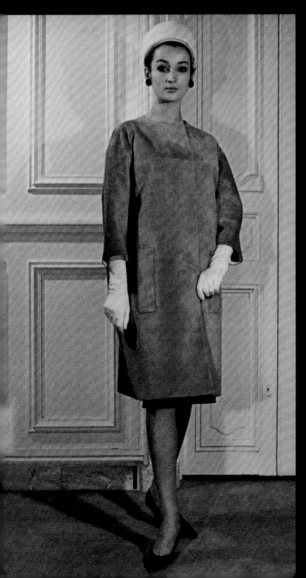

BREAKFAST AT TIFFANY'S

The 262 designs in this collection represented a continuation of Hubert de Givenchy's signature style, which he was constantly seeking to perfect.

The generous coats were shorter than the dresses, leaving the hems to peek out. They featured broad martingale belts that were knotted and hung down at the back, or fastened around the hips at the front, or gathered the voluminous fabric into pleats. The day dresses were embellished with fringing and long leather belts.

The evening dresses featured a slightly higher waistline. Their bodices were fitted around the bust, while the skirts, shaped like upturned tulips, had a line of pleats down the lower back. The asymmetrical necklines that appeared on a number of evening gowns sparked comments. The fronts of the dresses were simple, while the backs were voluminous, embellished with bows, flaring out into capes, or plunging low to leave the wearer's back exposed.

The loungewear designs included black chenille trousers. The collection was a celebration of different fabrics, a notable example being a satin sheath dress with black velvet hearts and a length of material that wrapped around the wearer like a stole (see p.134, left).

While some of the tall pillbox hats were made of fur, others featured ostrich feathers that wafted with every step. The evening dresses were also embellished with ostrich feathers, as well as long pheasant quills that looked like strokes of black ink.

Audrey Hepburn chose three dresses, one coat and several accessories from the collection to wear in Blake Edwards's film *Breakfast at Tiffany's*, which began shooting in October 1960. In the opening scene, she wore a black satin evening dress with a cut-out back (see p.137 for similar) that has since become iconic.

A.S.

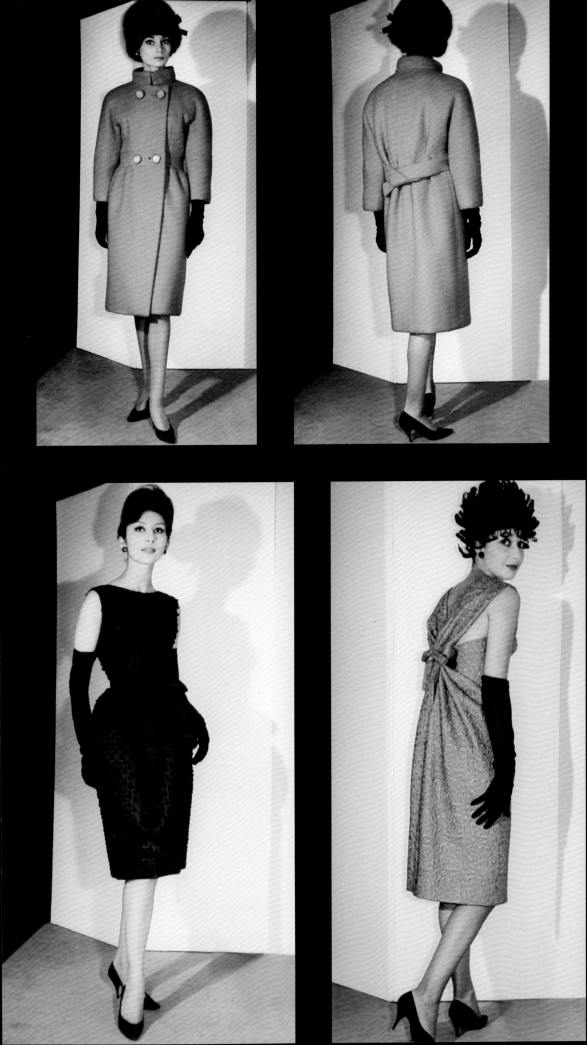

BLURRED FLORAL PRINTS AND OVERSIZED EMBROIDERIES

Building on the previous two seasons (see pp. 126 and 132), this collection was dominated by rounded silhouettes.

The wide shoulders of the coats curved into batwing sleeves, and Hubert de Givenchy cleverly combined bias-cut and straight-cut fabric around the bust to create integrated capes and dickeys. The two-piece outfits featured jackets that were fastened at the side, large buttons embellished with passementerie, and rounded or pointed peplums.

Various shades of white and yellow dominated the daywear, while the eveningwear was an explosion of colours in unexpected pairings, such as black and mahogany, that went down a storm with the critics.

The collection saw a return to plant-based patterns. Whether realistic or stylized, they were printed on faille or layers of organza, creating a blurred effect that Givenchy would continue to play around with over the next ten years or more. The designer was a garden lover, and he made use of oversized embroidered flowers, stem-like rinceau motifs and sprigged patterns, which evoked the embellishments on Spanish shawls or ancient pottery. These patterns sometimes covered all of the dress, sometimes just the bust. Dress no. 3378 (see p. 141, right), worn under an ivory satin coat, was the basis for an outfit worn by Jacqueline Kennedy to the château of Versailles on the evening of 31 May 1961. This dress was the only French design that she wore during the American presidential visit to France.

In a surprising touch, Givenchy covered some of his outfits with black organdie feathers. This unusual detail was echoed on the large conical hats, some of which had ruffles of dark tulle, on the floppy wide-brimmed hats, and on one headpiece (see opposite, bottom left) that featured a long black organdie veil falling over the face.

A.S.

INNOVATIVE FURS AND LOUNGEWEAR TROUSERS

The day suits for this collection featured dickeys and surprising arrangements of buttons, details that harked back to the 1950s. Alongside the curving lines of Hubert de Givenchy's now signature generous coats, mackintoshes were a surprising new addition. These followed the line of the body more closely, and some hid impressive fur linings. The prevalence of fur, which was a recurring theme throughout the collection, was due to a new technique that allowed the designer to use the whole of the pelt, thereby reducing waste.

A little black crepe dress featured a draped bust and a plunging scooped neckline at the back. The use of rich fabrics and innovative details made the evening dresses stand out. One was made of bright pink brocade and boasted a cape trimmed with chenille in the same colour, which formed a strip of material around the hips. Another standout was an outfit in lime green *ciselé* velvet (see p.147, right), adorned with a huge flouncy stole that draped around the body.

This collection saw the triumphant return of tops, jackets and sweaters worn over dresses with pared-down silhouettes. They were richly adorned with crystals, pearls, chenille and strips of fur.

Trousers were a common sight in the loungewear designs – black velvet, straight legged, or with flounces around the shins – often worn with matching jackets. One highly original satin outfit included short wide-legged trousers, reminiscent of bloomers (see opposite, bottom right), with a border of fur that matched that on the large coat which could be worn over the top.

A.S.

DECORATIVE BUTTONS AND INSPIRATION FROM IRAN

Textured fabrics and large geometric checks emphasized the sophisticated cuts of the coats, as well as the semi-fitted mackintoshes with backs that fanned out into pleats. The daywear featured soft skirts that were carefully constructed with pleats, buttoned panel effects and tiered flounces. Box pleats appeared on the back or, more unexpectedly, the front of garments.

Buttons sewn onto the backs as embellishments gave the impression that the coats had once featured a martingale belt.

The supple leather belts that had been a feature of Givenchy's collections for many seasons marked the natural waist. Many designs were made of intricately textured fabrics (ottoman, quilted, embossed, damask) and boasted silhouettes that billowed out at the back.

A number of the outfits and dresses were covered with tiny whimsical prints such as dashes or small ink stains, doubtless inspired by the exhibition '7,000 Years of Art in Iran' that was held at the Petit Palais in Paris from 13 October 1961 to 8 January 1962 and featured archaeological finds, ceramics, fabrics, rugs and miniatures dating from the Neolithic era to the 18th century. The evening gowns had elaborate tiered backs, or were left open at the back to reveal a heavily embroidered bustier underneath.

However, it was the loungewear designs that sparked the most passionate response. Most of these outfits were composed of two separate garments – a pair of trousers and a sumptuous house-coat – but one design combined these into a single piece (see p.155, left): trousers with an integrated cape made of embossed fabric and an embroidered dickey.

Ten years after Hubert de Givenchy's first catwalk show, buyers and press alike gave this collection a standing ovation. Eugenia Sheppard wrote in the *New York Herald Tribune* that the collection was 'the most elegant he has ever done'.

A.S.

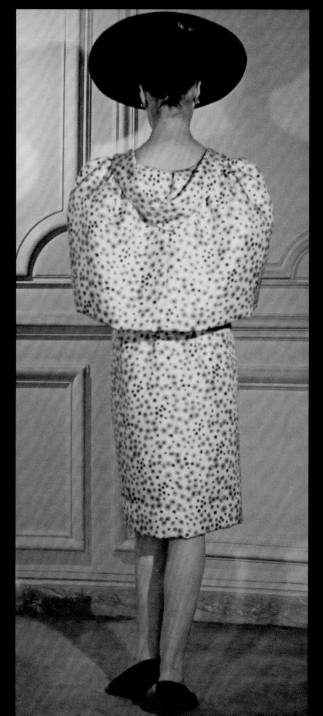

DRAPED DRESSES AND INFANTA DRESSES

For the first time in many years, Hubert de Givenchy's collection featured clothes that hugged the body and – unlike the sack dresses that he had been designing since winter 1955 (see p.74) – emphasized the wearer's feminine curves. These dresses were worn under narrow frock coats that were slightly fitted around the bust. Some of the evening coats exaggerated the waist and hips, forming a vase-like shape that was nipped in tight at the hem.

As well as the generous coats, which had been a signature look in Givenchy's collections over the past few years, there was a number of fur coats. While fur had mainly been used on details the previous winter – with designs adorned with strips of fur or furred hems – this collection featured 22 different types of fur, ranging from sable to ocelot, across both daywear and eveningwear. Givenchy even developed a kind of pony-skin leather printed to look like zebra or leopard skin. There was also a plastic mackintosh lined with mink.

The majority of the daywear designs featured a high waist at the front and a lower waist at the back. In his eveningwear, Givenchy returned to the draped approach that he had favoured in the 1950s, swathing the body in heavy black silk crepe with floaty trailing fabric and low scooping backs, which were attached to the collar with lengths of ruffled fabric.

Infanta dresses made from sumptuous brocades and brightly coloured damasks added an even more sophisticated touch. They were adorned with flounces and ruching around the neckline, cascading down the back in some designs and adding volume to the front in others.

One unexpected design was a hostess outfit in white satin, composed of a bodice top and wide draped jodhpurs worn over a pair of narrow trousers. At first the outfit was entirely concealed by a cape, heightening the sense of surprise when it was revealed (see p.159, left and right). The cape was covered in life-sized tiger lily flowers made of velvet overlaid on a satin background.

A.S.

EXQUISITE HOSTESS DRESSES

'To see a Givenchy collection is to know what many of the world's best-dressed women will be wearing this spring,' wrote Jeanne Molli in *The New York Times*.

The collection was built around new kinds of shirt dresses. One of these, fastened with buttons down the front, was made of bias-cut linen and had a diamond-shaped cut at the lower back (see opposite, top and bottom left). The waistline sat slightly higher and was once again emphasized by supple leather belts.

The evening dresses featured many cloqué fabrics with shimmering raised patterns. Some of the pieces were draped to look like waves crashing down towards the hem of the dress, which was fastened at the front. The ruched flounces that had featured in the previous season's collection (see p.156) appeared again here, emphasizing the necklines.

Hostess dresses once again made the headlines. Adorned with large collars, they were buttoned up at the front, with busts that were tight to the waist and then flared out over the hips. Some featured a regal cape-like back. While Hubert de Givenchy liked working with luxurious fabrics, he also continued to develop the cuts of his designs, and the new variations that he created confirmed his status, along with Cristóbal Balenciaga, as one of the major influential designers of the early 1960s.

A.S.

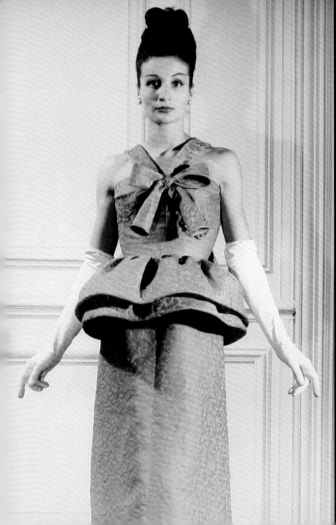

HINTS OF THE BELLE ÉPOQUE

The coats for this collection were cut on the bias at the front and adorned with storm flaps at the back. Optical illusions created by the checked patterns emphasized the cuts. A smaller version of this grid pattern also appeared on a reversible coat made of mohair with a dipped lambskin lining (see opposite, bottom left). A leather hat shaped like a tall riding helmet completed the outfit and testified to the importance of animal hides in the collection. There were pillbox hats, caps, boaters, top hats and oversized riding hats made from all kinds of furs and even worn with evening dresses.

A suit made of velvet calfskin was followed by two rust-red snakeskin mackintoshes and a third mackintosh made of satin ciré printed to look like crocodile skin (see p.170, left). The linings were made of fur or printed pony-skin leather. Cloaks and short capes – some straight, others curved – were worn over a number of designs across the collection. There were not many instances of embroidery, aside from the now-signature embroidered bodices and jackets; one satin evening gown was embellished with three-dimensional sprigs of plastic flowers (see p.173).

Although in 1955 Givenchy had been the first couturier to present loose-fitting dresses that floated away from the body – an approach that had since been adopted by his contemporaries – he now moved away from this silhouette in favour of more fitted designs. For the time being, he also resisted the trend for long boots and textured tights that had taken over Paris.

Nathalie Mont-Servan wrote in *Le Monde* that the couturier may have been influenced by the recent exhibition of the works of Italian portrait artist Giovanni Boldini at the Musée Jacquemart-André, arguing that this might explain the emphasis placed on feminine curves and the 'Belle Époque' colour palette of brown, purple, magenta, dark green and black.

A.S.

THE RETURN OF
SURPRISING PRINTS

Hubert de Givenchy did not make any major
changes, presenting a collection that was largely in
line with the previous season (see p. 168). The suits
and dresses were nipped in at the waist by narrow
patent leather belts, while capes and storm flaps
adorned the backs of coats and mackintoshes.

For this summer collection, the couturier returned
to his earlier love of inventive, surprising prints.
Unlike the larger prints of his earlier collections,
this time he used tiny tomatoes or flocks of stylized
birds. Like the 'ink stain' stripes, all these motifs
were printed on dresses and outfits made of twill.

Linen dominated both the daywear and
eveningwear lines. In a nod to contemporary
fashions, almost all of the outfits included
tall rounded bowler hats, turbans or wide-
brimmed hats.

The smart daywear and eveningwear featured
large stylized floral motifs printed on rich Lurex
cloqué fabric. Givenchy used a favourite visual
trick of his, layering together organza and crepe
that were both printed with the same motif, which
meant that the pattern appeared blurred and
distorted (see p. 176, right). There were a few
touches of embroidery, on boleros and short capes,
and some designs were richly adorned with pearls
and crystals.

A.S.

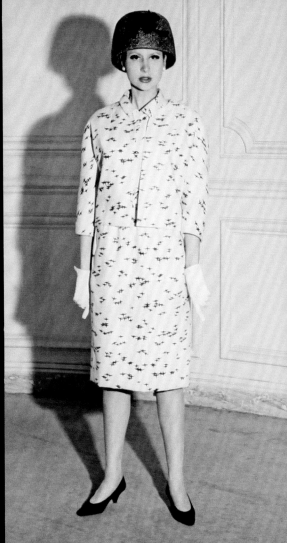

INTRICATE DRESSES AND LONG EVENING COATS

Fur, tweed and leather all featured on the daywear designs in this collection. There was a number of generous straight-cut woollen coats with checked patterns, while others stood out due to their elaborate wraparound batwing sleeves. Daytime coats and evening gowns featured short capes around the shoulders, and embroidery made a return on both the capes and the dresses worn underneath them.

For Hubert de Givenchy, eveningwear was an opportunity to showcase the simplicity of his cuts. The princess line returned on several dresses made of satin or cloqué lamé. These sleeveless dresses hugged the bust, waist and hips, then flared out gently towards the ground. Hems of skirts were adorned with ostrich feathers.

One innovative dress design, which testified to the dialogue between Givenchy and Cristóbal Balenciaga, featured a long skirt made up of two separate pieces of fabric that crossed over at the sides (see p. 182): the front piece was shorter and went up at the back, layering over the rear panel that tapered down to form a pointed train.

The long coats that reached the floor were made of an unusually wide range of fabrics: organza overlaid with guipure lace, sequined fabric, duchess satin, colobus monkey fur, and even suede, which was then an unusual sight in eveningwear. One straight-cut woollen coat with a suit collar was inspired by a man's greatcoat (see opposite, top right), while another, which had four patch pockets with flaps (see p. 180, left), was reminiscent of military attire such as safari suits.

Finally, sculptural hats provided the finishing touch for a number of cocktail dresses. These geometric designs featured fin-like or stalk-like details that pointed skyward.

A.S.

SILK GAZAR, STOLES AND JUDO JACKETS

As was his custom, Hubert de Givenchy presented a collection that seamlessly combined earlier experiments and new details. The variations on his signature looks, such as suede suits, supple leather belts, generous batwing coats, the heavy use of linen and the little black dresses with modest fronts and elaborate backs, were all popular with the public.

The couturier moved away from classic button fastenings on his jackets and coats, instead exploring designs where the two edges meet rather than overlapping, secured with finely crafted buttons and buttonholes made from loops of fabric. The cut of the dress bodices, which were made up of two pieces of material that crossed over and were secured with a knot at the side, was thought by some journalists to be inspired by the kimono jackets worn by judokas.

The eveningwear was dominated by stoles – some with pointed tips, others with rounded ends. These signature pieces draped around the shoulders in a cone shape and were reminiscent of the copes worn by Roman Catholic priests. They were worn over refined evening dresses embellished with embroidery details that also appeared on the long evening coats and the cocoon capes that were sometimes attached to the dresses.

Givenchy presented outfits made of silk gazar – an intricately woven fabric made of raw silk threads, which was both stiff and floaty. It had first been created in 1958 by the Zurich-based textile producer Abraham, in partnership with Balenciaga. This collection, like the ones that came before it, appealed to both journalists and buyers alike. André Courrèges, whose collections had been making headlines since the summer of 1964, had just caused a stir with his history-making collection, which was a true ode to modernity. By contrast, Givenchy's designs were more conventional, embracing classic elegance. They were the height of sophistication, as embodied by the world-renowned figure of Audrey Hepburn.

A.S.

MONASTIC INFLUENCE

The generous batwing sleeves on the belted coats of this collection were especially impressive when seen from the back. Once again, the bodices of the dresses were made of two pieces of fabric that crossed over (see p.184), this time at the back. Large capes, whether ornate or sculptural, shone when paired with simple, sophisticated cocktail dresses. The couturier also created intricate necklines on his little black dresses, with straps that crossed over at the front or back, secured by rhinestone buttons, or racer backs that revealed the shoulder blades – a detail that also featured on some of the evening dresses.

Inspired by the simple cuts of liturgical garments, Hubert de Givenchy presented stoles that resembled monks' copes, with raised collars. One of these boasted a long train at the back, with a border of wood-grouse feathers (see p.193, left).

Cocktail dresses and evening gowns in quilted Lurex dominated, alongside hostess outfits made from shimmering cloqué fabric. Trousers were limited to homewear, although other designers had been featuring them in their daywear collections since 1964.

Nathalie Mont-Servan wrote in *Le Monde* that Givenchy's collection was one of 'the most pared-down and refined in Paris, even in his choice of fabric and colours, which added a touch of monastic severity'.

A.S.

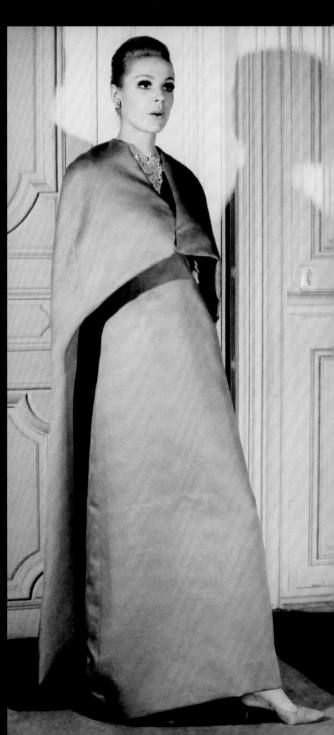

A RETURN TO THE SPIRIT OF THE TIMES

Hubert de Givenchy's silhouettes underwent a notable rejuvenation as he adopted some aspects of his contemporaries' ideas. The influence of couturiers such as André Courrèges was clearly felt in the shorter skirts that ended above the knee, the placement of flap pockets, the use of white gabardine wool for the dresses and coats, and the flat shoes worn with long knee-high-style hosiery made of white or multicoloured fishnet. This surprising material even featured on a day dress (see opposite, bottom right), worn with sunglasses – the first time these appeared in an haute couture collection.

The couturier played around with these new ideas, as well as with the possibility of eliminating the waist by adding two martingale belts at different levels on a straight-cut coat – one under the bust and one at the hips (see opposite, top left). He also made surprising use of PVC to create a pair of boots and a mackintosh that were both completely transparent, the coat revealing a short-sleeved dress worn underneath (see opposite, bottom left). Sophisticated, refined cocktail dresses made way for short dresses with bell skirts that were reminiscent of the clothes worn by little girls.

Givenchy created a layering effect with longer skirts that peeked out from underneath coats or tunics. He also used contrasting patterns and continued to experiment with transparent fabrics and blurring effects by layering printed organza over the top of crepe printed with the same motif, such as on a sheath dress embellished with large stylized flowers, worn with a chain necklace made up of oversized rhinestone-encrusted links (see p.197, left). Another dress, this one with blue and white sailor stripes (see right), caused a stir in high society circles when the Duchess of Windsor arrived at a party to find five other guests wearing the same dress.

A.S.

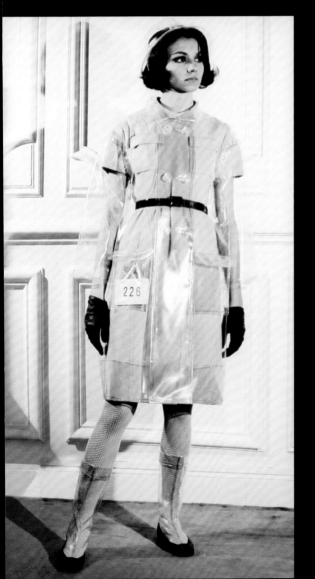

SPORTSWEAR

This was the first of Givenchy's collections
to feature sportswear and skiwear. One outfit
included a scarf printed with the names of the most
fashionable ski resorts (see right). The watchword
was comfort, with a number of dresses and coats
in the collection made of stretchy elastane-blend
fabrics. In the same vein, fitted jackets gave way
to blouson jackets worn over dresses, or large
shearling coats.

There was an emphasis on accessories. Leather
belts were fastened with metal buckles and rested
on wide yokes around the waist of the dresses.
Some of the coats were simply encircled by a
narrow strip of knotted leather. Headscarves and
helmets were made of matte or patent leather.
Whimsical multicoloured tights were worn with
flat shoes or boots – the first time these appeared
in an haute couture collection.

The evening dresses were more classic than
the daywear, building on the silhouettes from
Givenchy's earlier collections. Crepe sheath dresses
were worn with draped scarves that brushed the
floor or adorned with large rhinestone-encrusted
chain-link belts. Some of the more generously cut
dresses had scalloped edges, while the jackets and
boleros were covered with textured embroidery.
Givenchy also used PVC again (see p.194), this time
in black on a coat to be worn over a cocktail dress
(see opposite, bottom right).

This new direction was met with enthusiasm,
and journalists saw it as confirmation that the work
of 'leading couturiers' such as Hubert de Givenchy
and Cristóbal Balenciaga 'allows us to trace the
evolution of fashion', as Nathalie Mont-Servan
wrote in *Le Monde*.

A.S.

THE FIRST APPEARANCE OF BERMUDA SHORTS

Hubert de Givenchy opened his show with a series of suits featuring Bermuda shorts, the first time shorts had appeared as city wear. The designs were met with enthusiasm by some journalists, who saw them as a sign that Givenchy was returning to the originality of his early days. They celebrated this new look for a new generation of women who were moving away from Balenciaga's somewhat old-fashioned influence. These innovative suits appeared alongside suede button-down sportswear. All were worn with whimsical long socks.

When it came to cocktail hour, the couturier swapped the scalloped edges of the previous season (see p. 198) for zigzag edges around the collars and hems. A gabardine coat was printed with wide black and white stripes, creating a graphic effect (see opposite, top left), while Givenchy once again explored the optical illusions achieved by overlaying printed organza and crepe (see p. 138). Floaty crepe evening dresses were made of lengths of fabric draped around the body. The embroidered jackets and boleros worn over them were shorter than before, covering only the shoulders.

Givenchy did not embrace the vivid colours being used by many other designers, such as the bright orange that dominated the Paris fashion scene. Instead, he focused on vibrant but soft shades such as lemon yellow, azalea red and apple green.

Chain motifs featured prominently in the daywear designs – on buttonholes and on a dress with a printed pattern of ropes tied to form chain links (see opposite, bottom left). In the eveningwear they appeared in the form of necklaces, or the crystal-studded strap that held up a draped Nile green crepe design (see p. 205, top left). Givenchy was influenced by contemporary fashions and, although he wasn't setting new trends, he was playing with existing ones without veering into caricature.

A.S.

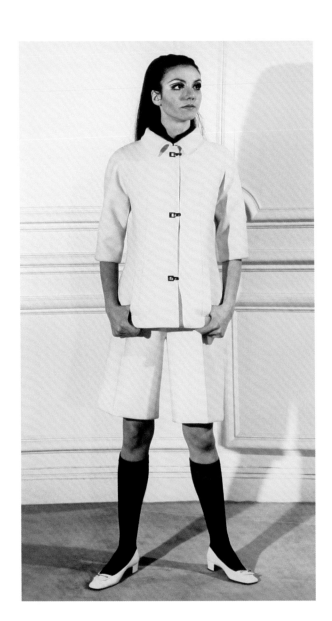

A RETURN TO ORDER AND SILK GAZAR

For the first time in 11 years, Hubert de Givenchy decided to open his doors to both journalists and buyers on the same day. The collection he presented was influenced by sportswear and gave pride of place to culottes, which were worn with long patent-leather or leopard-skin boots.

In a return to the surprising accessories that had made his name, Givenchy added pockets to belts and hats. The tall rounded hats had visors, and sometimes straps tied under the chin. The collection also featured a number of hoods, which provided the finishing touch to jersey dresses that zipped up at the front.

However, it was in the eveningwear that the couturier's inventiveness reached its peak. Givenchy returned to the peacock-tail silhouette (see p. 62) for his dresses and coats made of ivory satin with motifs of small rabbits, or giraffes and elephants, in lilac velvet (see p. 210). This last design was worn over a short jumpsuit, a garment that featured prominently throughout the collection.

Never before had Givenchy used silk gazar to this extent. This lightweight but sculptural fabric appeared in purple on an evening dress with a split skirt (see p. 209), and in raspberry pink on an apron-like coat cut in a highly innovative way (see p. 211, right): the coat passes under the arms at the front, then over the sides and is tied at the neck, framing the sumptuously embroidered bodice of the evening dress underneath. A short black silk gazar dress with a wide flared skirt featured a belt with a rhinestone-studded buckle (see p. 208, left). In the form of a heart, a common motif throughout the collection, the accessory also appeared at the bust of a generous charcoal-grey silk gazar dress (see p. 208, right).

A.S.

REVEALING CUT-OUTS

Linen beachwear outfits, made up of shorts and striped jerseys with buttons on the sleeves, were paired with sunglasses and headdresses inspired by ancient Egypt. They were shown alongside trousers and linen cropped tops that revealed part of the stomach.

The sexy look – a concept prized by a new generation in search of freedom – dominated the entire collection. Gloria Emerson wrote in *The New York Times* that 'the sexiest dress in all the Paris collections' was a bustier dress made of silky garnet-coloured Cigaline fabric with a horizontally draped bust that allowed the stomach to show through the translucent material (see p. 214, right).

Hubert de Givenchy maintained this tension between revealing and concealing by incorporating sensual cut-out sections into his eveningwear. There were triangular cut-outs under the bust or cut-outs along the sides of a black silk gazar dress. The couturier even presented an entirely backless dress, made of Cigaline in a warm brown shade folded over white crepe (see p. 215, left), the back consisting of nothing more than two wide straps running down the sides. In an ivory crepe evening dress, the wearer's stomach was only half-covered by sumptuous embroidery (see right). Similar embroidery featured across the entire collection in the form of embellished brassieres, which were sometimes reduced to strips of fabric across bare skin.

Although the collection featured a number of pairs of trousers, they were reserved for more casual spaces, appearing only on beachwear, 'hostess' outfits and 'casino' looks, rather than outfits designed to be worn in town. One pair, made of organdie embroidered with small light-coloured flowers, was worn under a transparent tunic, with a knotted belt showing through (see p. 214, left). In short and long versions (see opposite, bottom right), trousers were also covered in dark petals that quivered with each step the wearer took.

A.S.

DEDICATED TO CRISTÓBAL BALENCIAGA

In May 1968, Cristóbal Balenciaga announced that he was closing down his couture house. While shockwaves reverberated through the fashion world, Hubert de Givenchy, who was naturally heralded as his successor, welcomed the Spanish master couturier's clients and workers. Balenciaga's radical influence was clearly felt in this collection. Refinement and sophistication were characterized by the rigour of coats that boasted checked patterns or oversized houndstooth motifs.

The show opened with a design that was entirely the product of Givenchy's own imagination: a sheepskin leotard (see opposite, top left). This was called a 'body' and worn over a jersey bodysuit. It was the first in a series of 'bodies' designed to be worn as both sportswear and, more surprisingly, eveningwear – in the boldest move seen from the couturier in many years. Once again playing with layers and transparent fabrics, Givenchy presented a black velvet leotard that barely covered the wearer's body (see opposite, top right), worn under a large diaphanous dress embroidered with seed pearls.

Sections of embroidery with an almost organic feel, like coral, transformed the female body into a reef, such as in a romper suit and in a fitted jumpsuit worn under a large black velvet coat (see opposite, bottom left and right). The eveningwear boasted frills around the collar of monastic dresses, which followed the line of the body before flaring out at the hem. Ostrich feathers were also a common sight on the eveningwear, standing upright so that they wafted gently down, creating a cascade of ruffled feathers on a short tunic (see p.218, right). A heavy black crepe cape with an asymmetrical design that left one shoulder bare was adorned with black turkey feathers and Himalayan monal feathers on the hem. Some of the black sheath dresses, such as one with an embroidered detachable armband (see p.219, bottom right), also hinted at this diagonal line, highlighted by rhinestone strips. On another version, jewelled bands wound around the arms like snakes.

A.S.

BEACHWEAR AND THE G LOGO

The Spring/Summer 1969 show opened with beachwear. It was the first time that Hubert de Givenchy had shown a two-piece swimming costume, made of cotton and boasting two flounces (see opposite, bottom right). This was followed by shorts worn with espadrilles, tall straw hats and headscarves. For the yachting crowd, light-coloured oilskins – many of which were waterproof thanks to a vinyl coating – were worn over linen dungarees, while one jacket was fastened with a zip that carried an oversized anchor (see opposite, top right). For the first time ever, the couturier added his initial – a capital G – to a metal belt buckle (see opposite, bottom left).

The press praised a number of pleated organza dresses – a technique that appeared throughout the collection, from daywear to cocktail dresses. Silk gazar still had pride of place in the eveningwear, such as in a short black dress paired with a hat embellished with white camellias (see p. 222, right). This flower appeared again on the belt of a sheath dress, also made of silk gazar (see p. 223, right), with a wide horizontal collar that built on a silhouette from the previous collection. Camellias also featured on a pair of trousers (see p. 223, left), worn beneath a heavy crepe wraparound coat with a peacock-tail back.

Sculptural embellishments, made of multicoloured feathers, created curved lines on the forearm or shoulder.

A.S.

LEOPARD PRINT, CUT-OUTS AND EMBOSSED SILK GAZAR

The final collection of the 1960s reflected the spirit of the times. The younger generation was embracing its newfound freedom and questioning the relevance of haute couture, as it catered to only a handful of older, privileged clients. Since Cristóbal Balenciaga had left the scene (see p. 216), Hubert de Givenchy took it upon himself to defend the art. While his collections continued to surprise onlookers with their supreme elegance and their measured response to trends, the classic nature of his designs was sometimes criticized by the younger generation. However, Givenchy understood women and presented a number of clothes – trousers, shorts and skirts in a range of lengths – in an attempt to combat the lack of fixed reference points in a rapidly changing fashion world.

Long daytime coats, with hems that brushed the floor, were made of suede or leopard-print fabric. Leopard print also appeared on a pair of trousers in the daywear line (see opposite, top left), and in printed lamé for eveningwear (see opposite, right). Cut-out designs in floaty crepe revealed parts of the body and the back, or the side of the bust in one asymmetrical draped dress. The bodices were heavily embellished, covered in pearls and tufts of swan's down.

Givenchy used acid-green silk gazar for a sleek dress with a plunging scooped back (see p. 227, right). One design used a technique that imitated metal embossing to create a black silk gazar fabric covered with raised motifs. This was also used on a classic midi-length dress (see opposite, bottom left), an alternative to mini-skirts and maxi-skirts.

A.S.

THE WILD WEST AND EMBRACING SENSUALITY

The Spring/Summer 1970 show opened with a series of beachwear designs, including an outfit with a curtain-like skirt that could be parted to the sides to reveal a swimming costume underneath (see opposite, top left and right). This was worn with a straw hat that had hints of the American Wild West, an influence that appeared elsewhere in the collection in the fringing that decorated a number of designs. Hubert de Givenchy even presented a suede coat with fringing and lacing at every edge (see right).

Once again, the couturier embraced his love for animal prints, such as giraffe and zebra patterns. The summer dress that epitomized the feel of this collection was made of bright pink linen and had a fitted bust with a series of small vertical pleats that flared out when they reached the hips, giving the skirt greater volume (see opposite, bottom left).

Echoing the more seductive feel of the previous year's collection (see p.224), the couturier presented a number of skirts that were split high on the thigh for eveningwear. More modestly, there were numerous long dresses made of printed translucent silk, the hems embellished with a ruffle to add to their fullness.

Many of the smarter dresses featured large prints on organza with wide, irregular stripes in bold colours, which looked as if they had been painted with broad brushstrokes. These contrasted with the large raspberry-pink cyclamen flowers printed on white crepe in one outfit that consisted of a poncho and a pair of trousers (see p.230, top left).

The belts were embroidered, attached to the garment or simply placed around the waist. Some were covered with crystal drops, while one chocolate-brown Cigaline dress (see p.231, bottom right) featured long chains of embroidery that wrapped around the waist and joined at the neck to form a collar.

A.S.

LONG SLEEVELESS JACKETS AND THE RETURN OF SILK FAILLE AND TAFFETA

A common sight across many fashion shows, long sleeveless jackets that almost reached the floor featured in a number of Hubert de Givenchy's designs, across both daywear and eveningwear. Woollen or leather culottes with a trompe-l'œil box pleat completed the hunting outfits. While Givenchy had featured wide hoods on his eveningwear in the 1950s, now he added them to fur or suede coats. Figure-hugging sweaters with tight-fitting integrated hoods were worn underneath.

Checked patterns were still a common sight on both coats and skiwear, which were made of stretch fabrics printed with navy blue, green and red checks. These were worn with matching helmets and headscarves, and the eyes were hidden behind large sunglasses. The small vertical pleats that had featured in the previous collection (see p. 228) were seen again here on many designs, from bodices in the daywear line to velvet skirts for cocktail dresses. In the eveningwear, a pair of astrakhan fur trousers was worn under a black organza tunic (see p. 235, left).

While silk faille and taffeta had disappeared from Givenchy's collections during most of the 1960s, they appeared again here on dresses printed with miniature vintage motifs, such as small or large yellow squares on a brown background. The hems of dresses and skirts had large ruffles or, in the case of one velvet number (see p. 234, left), a chenille lattice motif that was similar to the decorations sometimes seen on furniture. A rich brocade in green and purple metallic Lurex thread on a black background added a touch of luxury to the eveningwear designs, in a collection that did not feature any embroidery.

A.S.

A TRIBUTE TO MARK ROTHKO

This collection was a hit with buyers and the press alike. *La Nation* celebrated the 'rediscovery' of Hubert de Givenchy's boldness, after a few seasons that his critics had judged too classic. The news agency Agence France-Presse wrote that the Spring/Summer 1971 collection was 'not at all conventional'. Shorts, with a 'romantic and erotic' feel, were everywhere, in both beachwear and eveningwear, in the form of pleated jumpsuits or worn under long skirts with wide slits at the front. Paired with blazers, shorts also made their first appearance as city wear.

Givenchy's designs played with graphic patterns to create optical-illusion-like effects, setting bands of black or dark blue material into outfits and coats made of white stretch fabric. Busts, sleeves and sides were literally cut in two, while one hat and coat combination was white at the front and entirely black at the back (see opposite, top left). Similarly, one dress was made from two pieces of crepe printed with different colours, which were joined at the front with a long seam down the middle. This penchant for graphic effects also showed through in certain prints, such as cross-hatched or painted checks. Givenchy's only concession to the 1940s nostalgia that dominated many of his contemporaries' collections was in the slightly wider, more structured shoulders of his jackets.

In contrast, Givenchy presented a series of floaty eveningwear garments printed all over with large flowers in vibrant colours on a black background. These designs delighted journalists, with some comparing them to Georges Seurat's pointillist paintings. Once again, the couturier played around with transparent fabrics and layering, presenting dresses worn underneath large organza capes. He followed the same principle with a second significant group of dresses, which were printed with wide horizontal blocks of solid colour and paid tribute to the American artist Mark Rothko, who had died the year before. A little later, with the help of his friend and client Rachel 'Bunny' Mellon, Givenchy acquired Rothko's painting *Untitled (Red-Brown, Black, Green, Red)*, completed in 1962, a notable example of Colour Field Painting.

A.S.

'A TRIBUTE TO BRAQUE AND MIRÓ'

After a spur-of-the-moment visit to the Maeght Gallery in Saint-Paul-de-Vence with Bunny Mellon, Hubert de Givenchy was inspired to design clothes that paid tribute to the work of Joan Miró and Georges Braque. Givenchy owned two of Miró's major paintings, *Blue I* and *Blue II*, the first two works in a huge triptych that was painted in Palma de Mallorca in 1961 and is now in the collection of the National Museum of Modern Art at the Pompidou Centre. Givenchy's homage to the Spanish artist took the form of two large coats, one made of blue silk gazar embroidered with black and white chenille stars (see opposite, right), the other made of purple suede and embellished with stylized appliqué motifs (see right). The couturier created a special faille fabric printed with the minimalist motifs that the artist was known for. As for Braque, a silk gazar dress with a large stole was embroidered with the bird silhouettes that were emblematic of the artist (see p. 243).

The daywear featured long sleeveless jackets that reached the floor, often made of thick suede. Double-faced wool allowed the designer to create coats without linings, with bands of green and pink fabric set into a black background. These stripes appeared again in the fringed flounces on an outfit featuring leather trousers. Givenchy's love of transparent fabrics came to the fore once again in a large black Cigaline evening coat worn over a sheath dress in bright green patterned fabric. While chenille had mainly been used on details over the last two seasons (see pp. 232 and 236), now it was used to create large Spanish shawls and garnet-coloured openwork dresses. The collection prominently featured trousers; in one outfit (see p. 242, right), they were paired with a top that had a low-cut draped satin bodice and a cut-out porthole back.

A.S.

BELL-BOTTOMS AND HANDWRITTEN STRIPES

The Spring/Summer 1972 show opened with sailor suits in the colours of the French flag. A perfectly streamlined pair of blue linen bell-bottom trousers was worn with a brassiere that was as short as its sailor collar was wide (see opposite, top left and right). Denim made one of its first appearances in haute couture, in an outfit with a tiny denim brassiere embroidered with red crabs. One bodice was long at the back but left the stomach bare (see opposite, bottom left); it was worn with a belt made of two lengths of fabric fastened with a buckle in the shape of an anchor. Finally, the couturier played around with sailor stripes on one coat made of stretch fabric, rotating them so they ran in a different direction at the pockets.

With a knowing nod to the early days of his career, Hubert de Givenchy added a touch of humour in the form of multicoloured stripes that 'announced their colour', as the newspaper *La Nouvelle République du Centre-Ouest* put it (see right). Each horizontal stripe on the block-colour ottoman fabric background had the name of its shade written on it. A long dress announced its 'chartreuse', 'lemon yellow' and 'lilac' stripes. On a red outfit, the words 'Été 72' [Summer '72] appeared in a delicate repeating pattern (see opposite, bottom right).

An evening dress made of organza with a pink gingham print had a long flounce with blind tucks on the hem, which changed the pattern so that the checks formed lines instead (see p.246, right). A dress with an asymmetrical neckline and only one sleeve was covered with red, orange, purple and white flowers on a black background, while another outfit that boasted a collar embellished with frothy ruffles had a marbled-effect pattern. Finally, black or printed silk gazar was used to create dresses with large sculptural collars.

A.S.

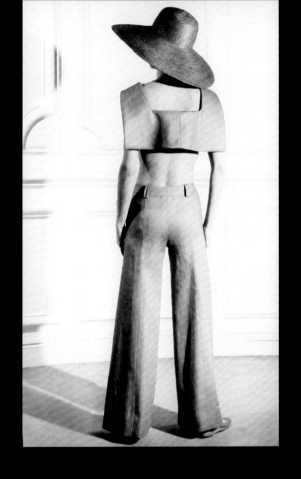

HOMAGE TO CRISTÓBAL BALENCIAGA

Hubert de Givenchy dedicated this collection to his friend and mentor Cristóbal Balenciaga, who had died on 23 March 1972. Givenchy explored new technological advances and opened his show with skiwear. He paid particular attention to metal fastenings: zips with large circular pull tabs, buttonholes with gilded metal clasps, and a new kind of metal popper made of rings and decorative snap fasteners closed by pressing on the side. In a nod to the 1940s, many coats were either entirely covered in fur or had fur sleeves, which made them wider in the shoulders.

The patterns had an increasingly graphic feel. Oversized rectangles or squares of fabric were set into the double-faced wool coats, and a 'photo negative' effect was created by repeating these in contrasting colours on the dresses worn underneath. Checked patterns continued to feature prominently, this time on sheath-style evening dresses inset with large squares in increasing sizes, worn with a medieval-style plaited hairpiece created by the hairstylist Alexandre de Paris.

Silk gazar and zagar were used on a number of evening dresses, including one with a cape that stood up around the face, fastened with ribbons of the same material that tied at the back (see p.251). Coats and dresses were also decorated with large panther silhouettes in yellow, green or blue.

The couturier worked with Lesage to develop a new kind of embellishment made of small rectangular mirrors with studs at each corner (see p.250). These decorated the seams of long evening dresses made of gold cloqué fabric, and entirely covered some jackets, like armour. Finally, Givenchy created distinctive flowers in multicoloured sequins for a coat that was worn by Brigitte Bardot in Roger Vadim's 1973 film *Don Juan, or If Don Juan Were a Woman*.

A.S.

REVEALED WAISTS, THE 'FLOWER WOMAN' AND A TRIBUTE TO AFRICAN ART

'A funny thing happened at Givenchy's salon this morning. For the first time in his career Givenchy himself, in his white work jacket, came out at the end to take a bow... It was the only way to get rid of the cheering, clapping crowd,' Eugenia Sheppard wrote in an article for the *International Herald Tribune*.

Most of the designs, across both daywear and eveningwear, were made up of two separate pieces and revealed the stomach, or even the navel. Linen brassieres designed to be worn on the beach gave way to blouses that left the waist bare, designed to be worn in town. These were partly hidden under short spencer jackets, while large printed capes hid daring brassieres. Even the wedding outfit that closed the show featured a brassiere (see p.255, right) worn under a more chaste-looking jacket.

Building on the 'photo negative' contrasts from his last collection (see p.248), Hubert de Givenchy added insets made up of strips of fabric, zigzags or tiered pyramids. These were set into the bottom of a coat and repeated on the skirt of the dress worn underneath it, often in contrasting colours that added to the virtuosic effect. These inventive touches were echoed on the edges of jackets and the hems of skirts, which were notched or scalloped. There was also a number of flowing, pleated designs throughout the collection.

The couturier also paid tribute to African art. Its influence was keenly felt in the patterns of squares and triangles, as well as the colour combinations of brown, white, beige and black.

With his large floral prints, Givenchy offered a new take on the classic theme of the 'flower woman', inspired by the heart notes of Oriental rose, lily of the valley and jasmine in the fragrance Givenchy III.

A.S.

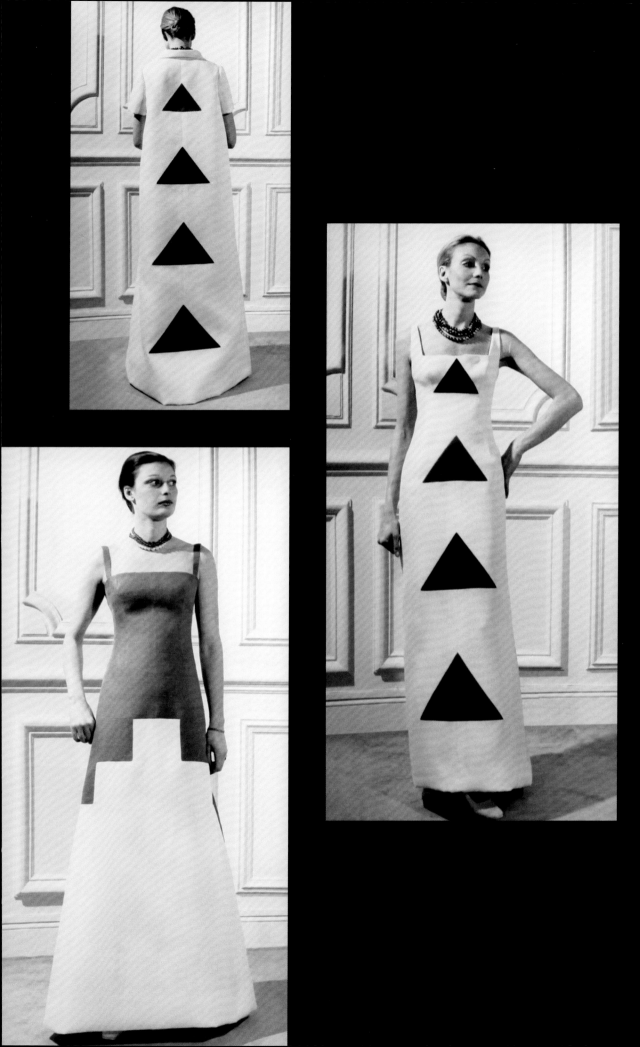

'COBRA' SNAKESKIN AND THE BATTLE OF VERSAILLES

Hubert de Givenchy presented a collection made up of soft lines, with dresses that subtly highlighted the shape of the body before the pleated skirts flared out towards the bottom. In the daywear, jersey coats and suits, as soft as cardigans, featured padding and topstitching. They had fur around the wrists or collar, as did a fir-green suede calfskin cape. In the eveningwear, 'Sultana'-style floaty muslin dresses were – on closer inspection – revealed to be jumpsuits with voluminous trouser legs down to the ankles. Drawing inspiration from the work of Mariano Fortuny, Givenchy used pleated Bucol lamé fabric in a variety of colours to create sheath dresses that accentuated the wearer's figure.

Snakeskin, referred to as 'cobra', featured prominently throughout the entire collection – on jackets, belts and coats. It was often red and, when evening fell, shimmered with hints of gold, silver or platinum. Long evening coats were entirely covered in this scaly snakeskin, while strips of it also adorned the hems of capes and muslin dresses. It was the first time that Givenchy had used this kind of snakeskin in his collections, and it also appeared in print form, in a range of sizes and colours, on wool for daywear and crepe for eveningwear.

Some of the looser, more flowing designs were shown on 28 November 1973 at the Royal Opera in the Palace of Versailles, as part of the fashion show that later came to be known as the 'Battle of Versailles'. Givenchy took part in the event to raise money for the château's restoration, presenting his dresses alongside designs by four other Parisian couture houses, competing against five American designers.

A.S.

MEMORIES OF THE 1930S

Conscious of how nostalgia for the 1930s was influencing contemporary fashions, Hubert de Givenchy presented a collection full of references to that era. From jersey suits with generous trousers and garden-party dresses with large floral prints to floaty, diaphanous evening gowns, all the designs evoked the late interwar period in their silhouettes, their fabrics or their embellishments.

Pinstriped daywear outfits, sometimes paired with a fur scarf, evoked the clothes worn by gangsters, while graphic patterns appeared on wide-legged trousers made of floaty crepe, which were like beach pyjamas.

There was almost no embroidery, with Givenchy instead opting for textured surfaces, such as fine tulle with a pattern of raised dots, or tulle embellished with motifs outlined in thick thread. The layered prints that were now characteristic of the designer appeared once again, in the form of organza dresses with multicoloured floral motifs worn over a crepe base layer with the same pattern.

A.S.

THE RETRO LOOK CONTINUES

In his daywear, Hubert de Givenchy presented a number of leather designs, including a short tunic dress that was reminiscent of a djellaba. Made of burgundy suede calfskin, it was embellished with braid and paired with a matching hat and long soft leather boots (see right). English tweed made a notable appearance, emphasizing the return of capes as daywear, sometimes fused with a coat.

The 'retro' feel that harked back to the fashions of the 1930s (see p. 258) was more popular than ever. Drawing inspiration from Jeanne Lanvin, Givenchy covered the sleeves and skirts of his floaty dresses with tiered flounces of crepe, while crepe georgette designs with clever geometric cuts brought to mind the work of Madeleine Vionnet. Evening dresses with integrated capes left the back and shoulders bare, while lingerie was the inspiration for the lace insets on a black velvet dress, which built on the couturier's playful experiments with transparent fabrics. White satin outfits that boasted impressive fox-fur collars evoked the fashions of Hollywood's Golden Age.

Journalists commented on the return of short shirt dresses that were loose around the waist. Their bodices, inspired by 'peasant blouses', had generous raglan sleeves that were nipped in at the wrist. They were made of muslin printed with an ombré pattern in shades of almond green or orange. This technique was also used on two groups of floaty muslin evening dresses. In the first group, the transparent fabric was layered over a bright orange base covered with sequins in gradually shifting shades. The second group was adorned with South African ostrich feathers that had been sorted according to colour so that they formed an ombré pattern. Finally, exceptionally long tassels – hanging loose or twirling about – decorated hems, the long flared sleeves of dresses, or the edges of large triangular wraps made of crepe, inspired by Manila shawls.

A.S.

FLUIDITY AND THE RETURN OF EMBROIDERY

Hubert de Givenchy presented an understated, classic and charming collection for Spring/Summer 1975. He accentuated the waist of daywear dresses with insets and leather belts. He had experimented with featuring his logo on clothes since the late 1960s (see p. 220), and here he decorated the busts of his blouses with the letter G, on both daywear and loungewear designs.

Muslin and organza dominated the eveningwear collection. Knife pleats meant that the dresses were fitted around the waist and hips, then opened out to give the skirts greater volume. Givenchy moved away from 'retro' fashions that evoked the 1930s, although he retained the fluid feel. One striking characteristic of this collection was the kimono-style look of sleeves, which here were gathered at the top and draped down.

Large multicoloured floral prints provided the light, bright touch necessary for a summer collection. However, the couturier also developed more unexpected motifs, inspired by marbled paper, which he used on both daywear and eveningwear.

After avoiding embroidery for his last few collections, Givenchy reintroduced it in the form of reversed-out tulips, embroidered by Lesage, or flames around the waist and hem. The modest, angelic wedding dress that closed the show (see opposite, right) had large flared sleeves and was crowned with flowers in every colour.

Givenchy saw himself as a defender of traditional haute couture. Building on his previous collections, he defined a classic elegance that appealed to his loyal client base of more mature women, many of whom were – partly thanks to him – among the most elegant women in the world.

A.S.

TASSELS AND A SHEATH DRESS WITH SPLITS

In response to the changing times of the 1970s, Hubert de Givenchy presented women with clothes that were flexible, comfortable and easy to wear. In a nod to modernity, classic suits gave way to jersey outfits of all kinds. Both classic and iridescent jersey fabrics were used to create sweaters and dresses that highlighted the shape of the body without restricting it. Large poncho-like capes, fastened with poppers down the sides, served as waterproofs. Lined with Loden fabric, they were paired with jumpsuits that created a long, slim silhouette, which was the dominant look of the collection. The bust was often gathered with smocking down to the hips.

Soft scarf-like jersey headdresses wrapped around the head, hung down the back and flared out, sometimes embellished with silk tassels. Tassels were a common sight throughout the collection – at the ends of scarves, on the hems of long tunics, or entirely covering the skirts of evening gowns. Embroidery appeared again, on jackets covered with butterflies or as simple crosses on the hips, adorning the belt of an evening dress.

The highlight of the collection was a black silk jersey evening dress with splits all the way up the sides and on the sleeves, so that the skin showed through the criss-crossed braids of gold laminette embroidered by Lesage (see opposite, bottom right). Jerry Hall wore the dress for a photoshoot with Norman Parkinson at Versailles for British *Vogue*.

A.S.

MEMORIES OF NEW YORK AND HAMMAMET

Shortly before this collection debuted, Hubert de Givenchy told *Women's Wear Daily* how profoundly he had been influenced by the exhibition 'American Women of Style', curated by Diana Vreeland at the Metropolitan Museum of Art in New York. He mentioned an evening dress designed by Mainbocher, which dated to around 1945 and had been worn by Millicent Rogers, and said, 'My long, pleated skirts for evening are very reminiscent of this style.' In the same article, he spoke about designing tunics that were cut 'like long T-shirts'.

The daytime silhouettes were floaty, typically made up of a billowy top and a straight pleated skirt, with the hips marked by insets, or embroidery in eveningwear. The suits and outfits were not matching, but their contrasting fabrics and colours resonated with each other.

Inspired by a recent trip to the Tunisian town of Hammamet, the couturier opened his show with kaftans and djellabas. These references to Berber traditional dress were picked up elsewhere in the collection by turbans and generous hoods. This hood effect also featured on an evening dress worn underneath a loose coat (see opposite, left), an outfit that played with layering printed organza with navy blue, brown and white stripes, all created by Beauclère. Two other sheath dresses – one made of dyed jersey (see right), the other of embroidered blue crepe (see opposite, bottom right) – were worn with a simple sleeveless bolero with an ingenious cut that allowed it to drape over the head. For more relaxed evening looks, large capes were worn over brassieres and long skirts printed with delicate repeating floral motifs.

This refined, simple collection epitomized haute couture in the second half of the 1970s: elegant designs that catered to an exclusive clientele, rather than spectacular ground-breaking creations.

A.S.

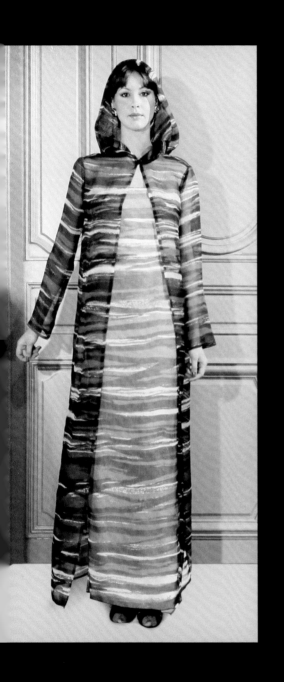

RUSSIAN COSTUMES

The catwalks of Paris were rife with dramatic
tension. The floaty, lightweight silhouettes of
the previous seasons were no more, replaced by
voluminous designs in a variety of lavish fabrics.

Hubert de Givenchy's silhouettes were inspired by
Russian folk styles. Large triangular fringed shawls
wrapped around the shoulders, while headscarves
covered the hair from morning to night, sometimes
worn under fur-rimmed hats. For daywear, large
coats made of woven leather or dyed wool were
paired with long boots. A number of short boleros,
some of which were sumptuously embroidered,
were worn over printed muslin blouses. The waist
was accentuated by long insets that started just
under the bust and reached the hips, or by belts
that were draped or trimmed with elaborate
passementerie edging.

This new direction, which was also evident in Yves
Saint Laurent's collection, may have been inspired
by the theme of the winter exhibition curated by
Diana Vreeland at the Costume Institute at the
Metropolitan Museum of Art in New York, which
was entitled 'The Glory of Russian Costume'.

Many designs featured tunics worn over long skirts,
some of which were embellished with long tassels.
Along with the ever-present velvet, generous skirts
made of taffeta – a fabric that had somewhat fallen
out of fashion since the 1950s – added a romantic
note that was appreciated by journalists. This lavish
collection contributed towards the international
press's renewed interest in the French haute
couture scene, which they recognized for its
innovation and creative experiments.

A.S.

'A LIGHT ... ULTRA-ROMANTIC COLLECTION ... WITH BRIGHT, CHEERFUL COLOURS'

The romanticism of the previous season (see p.268) found a new expression that was once again popular with the press. Short boleros, billowy sleeves and generous, diaphanous skirts sat alongside distinctive prints and floral motifs. Some of the day dresses, made of crêpe de chine, were printed with stripes of flame designs inspired by ikat, traditional textiles created on the island of Sumba in Indonesia.

The eveningwear featured low-cut necklines that left the shoulders bare and were adorned with small ruffles and flounces. Strips of passementerie trimming decorated the edges of coats and the hems of skirts, or formed a wide, supple, bodice-like belt that accentuated the waist. Lightweight silk gazar by Abraham (see p.184) made a noted comeback on more structured, printed dresses and skirts.

In a tribute to Spain and the Manila shawls worn by flamenco dancers, a red dress was embroidered all over with floral scroll patterns (see opposite, bottom left). Its skirt ended in very long braided silk tassels, which also appeared on the large shawl that accompanied it. Short boleros were adorned with silk thread tassels that looked as if they had been taken from a bullfighter's jacket. There was a certain bohemian feel to other eveningwear designs, which featured ornate belts decorated with dangling gold chains.

The audience gave the collection a resounding standing ovation. The press also praised the freshness of the fruity colours: apple green, tomato red, melon pink.

A.S.

LOOKING TO ASIA

While this collection built on the boleros, tunics of varying lengths, generous blouses and luxurious fabrics of the last few seasons, Hubert de Givenchy found a new source of inspiration in Asia. Jackets with mandarin collars were covered with scroll motifs inspired by the traditional patterns used on Chinese furniture. These complex pieces were made of suede with insets of Swakara astrakhan fur or Saga mink. Sometimes their wide sleeves were made of fox fur.

These repeating motifs were also printed on muslin wool for daywear and appeared in the form of embroidery on eveningwear designs. Slightly pointed hats once again evoked Chinese miniatures. Day dresses and coats had a narrow bust achieved with pleats that flared out from the waist to create a more generous skirt. Responding to contemporary trends, Givenchy presented a series of culotte-dresses. These were very popular in ready-to-wear fashions, and Givenchy's designs were made of printed muslin wool and worn with long dark leather boots.

Just as the two designers' Autumn/Winter 1976–1977 collections had both been inspired by Russia (see p. 268), once again Yves Saint Laurent's collection had a similar theme, with an Asian influence. This caused some speculation as to which designer had first had the idea. When asked about this, Givenchy replied that the couturiers both used the same fabric suppliers, who offered lavish fabrics with a similar aesthetic to every couture house, and this was reflected in their collections.

A.S.

'THE RETURN OF A CLASSIC APPROACH WITH VERY SIMPLE SHAPES AND FABRICS'

After the relative exuberance of the last few seasons, this show had a more subdued feel. The simplicity of the designs encapsulated Hubert de Givenchy's constant search for refinement.

The soft, floaty silhouettes were enhanced by sophisticated details. Fastenings were often replaced by elaborate passementerie braids with fringed tassels, which appeared on hats too. Braid also decorated edges and hems, while the intricacy of surprising topstitched embellishments was only fully appreciated by true experts. The generous sleeves of a printed muslin evening coat with a pattern of satin rectangles, as lavish as any 19th-century design, were decorated with knots of braid on the arm. Inspired by ready-to-wear fashions, the coats had structured shoulders, hinting at the broad-shouldered silhouette that would come to dominate the next decade.

Printed organza evening dresses flared out in tiered bands of cloqué fabric. The ruching around the necklines built on the romantic silhouettes of previous seasons. Long sheath dresses made of muslin, crepe or jersey, with simple, refined silhouettes, were embellished with sections of mesh fabric that let the skin show through, and sometimes worn under large capes. One of them (see opposite, right), in royal blue muslin, was short at the front and long at the back, embroidered with gold stars.

A.S.

'AN ULTRA-SOPHISTICATED COLLECTION'

This collection pointed towards fashions of the 1980s, featuring designs for the 'female senior executives' that American studies had recently predicted would begin to appear, and who, according to Nathalie Mont-Servan in *Le Monde*, would have to 'wear plain, neutral suits in order to be taken seriously'. Hubert de Givenchy rose to the challenge, opening his collection with a series of suits with clean silhouettes that emphasized the shoulders, minimized the bust and created narrow hips.

Large 'blade-like' feathers sliced day hats in two, or stood upright on evening hats. Plumes were also used to embellish belts or accentuate the shoulders. Sable muffs, impressive fox-fur coats, and broad lynx collars and hems inspired by Hollywood icons of the 1940s created exaggerated silhouettes, as did an impressive fur hat struck through with a rhinestone feather (see opposite, top left).

A short cape made of black fox fur had the heads still intact, with the eyes embellished with rhinestones (see opposite, top right). This was worn over a fishtail dress with a bust made entirely of tulle dotted with crystals (see right). It bordered on indecent, leaving the breasts almost bare, with only the nipples covered by velvet stars. Many of the designs featured seductive transparent sections like this. The most extreme example was a velvet sheath dress with asymmetrical cut-outs that revealed half of the body (see opposite, bottom right). It was later adapted to be worn by Audrey Hepburn in Terence Young's 1979 film *Bloodline*. The eveningwear featured voluminous satin tulip skirts, many of which had thigh slits and revealed underwear with rhinestone designs.

Recalling 'the years of true haute couture', the show was awarded a Golden Thimble, a prize created in 1976 to celebrate the best collection in Paris.

A.S.

'LOVE' PRINTS
AND TROMPE-L'ŒIL
RIBBONS

This new collection, heavily influenced by
the fashions of the 1940s, was the height of
sophistication. The broad-shouldered silhouette
of the plain suits was exaggerated by pleats at the
shoulders and strap seams. The nipped-in waist
was accentuated by short bodices with rounded
hips. The skirts were straight-cut, sometimes
even gently nipped in at the hem.

These clean lines were softened by multicoloured
designs, with the word 'Love' printed on beachwear
and daywear. Other motifs included lily of the valley,
clouds and doves that looked as if they had been
painted by hand.

The collection also featured a number of trompe-
l'œil printed motifs. The exclusive bow and ribbon
prints on some daywear outfits referenced the
motifs that had made Elsa Schiaparelli's name
in 1927, but it was after dark that these features
truly came into their own. In the eveningwear,
large ribbons, tied into bows or loosely draped,
decorated the bust like a tie, or nipped in the skirts
of extravagant colourful designs. Sometimes they
encircled the hips, held in place by chains, which
were also used to secure another dress that was
constructed from draped swathes of muslin.

The legendary photographer Cecil Beaton was
invited to view the show, which he described
in *The New York Times* as 'delicious, great taste,
good fun'. Hubert de Givenchy was playing his part
in the inventive revival of Parisian haute couture,
stimulated by the burgeoning creativity of new
ready-to-wear designers who would come to
dominate the 1980s.

A.S.

ODE TO
BLACK WOMEN

For this show, Hubert de Givenchy chose to use almost exclusively Black models. He presented a dramatic collection, both in terms of the voluminous silhouettes and the motifs used. Across both daywear and eveningwear, the dominant silhouette was starkly geometrical, with square shoulders, leg-of-mutton sleeves that were nipped in at the wrists, and long bodices that flared into a triangle shape over a narrow skirt.

Black velvet reigned supreme across the collection. It was used to make dresses with long trains and puffy fabric or bustles around the hips. Jackets were made of quilted lamé Lurex with pink, gold and black stripes, while the eveningwear featured scarves draped around the body in criss-cross shapes to accentuate the hips.

Feather motifs were everywhere. The daywear featured pheasant feathers printed on crepe. In the eveningwear, a large, exaggerated ostrich feather had an almost threatening feel. Printed in acid pink or green on a black background, its outline was reminiscent of photograms, and it covered the designs almost completely.

The trompe-l'œil prints harked back to Hubert de Givenchy's early collections. A delicate repeating pattern of fox heads (see opposite, right) echoed the cat heads of the Autumn/Winter 1952–1953 collection (see p.34). Fur stoles were once again a prominent feature, wrapped around the neck or appearing in the form of a stylized print on eveningwear.

Among these animal motifs, one design featured an embroidered blue lamé tiger that wrapped around a sheath dress, its jaws poised under the model's throat (see right). Lips in gold lamé on the leg-of-mutton sleeves of another dress gave a softer feel to the end of the show.

A.S.

GRAPHIC BY DAY, FLORAL BY NIGHT

The daywear for this collection featured suits with graphic black-and-white effects: pinstripes, lapels trimmed with braid, pocket flaps. Once again playing with the 'photo negative' effect (see p.248), Hubert de Givenchy added white pocket flaps to a black coat, then reversed the colours on the white dress worn underneath, which had black pocket flaps. Jackets had lapels in colours that matched their blouses or bustiers, while the designs were topped off with lacquered straw boaters. Optical illusions achieved through diagonal stripes with ingenious cuts appeared on a number of day dresses and were repeated in embroidery form on 'geometric' fishtail evening dresses.

Taking up the classic theme of the 'flower woman' once again (see p.252), Givenchy used a range of impressive motifs that drew on many different flowers: roses, carnations, poppies, sunflowers, tulips, pansies. Whether stylized or realistic, printed or embroidered, they provided an explosion of colour on both day and evening dresses. Some were delicate repeating patterns, while others were large single flowers 'in the style of Rousseau'. The flowers appeared on pleated organza evening gowns, dresses with asymmetrical collars and only one sleeve, and 'anemone' dresses with asymmetrical 'petal' skirts.

Givenchy presented a classic collection that captivated his most loyal clients.

A.S.

REFERENCES TO THE RENAISSANCE AND TO MARIANO FORTUNY

This collection opened with a group of 'schoolgirl' frock coats with fitted busts, raised sleeve caps, exaggerated hips and flared skirts. These were followed by culotte-dresses with inset dickeys bordered by ruffles. Suits once again featured padded shoulders. Daywear suits were plain, while those designed to be worn at cocktail hour were made of black velvet.

The collection built towards the spectacular eveningwear designs. This season, Hubert de Givenchy drew inspiration from the silhouettes and fabrics of the Italian Renaissance to create floaty dresses with doublet-style bodices, made of black velvet or embellished lamé cloqué fabric. They had puffy sleeves and flared skirts made of figured lamé, while the low neckline was bordered with ruffled frills or strips of fur – mink and sable – which echoed the clothes worn in 15th-century paintings.

However, it was the dresses inspired by the work of Mariano Fortuny that were the 'jewels of the collection', according to the press release. These were a group of sheath dresses that reimagined the Venetian designer's signature pleats in panne velvet that was printed, crinkled or embossed with cut-out patterns. The motifs created by Fortuny, who had himself been inspired by the notion of Oriental luxury prevalent in Renaissance-era Venice, appeared on both daywear and eveningwear. Arabesques and scroll motifs were printed on loose muslin jackets embellished with gold or silver beads, while trees – a motif that recurred throughout the Venetian designer's work – were embroidered on the front of bodices.

High ruffs framed the face, while taffeta dresses in shifting shades of gold or bronze, which looked as if they had acquired a patina over time, boasted generous skirts embellished with appliqué.

A.S.

'HOMAGE TO AMERICA'

Hubert de Givenchy abandoned the luxurious feel and complexity of his previous collections, instead embracing a new kind of simplicity. He broke with tradition in naming this collection 'Homage to America', in tribute to 'the America of Broadway musicals … of youth, of dynamism, of a certain renewal'.

The collection was full of soft fabrics that did not restrict the body in any way. The designs were billowy, embellished with bow collars, ties and scarves. This collection also saw the return of the shirt dress, with a straight cut that didn't accentuate the waist, as well as the return of trouser suits.

The collection stood out through its use of prints that had been created especially for Givenchy. Although they included stylized flowers and irregular stripes, these gave way to animal prints that dominated both daywear and eveningwear. The couturier's prints evoked a true menagerie of animals – zebra, leopard, Dalmatian, tortoise and giraffe – all in black and white. This contrasting colour combination dominated the collection, especially the 'cocktail pyjamas' that made their first appearance here (see opposite, top), catering to the needs of the jet set who, although they were a symbol of the decade, were beginning to see the end of their glory days.

In the eveningwear, these prints accentuated the female body in fishtail dresses made of bias-cut satin, faille or silk gazar, often with asymmetrical necklines. Embroidery was more discreet, building on the animal motifs, while garden-party dresses were embellished all over with flounces and ruffles.

A.S.

THE FIRST COLLECTION AT THE GRAND HÔTEL

For the first time in his career, Hubert de Givenchy ventured out from his own premises, instead holding his show in the lavish auditorium of the Salon Opéra at the Grand Hôtel. Inspired by his surroundings, the couturier's designs took on a more lavish feel.

Described by Nathalie Mont-Servan in *Le Monde* as a true 'firework', the eveningwear was organized into two main themes. The first was a romantic style that evoked the silhouettes of the female characters in Marcel Proust's *In Search of Lost Time*. The generous, rustling skirts made of shimmering bronze taffeta featured swathes of draped fabric, apron-style effects or black velvet trains edged with flounces, while the impressive leg-of-mutton sleeves faithfully evoked the fashions of the late 19th century.

The second theme running through the collection was once again inspired by Asia (see p. 272). Lamé tunics covered in gold piping motifs inspired by Chinese marquetry were inset with generous velvet dickeys and worn over a black velvet sheath dress. The jackets – all embellished with gold – were worn with loose trousers, while the sumptuous evening gowns featured geometric patterns in shades of copper and bronze. Often appearing as details, mink was also used to create a jacket with a mandarin collar fastened with passementerie frogging; its lamé sleeves were embellished with leaf designs in fur.

Celebrated by the press, Givenchy's creations 'represented the kind of grandeur that haute couture stands for and, as soon as the bride appeared (in a square neckline dress with white mink at the wrists and the hem), bravos erupted from the audience. They were deserved,' as Bernadine Morris wrote in *The New York Times*.

A.S.

'THIRTY YEARS OF COUTURE'

To celebrate the thirtieth anniversary of his couture house, Hubert de Givenchy dedicated his collection to Audrey Hepburn. The show pointed forward to the retrospective of Givenchy's work that was to take place at the Fashion Institute of Technology in New York, picked up on the historical themes of his previous collection (see p.294) and presented new interpretations of his most famous silhouettes.

Givenchy presented printed muslin shirt dresses, in a nod to the designs that he and Balenciaga had debuted in 1957, which did not accentuate the waist and therefore did away with the need for a corset (see p.98). A strip of fabric around the knees nipped the skirt in and created a slightly tapered silhouette. Embodying a greater sense of freedom, Givenchy also presented a series of suits featuring turned-up Bermuda shorts with thin stripes.

One version of the shirt dress, which Bernadine Morris described in *The New York Times* as 'the youngest and the most contemporary', featured a bubble silhouette. The generous fabric was draped around the bust and sometimes nipped in at the hips by an embroidered inset. Made of floaty muslin or organza, these bubble skirts were voluminous at the front, as seen on a bright pink patterned evening gown made of gauzy organza.

The cocktail dresses were reminiscent of those worn by Audrey Hepburn in her most famous films. They were short, with narrow busts and puffy skirts. The cotton blouses of Givenchy's first collection (see p.26) were reinterpreted in the form of 'the new elevated blouse', embroidered all over with flowers and Oriental-inspired motifs.

The evening dresses were tight-fitting, accentuating the wearer's figure. Flounces were gathered into puffs and bustles at the back to create dramatic silhouettes. Sometimes the voluminous fabric was secured on one shoulder or on one hip, giving the silhouette asymmetrical flounces.

A.S.

WINTER SPLENDOUR

The simplicity of summer was complemented by
the opulence of the winter collection, following
a new custom adopted by Hubert de Givenchy.

Inspired by the shirt dresses that had made
a triumphant return in the previous season's
collection (see p. 296), the couturier added tiered
flounces onto his jackets and coats in order to give
them greater volume. He gave leather an haute
couture twist in the form of smart coats entirely
covered in gold.

When it came to cocktail hour, jackets made of
black velvet – his favourite material – were worn
with striped taffeta skirts in iridescent colours,
creating a stark contrast. The cocktail dresses
were almost all made of black velvet and featured
puffy skirts. Their leg-of-mutton sleeves were
sumptuously embellished with feathers or appliqué
motifs with kiss-curl edges. One of these designs,
in broderie anglaise, was made up of small hearts
in two different shades.

Velvet, embellished with a range of printed gold
motifs inspired by Mariano Fortuny, was used to
create sheath dresses with wide shoulder pads
adorned with heron feathers. These feathers
featured prominently on the shoulders of cocktail
coats and on grand evening gowns. Sometimes they
were used to accentuate the seams of embellished
bodices. The skirts were flared or puffy, with
swathes of taffeta secured by black ribbons.

A.S.

'A REAL SUMMER COLLECTION'

The new season's collection prominently featured
a range of prints freely inspired by the paintings of
Henri Matisse and Raoul Dufy, with their colourful
palettes of soft, radiant, sunny shades. Stylized
plants and flowers – such as palm trees, a reference
to Dufy – appeared on short dresses, which drew
on fashions popular during the Occupation. This
inspiration also came through in the square or
sweetheart necklines, as well as the narrow waists
counterbalanced by broader shoulders, creating a
V-shaped bodice.

This season, sleeves were bigger than ever before.
Sleeve caps were raised. Short, puffy sleeves were
nipped in above the elbow or blossomed into wide
petal-like shapes. All of these designs accentuated
the fashionable wide-shouldered silhouette. One
dress, in particular, was inspired by Matisse's
painting *The Romanian Blouse* (1940), represented
by three different versions (see right, for example);
the designs on the blouse were precisely copied
and printed in the correct proportions for the dress.

The grand evening gowns were also belted.
A number of them took up the prints inspired by
the two painters, or were embellished with intricate
embroidery in floral or stylized motifs. Flamenco-
style dresses with long trains boasted flared
skirts that were covered all over with petals
or wide flounces that quivered with each step
the wearer took.

Like his contemporaries, in this collection Hubert
de Givenchy was developing and reinterpreting
his most successful silhouettes and motifs from
the past. He left the experimenting to the ready-
to-wear designers.

A.S.

FOR THE TRAVELLERS

Perhaps inspired by his recent trip to Japan, where he presented his new collections alongside older designs from his archive, Hubert de Givenchy dedicated this collection to women who travel.

In the daywear, trouser suits took the place of skirts, often paired with a tall fur hat. Generous, floaty shirt dresses appeared again, even as cocktail dresses. One of them, made of black velvet, had a cut-out front with a large embellished muslin rosette that allowed the stomach to show through the material. The broad shoulders of suits and dresses were accentuated by adding insets of embroidery or fur.

Once again, the couturier embraced graphic effects. The bodices of cocktail dresses were divided into asymmetrical pieces of black velvet and bias-cut white satin in a wrap-over style. The eveningwear consisted of sheath dresses, which Givenchy said were more practical for travelling. These also had a graphic feel. One was embellished all over with sequins that looked like raindrops tracing vertical lines as they fell (see opposite, bottom left). Other velvet dresses were embellished with large dragonflies on one hip or large winged insects on a background of stylized sunray patterns reminiscent of Art Deco motifs. A short cape was made of pieces of black and white mink arranged in a sunray pattern.

However, the couturier did not completely abandon more voluminous designs, which he explored in the form of a long dress embellished with ruffles of sequinned tulle on the shoulders and hem (see opposite, right). A number of dresses had flared skirts made of taffeta that changed colour as it caught the light, which contrasted with the fitted bodices that were embroidered all over.

A.S.

A TRIBUTE TO MIRÓ AND 'MOSAIC' PATTERNS

Still embracing the shirt-dress silhouette of previous seasons, day dresses billowed out at the back. While navy blue was the dominant colour for the daywear, the collection's high point was the evening dresses.

This season saw Hubert de Givenchy once again working with Andrée Brossin de Méré, with whom he had first collaborated in the 1950s (see p.34). He commissioned a series of guipure lace designs from her, which Givenchy described as 'flower paintings', and used them on sheath dresses that were nipped in at the waist and knees in a style comparable with his earliest collections. These dresses were worn underneath generous, dramatic coats decorated with warp-printed motifs made up of large turquoise or golden-yellow spots created by the master weaver Abraham. Like the giraffe-print dress, these motifs also came outlined in black. Warp-printed motifs in golden yellow, blue or red on a white background additionally featured on evening dresses with detailed shoulders, a fitted bodice and skirts in the shape of upturned tulips.

Some of the designs paid tribute once again to the work of the artist Joan Miró (see p.240), in the form of satin with a speckled print designed to look like paint had dripped onto the fabric.

Mosaic-style embroidery embellished the bodices of evening gowns. Other embroidery motifs inspired by Hindu art were commissioned from Jakob Schlaepfer. India was also the inspiration for two asymmetrical dresses made of figured organza – one in blue, the other in bright pink (see opposite, top right) – which were draped around the body like saris.

A.S.

YSATIS

'Soft' and 'billowy' were the watchwords of this collection, which consisted of 150 looks. Classic masculine coats contrasted with furs created by Revillon in bold colours, from fuchsia and tangerine to jade green.

The dresses had a billowy feel due to their kimono sleeves, which had no seam. Once again, velvet reigned supreme, on both smart daywear and eveningwear. Hubert de Givenchy used it as a base fabric, setting it against richer fabrics, either in contrasting colours or with different textures in shades of the same colour. In one example, a black velvet cocktail dress featured strips of black smocked taffeta along the sides of the bodice and sleeves, and was embellished with a huge taffeta bow worn as a tie.

Short capes abounded, bristling with feathers or adorned with velvet lacework in leaf motifs. These were followed by generous draped boleros with batwing sleeves in multicoloured satin with stripes of velvet, or in velvet with gold lamé edging.

In a nod to the early days of his career, Givenchy worked some of the details that had first made his name into this collection. Large satin ribbons threaded through the skirts and were tied at the back. In a surprising inclusion that had rarely been seen since the 1970s, the backs of jackets were heavily embroidered, while dresses had low necklines and were sometimes edged with beaded tassels.

In the show's programme, Givenchy revealed that the collection had been inspired by his new perfume, Ysatis. He closed the show with a series of models, each carrying an oversized version of the perfume bottle perched on a velvet cushion. They wore luxurious long coats printed with palmette motifs in green and red, the signature colours of the fragrance.

A.S.

EXPERT EMBROIDERY AND BOUQUETS OF FLOWERS

Hubert de Givenchy presented a classic summer collection. The T-shaped silhouette emphasized broad shoulders and a narrow body, not accentuating the waist or hips.

Many outfits featured trousers, often worn with a short jacket and bustier. The bustier was often made of guipure lace, a fabric that featured prominently throughout the collection. It also appeared on evening dresses, embellished with ceramic beads, raffia, jet or coral.

There was a particular emphasis on cocktail dresses. These were soft and generous, cut like shirts or featuring belts fastened at the side. They had a range of printed motifs, from giant flowers to 'primitivist', graphic, simplified or stylized motifs created by Beauclère and printed on silk gazar. Dresses embellished with three-dimensional flowers in multicoloured guipure lace, inspired by Impressionist paintings, were shown alongside outfits with black and white stripes.

Evening coats made of silk gazar or warp-printed faille were worn with dresses embellished all over with paisley palmette motifs or black and white triangle patterns created by Lesage, Montex or Vermont. Even the journalists who were most familiar with the couturier's style acknowledged how exceptional these were.

As was traditional, the show ended with the wedding outfit (see opposite, bottom right). The bride wore a guipure lace ensemble embellished with delicate sprigs of lily of the valley, as well as a fascinator boasting a bouquet of these flowers, which had been a good luck charm for Hubert de Givenchy since 1953.

A.S.

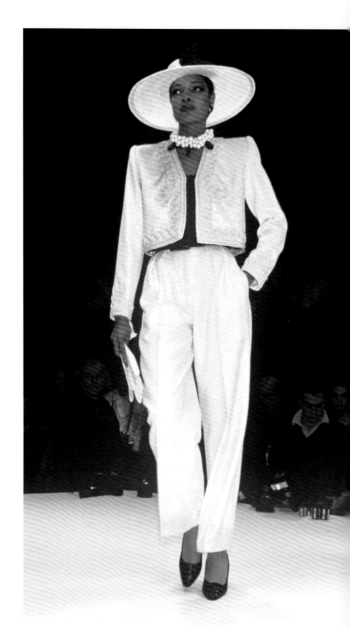

'ALL-PURPOSE' DAYWEAR AND A TRIBUTE TO MARLENE DIETRICH

Wool jersey was everywhere, on both daywear and eveningwear. Hubert de Givenchy described it as an 'up-to-date, young, sexy, skintight' fabric and used it to create short black dresses with contrasting geometric insets. Hood effects appeared on many daywear designs, and even on the 'sweater dresses' intended as eveningwear. These fishtail dresses revealed the influence of the latest contemporary designers, such as Azzedine Alaïa and Claude Montana. Givenchy was closely following developments in the fashion world, adopting trends and putting his own stamp on them.

This hood effect also appeared on coats described as 'all-purpose', which had large collars that covered the shoulders and formed a huge round hood that hung down the back like a cape. These coats were made of blue wool for daytime and black velvet for eveningwear, or from fur supplied by Revillon.

There was a renewed focus on cocktail dresses. Made of silk brocade or figured silk, they were wrapped tightly around the body, with the end of the fabric left trailing free from waist level, tied into large bows or secured by ornate belt buckles.

Tight-fitting evening dresses were made of leopard-print velvet panne. More voluminous evening gowns were embellished with a patchwork design of taffeta and satin created by Andrée Brossin de Méré, which evoked the facets of precious gemstones. Another dress, made of black tulle covered with multicoloured satin appliqué motifs in the shape of arrows and arabesques embellished with jet beads (see opposite, right), was later worn by Audrey Hepburn when she received a Fashion Oscar at the Palais Garnier on 24 October 1985 to acknowledge her faithful support of the house of Givenchy.

Finally, inspired by Marlene Dietrich, a grand evening gown swathed the body in a drape of blue muslin (see right), its generous kimono sleeves forming a cape that wafted in the model's wake.

A.S.

A TRIBUTE TO DIANA VREELAND AND THE 'INDIAN MOOD'

'Just as authors include dedications in their books,' Hubert de Givenchy announced in a public statement, 'I think that every collection should be dedicated to someone the designer likes or admires… I will dedicate this one to Mrs Vreeland, not only because of who she is, but also because of her passion for the world of fashion (contemporary fashions, but also the fashions of the past, of other countries, fashions that play with nature, climates, colours…).'

Throughout the eveningwear designs in this collection, the couturier paid tribute to Diana Vreeland, the former editor-in-chief of *Vogue* magazine, and celebrated the success of her exhibition 'India!' at the Costume Institute at the Metropolitan Museum of Art in New York.

The first trouser suits featured embellished jackets with a brightly coloured crepe georgette scarf draped over the top and wafting behind. Sometimes the scarf was an extension of the draped material that formed the bustier worn underneath. Swathes of lamé crossed over the bust, while Givenchy also made use of unexpected colour combinations. The bodices of dresses wrapped around the bust, with a length of fabric left trailing at the back. Directly inspired by saris, these designs were examples of an important influence that the couturier referred to as the 'Indian Mood'.

Many of the designs featured embroidered palmette motifs, while Andrée Brossin de Méré also used large palmette shapes appliquéd onto patchwork designs in iridescent lamé. Cut-outs revealed the skin and were the inspiration for capes that left the shoulders bare.

While the models, most of whom were Black, walked the catwalk in absolute silence as usual, Bernadine Morris reported in *The New York Times* that '[t]he collection was greeted with thunderous applause and the first bravos of almost a week of showings'.

A.S.

REPTILES AND CHAINS

Hubert de Givenchy was heavily inspired by reptiles, which showed through in the form of snakeskin and lizard prints on a red or green background, used on dresses that gently hugged the body. Real lizard skin and water snakeskin were used on accessories, boots and belts, but also on trousers and jackets with padded shoulders, made of patent black cobra snakeskin.

Once again, cocktail dresses in figured taffeta and velvet dominated the collection. These short dresses were loosely draped and secured by a belt at the waist. Cape effects were common on frock coats made of grey serge, and also appeared on a black velvet evening gown with a large white satin skirt with gold polka dots. Lavishly embroidered cardigan-like jackets were worn over soft satin sheath dresses. The collection also featured puffy velvet and satin dotted with jet beads or gemstones, on pink boleros and dresses with balloon sleeves.

Many of the dresses had bodices made of transparent fabric that allowed pieces of fur, intricately embellished with leather and gold or bronze lamé, to show through. The show closed with a series of princess dresses. These had simple lines but were made from sophisticated fabrics such as double-faced satin, and they often featured plunging backs. Finally, necklines were embellished with wide, flat-link chains, some of which were studded with rhinestones. Chains also appeared in the form of velvet appliqué motifs on a cocktail skirt made of tulle with a delicate pattern of raised dots.

A.S.

'1987 = HAPPINESS'

Drawing inspiration from contemporary fashions and the creations of ready-to-wear designers, the daywear in this collection was unexpectedly edgy. Gold and silver oval rivets accentuated the seams and edges of jersey dresses, coats, and narrow suits made of brown or green patent lambskin.

The day dresses and cocktail dresses featured classic prints with springtime themes such as butterflies, birds and flowers. However, the supple draped leather belts that Hubert de Givenchy had favoured since the late 1950s also made a notable comeback.

The collection did not feature many trousers, and these were limited to evening outfits in rich Lurex brocade. The eveningwear was unusually varied and paid tribute to all the Parisian craftspeople who created exceptional embroidery and fabrics. Givenchy's admiration for these artisans shone through in the ceramic bead embellishments on jackets and the bodices of dresses, some of which combined animal hide with organdie or faille.

Broad multicoloured stripes printed on silk gazar by Abraham featured on suits and strapless sheath dresses, which were fastened with buttons down the back, but also on evening coats, which made a reappearance after being absent for several seasons, now worn over low-cut dresses. These dresses were often strapless fishtail designs made of silk gazar in a single colour. One of them, however (see opposite, bottom right), was part-orange and part-black, and decorated with large bows around the neckline, which were a common feature throughout the collection.

For the first time, the show was set to music, and Givenchy closed the presentation with two wedding dresses, one in pink, the other white.

A.S.

'HOMAGE TO CHRISTIAN BÉRARD'

Inspired by a recently published monograph by Boris Kochno, this collection paid tribute to Christian Bérard, nicknamed 'Bébé', thanks to whom a young Hubert de Givenchy was employed at the very beginning of his career by fashion designer Robert Piguet.

Taking inspiration from Bérard's drawings, the backdrop to the catwalk show was decorated with a repeating pattern of faces painted on a pink background, a design that was echoed on the programme. This tribute to the artist, who was associated with the Surrealist movement, also came through in the aesthetic of the couture designs. Prints made up of large diamonds in purple and red inspired by the commedia dell'arte, tall suede Turkish-style chechia hats, sculpted velvet headpieces and certain motifs such as twisting vines recalled the work of Elsa Schiaparelli.

The names given to colours used in the collection also evoked the major figures and works in the literary and artistic movement: 'Bébé pink', 'Beauty and the Beast black' (named for Jean Cocteau's 1946 film), 'Marie-Laure purple' (in memory of Marie-Laure de Noailles, a friend and patron of the Surrealists).

But Bérard's drawings were the main inspiration for the prints and embellishments. Repeating patterns of faces, vignettes, bows and shining suns, with painted outlines in India ink, all evoked the artist's illustrations for *Vogue* from the 1930s onwards.

Cocktail dresses made way for extravagance in the form of sumptuous fabrics. The evening dresses were often short and had longer pieces of fabric trailing at the back, creating a sense of movement that was echoed in the large petal-like collars.

A.S.

'BODY LINE'

'Givenchy is a traditionalist who varies his look just enough to keep in step with the times but not enough to make any woman feel uncomfortable,' Bernadine Morris wrote in *The New York Times* after viewing his collection.

Dubbed 'Body Line', the dominant silhouette in the collection was narrow and tight-fitting. The colours of the dresses, most of which were short, matched the stockings. Day dresses had buttons down the front, like close-fitting cardigans, and their edges were accentuated with braid in contrasting colours.

Leather was once again a common feature on daywear. Short dresses made of dipped lambskin were fastened down the front with buttons or laces with gold metal eyelets. Suits with padded shoulders also made a comeback.

The eveningwear featured a number of embellishments, from ceramic beads to passementerie and sequins. The influence of Christian Lacroix, who had presented his first collection the previous season, was clearly felt in the pairings of patterns, such as polka dots and stripes, and in certain designs that featured voluminous fabric around the shoulders.

The simple cocktail dresses boasted a number of luxurious prints, which also appeared on the evening gowns. The designs were covered with 'a garden of flowers', as the couturier described it. Sweet peas, anemones, lilacs, poppies or wisteria – whether miniature or enlarged, blurred by warp printing or sharp and stylized – made up huge bouquets of three-dimensional embroidery. Even the very short wedding dress (see opposite, bottom right) was entirely covered in sprigs of lily of the valley, which also appeared on the accompanying headpiece.

A.S.

MEMORIES OF ELSA SCHIAPARELLI

Hubert de Givenchy closed the week of fashion shows with a stunning collection dominated by bold colour combinations that were heightened by shimmering satin.

The colour palette was clear from the very first designs. A suede leather coat in electric blue was embellished with tassels and worn over a comfortable day dress in dark red wool jersey (see opposite, top left). The supple leather belts that had featured in many of Givenchy's recent collections became stiffer and wider here, covering the waist completely.

Elsa Schiaparelli's influence was clear in the velvet chechia hats and conical draped satin turbans. The trompe-l'œil that the Italian couturier would have embraced also appeared in the form of a bolero dress in dark purple velvet with a shocking-pink satin dickey, its edges highlighted by ruffles (see opposite, bottom left).

A number of fitted dresses with padded shoulders also testified to the influence of fashions from the late 1940s. These dresses were buttoned down the front and the fabric was tightly wrapped around the hips, while scroll motifs were embroidered on the jackets of a number of evening suits.

Givenchy embellished the front of brightly coloured satin cocktail dresses with black or dark blue velvet dickeys in abstract shapes with scalloped edges. These unexpected colour combinations reached their high point in a series of draped dresses that combined bright green with shocking pink and an intense shade of blue.

Bustiers were a prominent feature. These often had plunge necklines, formed an integral part of the sheath dresses, and were embellished all over with sequins. One was worn under a dramatic cape-coat in dark purple reversible satin. Finally, the dickey trend culminated in a series of satin heart shapes appliquéd and embroidered onto the bodices of smart dresses, and the dickey on the wedding dress.

A.S.

'HOMAGE TO PARIS'

Hubert de Givenchy dedicated his collection
to the French capital city, and 'to her beauty,
to her women, to her artists, to her elegance'.

The show opened with a number of bold suits
made of black leather. They featured wraparound
skirts and their edges were trimmed with electric
blue or red leather. One jacket, worn with trousers,
was covered with white stripes. A series of more
pared-back suits featured diagonal pocket flaps
with gold buttons. Elsewhere, Givenchy spelled
out his name in metal on a leather jacket (see
opposite, top right) and suit.

Once again, the couturier was inspired by animals,
with giant tortoiseshell scales appearing as large
prints or sometimes in the form of patchwork.
These were also the source for the complex
embellishments on bodices and boleros which,
combining mother-of-pearl and ceramic beads,
were reminiscent of 'nymph shrines', artificial
caves with baroque decorations inspired by
nature, often built around a spring or fountain.

The collection had a romantic feel, which was
heightened by the music that accompanied the
show. The models wore floaty muslin dresses, in a
single colour or with large flower prints, the fabric
wafting behind them as they walked. In another
highlight of the collection, Givenchy adorned his
creations with butterflies, printed or skilfully
embellished with pearls, gold and sequins.
A three-dimensional butterfly (see opposite,
bottom right) covered the entire bodice of one
muslin evening dress in an intense shade of blue.

A.S.

NATURAL-FEELING DRAPED SILHOUETTES

Classic suits – always with padded shoulders, and often with belts – were worn under capes, which were a prominent feature throughout this collection. Daywear capes were made of suede or wool, smarter capes of angora, and eveningwear capes of rich brocade, lamé or charmeuse.

Buttons were an important feature on many outfits: discreet but beautiful buttons on the wrists of jackets, and larger enamel buttons on eveningwear. Elsewhere, they were used to secure the diaphanous dresses that were the stars of the collection. These were draped around the body in a natural-feeling way, barely skimming it. Made of a single piece of fabric, they formed floaty capes at the back.

Long silk tassels adorned the splits of wraparound dresses and covered the seams of sleeves, while highlighting a sense of movement. In one eveningwear outfit, paired with a modest suit jacket, they also formed a skirt that allowed the legs to show through as the model walked.

Sumptuous embroidery covered boleros or insets of chenille, velvet, passementerie or beads. Sometimes it was used to embellish the edges of long jackets that reached all the way to the floor, with a palm-tree design that evoked the lavish embroidered clothing worn by men in the 18th century. Broad belts nipped in the waists of evening dresses with wide sable-trimmed necklines that left the shoulders bare.

A.S.

'HOMAGE TO MARLENE DIETRICH'

Hubert de Givenchy dedicated this collection to Marlene Dietrich, who had been a friend of his since the 1950s. Her song 'Johnny' opened the show, while the many wide-brimmed hats that featured in the collection were a nod to the actress and singer, who had retired to lead a quiet life in Paris.

The first outfit was an allusion to the Bettina blouse that, paired with a tobacco-brown skirt, had made Givenchy's name in 1952 (see p. 26). Thirty-eight years later, the ivory blouse in this collection was made of linen rather than cotton, and it was worn with a pair of leather shorts instead of a skirt, showing the extent to which the couturier had been influenced by sportswear (see right). The outfit was completed by a belt and a boater.

The square-shouldered silhouette persisted in the refined suits made of light-coloured gabardine with gold buttons. These buttons also appeared in diagonal lines on black or mahogany linen dresses.

Large floral prints on brightly coloured backgrounds evoked the gardens at Giverny in springtime and paintings by Monet. Poppies, daffodils, irises and lily of the valley covered smart dresses. Cocktail dresses and evening gowns featured large petal-like collars that framed the face. These dresses were all asymmetrical, often with diagonal hems. The draped fabric was secured on one hip with large bows, while lengths of faille wrapped around the chest and came together at the back in a huge puff of fabric.

The floral motifs gave way to foiled lamé jersey dresses with wide, shiny, metallic belts. A white crepe sheath dress had splits along the sides, with criss-crossed strips of fabric trimmed with gold.

Finally, the super-short wedding dress (see opposite, bottom right) was covered all over with an array of pastel-coloured flowers created by Lemarié, and secured at the waist by a simple pink satin ribbon.

A.S.

'A TRIBUTE TO QUALITY AND LUXURY'

Hubert de Givenchy wanted to acknowledge all the people who worked behind the scenes in the haute couture world in Paris. Firstly, he thanked his ateliers and his couture *premières*, including Gilberte Thomassin, who had been with him since leaving Balenciaga and who was now retiring. He also celebrated the fabric suppliers, featuring a luxurious range of brocade, gauzy metallic fabrics, gabardines and failles that changed colour as they caught the light – all fabrics that combined a lightweight feel with a sense of luxury – in shades of gold, amber, brick red or imperial green.

The daywear celebrated the work of tailors with a new kind of loose stand-up collar that revealed the bow necklines of diaphanous blouses worn underneath, while coats were covered with python or cobra snakeskin. Asymmetrical designs featured heavily, with capes that hung down on one side, off-centre rows of buttons, and wraparound skirts that revealed the legs. Whether short or long, the skirts' hems were tucked under at the front and trailed down at the back.

One dramatic evening gown combined different fabrics in an innovative pattern (see opposite, bottom left). The shoulders were left bare, with balloon sleeves hanging down, while the generous skirt was made up of alternating squares of black velvet and lace in increasing sizes.

Givenchy also paid tribute to the embroiderers, whose skill was evident on the pockets and peplums of strict black satin jackets and dresses that were sumptuously embellished with gold (see right), evoking Schiaparelli's designs from the 1930s. Finally, the couturier highlighted the craft of feather workers, using two crossed black bird-of-paradise feathers to adorn the asymmetrical neckline of a dark charcoal-grey satin sheath dress (see opposite, right), while the hats were embellished with plumes of pheasant, cockerel and ostrich feathers.

A.S.

'GIVENCHY: 40 YEARS OLD!'

The show opened with five models wearing navy
blue suits with white details around the collar and
on the pockets (see, for example, right). These suit
jackets with padded shoulders were paired with
modest skirts or trousers. However, the buttonholes
were embellished with piping in a contrasting
colour – white on navy blue or red – on suits
made of lambskin that had been dyed red or black.

This spring collection celebrated 40 years
since Hubert de Givenchy had founded his
couture house. It featured traditional prints in
bright colours, which adorned smart day dresses
as well as evening gowns. Classic prints such as
butterflies, fruit and stylized flowers contrasted
with surprising undulating stripes in bold colours,
while some coats were made from ottoman fabric
printed with vibrant palmette motifs, inspired by
Léon Bakst, the designer for the Ballets Russes
(see opposite, top left).

The evening dresses were light and floaty.
Brassieres decorated with only a few embroidered
details left the stomach bare, partly covered by
an asymmetrical cape that testified once again
to the enduring influence of saris (see opposite,
bottom left). Petal-like flounces adorned generous
organza skirts, as well as the necklines and hems
of babydoll dresses.

Givenchy also presented a new twist on the
peacock-tail cut, with a short skirt at the front and
a longer train with a rounded hem at the back. It
appeared on a satin organza dress with a plunging
back held in place by two large bows, as well as
on the wedding dress (see opposite, bottom right)
in pale pink organza embellished with garlands
of flowers.

A.S.

FORTY YEARS OF CREATIVITY

Following on from the previous collection
(see p. 332), and in parallel with the exhibition
'Givenchy, Forty Years of Creativity' that opened
on 21 October 1991 at the Palais Galliera in Paris,
this show continued to celebrate the fortieth
anniversary of the house of Givenchy. 'Forty years
have gone by all too quickly, filled with youthful
dreams, passions and great joy,' the couturier
commented. 'I have participated in and outpaced
many changes … always living fully with the times.'
To mark the occasion, two huge photographs
taken in the 1960s by Tom Kublin framed the
white catwalk.

The daywear featured a silhouette that no longer
emphasized the shoulders as strongly. Coats took
centre stage once again, often in the form of frock
coats in subtle colours such as blue-grey, almond
green and absinthe green. Backstage, Hubert de
Givenchy said that he had been influenced by
Audrey Hepburn's outfits in Stanley Donen's film
Two for the Road (1967). Most of the jersey day
dresses had a draped collar – a sophisticated detail
that allowed them to be worn at cocktail hour or
to the theatre. This was also the case with a number
of little black dresses.

The floaty eveningwear took a variety of different
forms. Long satin sheath dresses were worn under
generous green- or garnet-coloured coats, their
wrists trimmed with black sable (see right). Taffeta
that changed colour as it caught the light was a
prominent feature throughout the collection. An
evening dress with flashes of green and orange,
which was accompanied by a short cape, featured
a bustier embellished with curving motifs in
multicoloured beads (see opposite, bottom
right). Sheath dresses made of double-faced
satin had cut-out backs edged with black velvet
or embroidered with gold thread and embellished
with black beads. Another dress, made of black
satin (see opposite, bottom left), featured an
embroidered asymmetrical design that crossed
over the bust and covered one sleeve, outlined
by a strip of coral-coloured fabric.

A.S.

1952–1992

Both the daywear and eveningwear featured
short, flared skirts, while the jackets had narrower
shoulders. Most of the designs in this collection
were daywear. The show opened with a series of
navy blue outfits with white collars, pockets and
wrists. These were followed by simple gabardine
dresses, some of which were paired with generous
open coats that only fastened at the collar or had
edges that met but didn't overlap.

The cocktail dresses were the other high point of
the show. They still featured plenty of traditional
floral patterns, but these gave way to small graphic
black and white motifs, with polka dots, diamond
shapes and undulating wave forms. The short, puffy
skirts were voluminous without becoming heavy.
Finally, the designs for cocktail hour featured
trousers made of navy blue barathea, paired with
a transparent organza bustier edged with white
guipure lace.

Although this collection did not feature as
many eveningwear designs as other years,
the eveningwear did have more dramatic
embellishments that made use of a range of
materials, including raffia, ceramic beads and
iridescent sequins. Generous skirts made of
shimmering faille had their fabric gathered into
a puff around the waist – a feature inspired by
the 1950s that appeared on a number of designs
(see opposite, right).

The collection closed with four wedding dresses.
Each one symbolized a different decade of the
couture house, which celebrated its fortieth
anniversary with a beautiful collection that
more than met journalists' expectations.

A.S.

AUTUMN HARMONIES AND LAVISH EMBELLISHMENTS

The show opened with day suits made of suede and snakeskin. Some of these featured checked patterns created with pieces of suede in different colours, while others had python snakeskin details in shades drawn from the 'autumn harmonies' colour palette: brick red, caramel, hazel.

Short, generous coats with raglan sleeves were worn over wool jersey dresses with belts and cut-outs. The suit jackets, made from textured tweed in bright colours such as red and sapphire blue, had a new cut that created a longer silhouette and flared out slightly around the hips.

The cocktail dresses gave way to opulent eveningwear. Black reigned supreme, with different materials combined to achieve contrasting matte and shimmering effects. For example, a black velvet sheath dress had a long curved split that reached all the way up to the hip, edged with black satin. Another sheath dress, also made of velvet, had a longer skirt at the back, created by two trailing pieces of faille, one in absinthe green and the other in shocking pink.

Since the early days of his career, Hubert de Givenchy had enjoyed experimenting with asymmetrical designs. These appeared again here in the form of overskirts made of shimmering Ziberline that crossed over at the front in a wraparound style or were fastened with diagonal lines of buttons down the front or back.

Since the late 1970s, the eveningwear in Givenchy's winter collections had been the height of luxury. This show was no exception: drawing inspiration from goldsmithing, the embellishments that covered the boleros and the bodices of evening gowns added a touch of refinement, while some of the jackets (see opposite, top left) were adorned with frogging in silver hide embellished with gemstones.

A.S.

COLOURFUL DRAPED CREATIONS

Soft, light summer suits were worn over blouses
with prints in bold colours, some of which were
inspired by the stylized motifs of ikat fabric from
Southeast Asia. Broad multicoloured stripes –
similar to bayadere fabric, and created
by Beauclère – dominated the cocktail dresses
and evening gowns. The eveningwear was less
extravagant than in previous collections, but
impressed with its refined cut and details.

Hubert de Givenchy's talent for combining colours
had been clear from his first collection. Here he
used contrasting colours on a number of dresses
that left the stomach bare, once again inspired by
saris. One of these featured a sky-blue Moroccan
crepe top that contrasted with a mustard-coloured
skirt (see opposite, bottom left). Another dress,
made of sapphire-blue and egg-yolk-yellow
Moroccan crepe, had a length of emerald-green
crepe draped around the hips in the style of a
sarong – the rectangular piece of fabric wrapped
around the hips to form a skirt, traditionally worn
in South Asia.

One silk gazar dress featured a print of wavy-edged
checks (see right), a nod to the designer's use of
surprising motifs in his early years. More classic
embellishments featured on dresses with black
muslin skirts and T-shirt-style tops, covered with
mother-of-pearl and ribbons, and edged with
gold beads.

At the height of his powers, Givenchy remained
faithful to his own tastes. Bernadine Morris wrote in
The New York Times that, '[w]hile Mr. Givenchy is not
opening up any fashion frontiers, he makes clothes
that give a woman confidence. That aspect of design
has been somewhat overlooked this week.'

A.S.

JUMPSUITS AND THE 1940S

Hubert de Givenchy remained open to new ideas in his creative work, although he incorporated these into his designs in moderation. He surprised onlookers by making cocktail suits out of dark red or purple ribbed velvet (see right). These jackets, like those made of brocade and embellished with textured braid, were worn over satin blouses in shades of apple green, bright red or coppery yellow.

The headpieces evoked the extravagant fashions of the 1940s. Perched on top of the models' heads, fascinators made of frothy satin and velvet created an elongated silhouette.

The short black velvet dresses were adorned with ruffles of black satin at the shoulders or in diagonal stripes (see opposite, top left). These textured embellishments also featured on a short black satin dress that boasted a neckline edged with satin and velvet roses (see opposite, top right).

A revealing bodice, made of a mesh of red and black chenille velvet, was worn with a pair of trousers and a black barathea spencer jacket. This mesh approach, allowing the skin to show through, appeared on several designs, including a top made of bright pink chenille worn with a satin brocade skirt with a pattern of pink flowers on a buttercup-yellow background (see opposite, bottom left).

Drawing inspiration from his own designs of the 1960s, Givenchy created a number of jumpsuits (see opposite, bottom right), which represented a departure from the classic feel of his previous collections. One had a bustier embellished with sequins; another was made of dark green crinkled velvet that changed colour as it caught the light; while a third was made from draped chartreuse satin chiffon. The couturier also used this iridescent fabric to create diaphanous dresses in shades of emerald green or hazel.

A.S.

CLASSIC SUMMER STYLES

The jumpsuits that had appeared in the previous season's collection (see p. 342) featured again here, in lime green, Wallis blue or pale pink. They were paired with loose-fitting jackets that ended at the waist and were fastened with a single button. One of these jackets, made of silk with a brocade pattern in pink and silver laminette thread, was worn with a jewelled belt that hung loosely around the waist (see right). The light-as-a-feather suits and coats featured pockets with pointed tips and buttons that were either gold or matched the colour of the fabric.

The day dresses were made of crepe printed with leaf patterns or other traditional summer flower motifs. Alongside polka dots, multicoloured mosaic patterns and large paisley designs, these plant and flower motifs also brought a bright, acidic colour palette to the evening dresses. These gowns, made of organza or light silk gazar, were embellished with flounces at the wrists or along the hems. Their low necklines sometimes left the shoulders bare. The finishing touch was provided by oversized wide-brimmed hats and fascinators adorned with flowers that matched the dresses.

The eveningwear consisted of garden-party dresses or summer dresses, made of muslin or floaty organza. A long gypsy-style dress was covered in ruffles printed with a floral motif in various shades of pink (see opposite, left). While there were not many instances of embroidery, those embellishments that did appear had lost none of their usual refinement. One pale chestnut-coloured organza dress had a transparent muslin bodice that was embroidered with delicate white flowers and allowed the stomach to show through (see opposite, bottom right), while the ends of a large ribbon tied in a bow at the neck floated in the model's wake.

A.S.

FABRICS TAKE CENTRE STAGE

As Hubert de Givenchy wrote in the programme that accompanied the show, this collection was first and foremost inspired by fabrics. At a time when the world of haute couture was starting to be seen as outdated, and the media and younger generations were losing interest, Givenchy – a respected establishment figure – saw himself as a champion of the industry. With this in mind, he used only the most exclusive fabrics: from the softest wools to textured bouclé and tweed in his daywear, to silk gabardine and silk gazar 'that glittered with jet or gold' in his eveningwear. The couturier created a luxurious, opulent feel while remaining faithful to the unpretentious but impressive designs that had made his name.

Sumptuous furs – nutria, beaver, sable, marmot, fox and mink – were used to make oversized stoles, scarf-hats, tie-like creations and sculptural hats. These added a touch of drama to the belted wool jersey dresses and suede suits, their pocket flaps featuring the pointed tips that Givenchy had favoured since the 1950s.

Bows were a prominent feature across the day dresses and evening gowns. They accentuated a low-cut neckline, appeared in a row down a bodice, or drew the eye to the small of the back. Sheath dresses, which Givenchy described as the type of eveningwear most suitable for the times, were made of all kinds of fabrics, from a black satin dress with leg-of-mutton sleeves to a bright red organza design embellished with sparkling sequins. Whether short or long, the black velvet sheath dresses had wide low-cut necklines embellished with sequin-covered lace.

A.S.

HOMAGE TO MADAME GRÈS

Hubert de Givenchy dedicated a number of designs in this collection to Madame Grès. The couturier wrote in his press release, 'I thought that in dedicating several styles to her … to the image of her great simplicity and her technique, this could be my gesture of friendship, admiration, and affection to her… That is why I wanted to finish this spring collection thinking of her…'

Givenchy learned of Madame Grès's death in an article in *Le Monde* in December 1994, a year after she died. Overwhelmed by debt, she had tragically been forced to retire in spring 1988. Before leaving, she called Givenchy and asked him if she could borrow some clothes boxes, as she didn't have any left to deliver orders to her last clients. She came to thank him in person, giving him the last ever design that she had created, in a box with the Givenchy label on it.

The couturier's tributes to Madame Grès took the form of several sheath dresses made of dark blue and white crepe, daring cut-outs, and floaty draped dresses made of red crepe. Madame Grès had wanted to be a sculptor and she worked with fabric as if it were stone, using pleats to avoid cutting the material. The show closed with a group of nine evening dresses created using this signature technique, which were met with a standing ovation. The floaty outfits evoked the purity of ancient Greek and Roman dress, as well as the mysteries of the Orient, with their tantalising drapery and revealing pleated brassieres, made of crepe georgette in shades of bright red, sapphire blue, slate grey, ivory and powder pink.

A.S.

HUBERT DE GIVENCHY'S LAST COLLECTION

A T-shaped catwalk and an ivory backdrop surrounded by huge photographs of past designs formed the pared-back set for Hubert de Givenchy's last show. The couturier dedicated this collection to his ateliers, his seamstresses and his dressmakers, as well as all the suppliers, from weavers to embroiderers, without whom he would 'not have been able to establish the brand of [his] couture house'.

The day dresses and suits, still with lightly padded shoulders, featured pockets and buttons placed in various different arrangements. The cocktail dresses had draped skirts that were gathered into large asymmetrical bows or puffs of satin or faille.

The two dominant silhouettes were each inspired by contrasting characters from Hollywood films. The 'Sabrina' line, named after the character played by Audrey Hepburn in 1954, consisted of cocktail dresses with a small bust and short bell-shaped skirt. In contrast to this child-like silhouette, the couturier created the 'Gilda' line, inspired by the femme fatale played by Rita Hayworth in 1946, which took the form of long figure-hugging sheath dresses. On both silhouettes, black reigned supreme, whether in faille or velvet, covered in lace or embellished with sequins in the shape of sharp claws.

For the finale, all the members of Givenchy's studio appeared on the catwalk wearing white jackets and were applauded by the audience, which was made up of famous faces, journalists, and designers such as Valentino, Yves Saint Laurent, Christian Lacroix, Paco Rabanne and Oscar de la Renta. Hubert de Givenchy appeared at the end of the procession with his assistant, Jeannette Malher. He left the catwalk to a standing ovation from the audience.

A.S.

JOHN GALLIANO

A SHORT BIOGRAPHY

John Galliano was born in 1960 in Gibraltar and moved to South London at the age of six. His father was English with Italian heritage, while his mother was Spanish, so he quickly felt at home in the cosmopolitan borough of Battersea, where he had his first encounters with the many diverse cultures that lived side by side.

Galliano began studying at Saint Martin's School of Art in London in 1981, graduating in 1984. His final show was an unprecedented success. Inspired by fashions that were popular during the French Revolution and the First Republic, his collection 'Les Incroyables' displayed such a high level of maturity and talent that the legendary fashion boutique Browns decided to display his designs in their shop window.

Galliano founded his own eponymous fashion label and presented his first collection for Spring/Summer 1985. Called 'Afghanistan Repudiates Western Ideals', it was highly praised for its marriage of East and West, combining a range of cuts, fabrics and techniques that would become hallmarks of his style.

Galliano drew on a wide range of references, reinterpreted historical styles and explored traditional dress from around the world, which he studied and admired. He was also passionate about the craft of haute couture, admiring the orientalist silhouettes of Paul Poiret and the austere designs of Madeleine Vionnet. He drew on the latter's iconic bias-cutting technique from the 1930s, learning how to emulate it and applying its subtleties to his ready-to-wear designs.

Embracing a total artwork approach, he believed that the staging of his catwalk shows was as important as the clothes themselves. His spectacular shows had clear narratives and were always carefully orchestrated to evoke a particular emotion in the audience. Every model played a role inspired by famous, often scandalous women throughout history.

The Spring/Summer 1988 collection, which paid tribute to the character of Blanche Dubois as portrayed in Elia Kazan's film *A Streetcar Named Desire* (1951), earned Galliano a British Designer of the Year Award from the British Fashion Council.

At the invitation of the Paris Fashion Federation, he presented his collections in the French capital, where he moved in March 1990, encouraged by the enthusiastic response to his shows. Despite financial struggles, he enjoyed the support of his peers, notably Azzedine Alaïa, who offered to host his show at his own premises, and influential figures such as São Schlumberger, who opened the doors of her private mansion to host Galliano's show in March 1994. This collection, which featured a number of more restrained designs, focused on exquisite details and embraced an haute couture approach inspired by 1950s silhouettes. It earned him another British Designer of the Year Award.

On 11 July 1995, one hour after Hubert de Givenchy's last show, John Galliano took over as artistic director of the haute couture collections and the luxury ready-to-wear line 'Givenchy couture'. For the first time, Galliano's talent and unbridled creativity would be measured against the yardstick of haute couture.

But his tenure at Givenchy lasted only one year. After many weeks of suspense and rumours, on 14 October 1996 he was announced as the new creative director of Christian Dior. The appointment was a dream come true, and Galliano transformed the image of the historic fashion house, while also designing for his own eponymous label. His baroque haute couture and ready-to-wear shows made history, displaying a range of technical wizardry all driven by the force of Galliano's own personality. They made him a leading light of the 2000s fashion world.

Retired from media and design since 2011, Galliano was appointed artistic director of Maison Margiela in 2014.

Alexandre Samson

'THE PRINCESS AND THE PEA'

Later named 'The Princess and the Pea' by *The New York Times*, the collection opened with a 6-metre-high pile of mattresses. Two models were sitting on the top, wearing dresses with extremely long trains (see opposite). This dreamlike vision introduced the first of five themes around which the show was structured. Called 'Mauve', it featured a series of ballgowns made of satin or taffeta with stripes in an 'arrow-head pattern in shades of mauve and truffle' or 'lilac and bitter chocolate' (see right).

The next theme – 'Cut-throat Black and Ecru' – featured suits and outfits made of barathea, with draped fabric and tuxedo collars. Looking through the couture house's archives, John Galliano was inspired by one of Hubert de Givenchy's designs from 1957, which featured a length of fabric draped over the body and hanging in a loop at the side (see pp. 92 and 98), and he used the idea on a sheath dress (see p. 356, right). He was also inspired by the barathea jumpsuit that Hubert de Givenchy had presented in 1993 (see p. 342).

The theme 'Rose Pink – Oriental Kitten' consisted of a series of opera coats inspired by Paul Poiret, made of ruffled muslin or ash-grey Ziberline (see p. 357, bottom right). One blouse, called 'white organdie French maid's blouse', was a nod to the iconic Bettina blouse. The theme 'Green' (see p. 358) consisted of three designs: 'Dry Martini with a twist of lime', 'Shaken' and 'But not stirred' – three short dresses with wide skirts, in shades of absinthe green, inspired by the 1950s. The final theme, 'Orange', combined the sack dresses of the 1950s, made of bright orange ottoman fabric, with red saris embroidered with gold (see p. 359).

Hubert de Givenchy's classic, chic style made way for a spectacular, carefully orchestrated show, a symbol of the regeneration that was needed to bring haute couture into the modern world. Even if there were a few technical issues, and the abundance of themes was a little overwhelming, it was clear that this first show held the seeds of a bright and promising future.

A.S.

'THE RAIN IN SPAIN STAYS MAINLY IN THE PLAIN'

In a nod to this collection's Spanish influences, John Galliano opened the show with a recording of Audrey Hepburn's voice reciting, 'The rain in Spain stays mainly in the plain', from the film *My Fair Lady* (1964). Three models then emerged from openings in a long curtain, accompanied by the kind of fanfare usually heard in the bullring.

The lavish embellishments of bullfighters' outfits were combined with the classic features of suits. One grey wool jacket boasted epaulettes made of gold sequins (see opposite, top right), while the high-waisted, tight-fitting skirts and trousers had pinstripes and strips of black satin down the sides, like tuxedo trousers. The tight white shirts were paired with narrow black ties, while a greatcoat-style cape with a wide collar was made of white wool (see right).

Echoing details that had appeared in his first haute couture collection (see p.356, bottom left) and in the pre-collection, Galliano – inspired by Givenchy's designs from the 1950s (see p.68) – added woollen bows to the pocket flaps of slim dresses and suit jackets.

Inspired by the dresses worn by tango dancers, the dramatic scarlet evening gowns contrasted draped fabric with damask kimonos and chiffon scarves with oversized peony prints. In a technique that he had used on many designs released under his own eponymous label, Galliano also added ruffles and flounces accentuated by bias tape in a contrasting colour at the edges, evoking flamenco dancers' outfits. Some of these featured large black and white polka dot prints.

A.S.

'JOSÉPHINE', 'WINTER ASCOT' AND 'BLACK NARCISSUS'

The first models took to the catwalk to the sound of the French national anthem mixed with 'Firestarter' by The Prodigy. The dark catwalk was divided down the middle by a scattering of wintry leaves, as if in a forest glade. This was inspired by the estate of the Château de Malmaison, the residence of Empress Joséphine de Beauharnais, whose romance with Napoleon Bonaparte, seen through the lens of Abel Gance's 1927 film *Napoléon*, had served as the inspiration for this collection.

The seductive empire line accentuated the body with transparent fabrics inspired by the extravagant fashions worn by the 'Merveilleuses', a subset of aristocratic women in the French First Republic. White tulle dresses subtly embroidered with braid or flowers in a needlework style known as *point de Beauvais* – the town where Hubert de Givenchy was born – had sumptuous trains made of 'pre-guillotine' red velvet. The headpieces were sometimes adorned with crystal drops, like chandeliers.

In a reference to Napoleon's military campaign in Egypt in 1798, the bust of a draped satin sheath dress, called Nefertiti, was adorned with the wings of the Egyptian goddess Isis (see p.366, top left).

The daywear was grouped together under the theme 'Winter Ascot', in homage to the elegant fashions worn at the famous British racecourse. The highly sophisticated suits and dresses were paired with extraordinary headpieces created by Stephen Jones. On one black dress (see p.369, left), Galliano carefully recreated the rose designs in tapestry-stitch embroidery that had featured in Givenchy's Autumn/Winter 1952–1953 collection (see p.34).

The final set of designs titled 'Black Narcissus' was a series of irresistible suits and cocktail dresses. Described by the designer as 'dangerously short', they featured an array of different blacks, in both matte and shiny fabrics. One inky black satin crepe coat had a ruff made of charcoal-grey flowers, while the model also sported an eyepatch (see p.369, bottom right). By drawing on a wide range of influences, John Galliano sought to step out from the shadow of Hubert de Givenchy.

A.S.

JANE AUSTEN IN MARRAKESH

For his final show at Givenchy, John Galliano opted for a simple set with a red carpet that the models walked down to the sound of singing and Moroccan drums. Inspired by Berber culture, the designer had tattoo-like symbols drawn in ink on the models' faces, navels or torsos, and had their hair styled in elaborate designs that looked as if they had been sculpted in clay. The collection drew on a diverse range of references, from the heroines of Jane Austen novels to the uniforms worn by the French Foreign Legion.

Generous shirt dresses made of white poplin were paired with black ties, with or without a blazer. References to men's clothing included an outfit made up of a shirt and tuxedo trousers with a red strip down the side (see opposite, right), and a black sheath dress with a white dickey (see opposite, bottom left), both of which had as the finishing touch a bow tie worn loose around the collar. Braid decorations inspired by late 19th-century fashions appeared on dresses, jackets and coats (see, for example, p.372, bottom left).

Black lace featured prominently, and the empire line from the previous season's haute couture collection (see p.364) also appeared again on a number of dresses, both short and long. The traditional costume of the Ottoman Empire was another notable influence, as seen on a formal coat made of striped linen with scalloped edges (see p.372, right), and in the Turkish-inspired carved metal jewelry.

The last of many influences that shaped this collection showed through in a series of floral motifs that evoked English chintz patterns (see p.373). The collection suffered by comparison to the successful show of Galliano's designs for his eponymous label, which he had presented a few days earlier. At the Givenchy show, the audience had a sense that the designer was distancing himself a little, which was confirmed when it was announced shortly afterwards that he was moving to Christian Dior.

A.S.

ALEXANDER McQUEEN

A SHORT BIOGRAPHY

The youngest of six children, Lee Alexander McQueen (17 March 1969 – 11 February 2010) was born in Lewisham, South London. He suffered abuse in his childhood and sought comfort in his mother, whose passion for genealogy sparked his obsession with researching his family history and Scottish roots.

At the age of 16, he left school and started work as an apprentice tailor at Anderson & Sheppard. This Savile Row institution dressed famous figures such as Mikhail Gorbachev and Prince Charles; McQueen once boasted about having made a jacket for the latter which he signed on the reverse of the lining with the words 'McQueen was here'.

He continued his apprenticeship at Gieves & Hawkes, where he learned to make military uniforms, then at Bermans & Nathans, which specialized in costumes for the stage. He then joined the studio of London-based designer Koji Tatsuno, before moving to Milan to train under Romeo Gigli.

In 1991, he returned to London to study fashion at Central Saint Martins College of Art and Design, where his final show was called 'Jack the Ripper Stalks his Victims'.

His first collection, in 1993, had a scandalous feel that would dominate his work throughout his career. In 1995, inspired by his roots, he presented 'Highland Rape', a metaphor for the English invasion of Scotland and the violence perpetrated by the English there. Transcending the dramatic historical events, he presented a collection of lace and wool designs slashed through by cut-outs that exposed the body. Both brutal and romantic, this provocative vision – offset by the clever cuts of McQueen's designs, in black or grey suiting fabric – became his calling card.

In 1996, he received the first of his four Best British Designer Awards and, on 15 October, he was named artistic director at Givenchy, in charge of both haute couture and the luxury women's ready-to-wear line. He rose to prominence on the international stage with his first haute couture collection, in January 1997. Its bold aesthetic was a shock to the system, eliciting negative responses as critics pointed to a lack of maturity and a mismatch between McQueen's unbridled creativity and the couture house's traditional image. McQueen decided to push the label in a new direction, de-emphasizing the iconic styles associated with the house of Givenchy and accentuating his own stylistic markers, thereby creating new signature looks. He freely combined elements of historical Western costume with traditional dress from cultures around the world, in spectacular shows that were always shaped by an original, imaginative narrative. He also greatly admired the craftsmanship of haute couture and drew on the discipline to perfect his ideas or generate new ones for his own eponymous label.

'Working at Givenchy helped me learn my craft,' McQueen later said. Over the course of 18 collections for Givenchy, his style grew more mature and refined, and he developed a lighter, softer touch.

In 2001, McQueen left Givenchy to concentrate on his own label and, backed by the French luxury group PPR, presented his collections in Paris from the following year onwards.

In 2003, the CFDA named him International Designer of the Year, while he was also honoured by the British monarchy as a Commander of the Order of the British Empire.

After presenting a series of extravagant, legendary shows throughout the 2000s, Alexander McQueen – left devastated by the death of his mother – took his own life in 2010.

Alexandre Samson

'SEARCH FOR THE GOLDEN FLEECE'

Alexander McQueen's first collection for
Givenchy was themed around the legend of Jason
and the Argonauts' quest for the Golden Fleece.
The designer had been inspired by the house of
Givenchy's 4G logo, created in 1967, as the meander-
like square design – made up of four hieroglyphs
resembling capital letter Gs – reminded him of
ancient Greece. A ram's fleece with gold horns
hung from a huge tree, while a harp could be
heard playing in the background, welcoming guests.
The figure of Icarus, a model wearing a huge pair
of outstretched wings, watched over the audience
from on high (see p. 378, top left).

In a nod to the house of Givenchy's traditional
colours, the collection was dominated by white and
gold. McQueen presented suits made of floaty white
crepe, with jackets that had criss-cross designs
and cut-outs at the back, allowing gold embroidery
or a sparkling metal dickey to show through. His
fascination with birds of prey inspired a series of
outfits covered all over with feathers, while one
model sported a stuffed eagle that had been
transformed into a headpiece by Philip Treacy.
The milliner based some of his hats on real
rams' horns, while others were made from
gold papier mâché.

The soundtrack was a song by Maria Callas, who
had played the character of Medea – the murderous
sorceress who became Jason's lover – in Pier Paolo
Pasolini's 1969 film. Some outfits featured sleeves
embellished with long trailing pieces of fabric at
the wrist, made of down and embroidered with
bees, inspired by the Napoleonic era. This martial
feel was also evoked by an armour-like dress
(see p. 380, left) and an Amazonian corset covered
with scroll designs inspired by the legendary armour
of Roman emperors (p. 380, right). In an allusion
to the fashion house's history, a blouse made of
double organza featured fresh rose petals and
leaves (see p. 378, bottom left). Dressed as sylphs,
in draped dresses with butterfly wings, two models
(see p. 381, top right) closed the show by taking
the fleece down from the tree, amid a shower
of gold sequins.

Although the collection was met with
incomprehension from some of the audience, it
represented a new direction for the fashion house,
drawing on the tension between the instinctive
aesthetic, storytelling talent and tailoring skill of
Alexander McQueen and the traditional image
of the Givenchy label.

A.S.

LADY LEOPARD

In this show, the models appeared from behind
revolving mirrors. Wearing tall, domed wigs cut
straight across at the nape of the neck or with
layers of different lengths, they stalked the cobbled
walkway and turned languidly around the many
metal columns that were a feature of the Halle
aux Chevaux, a former abattoir.

The models walked to the sound of 'Encore une
fois', an electro hit for the band Sash! in 1997.
The first suits had cape-like jackets made of black
dipped lambskin and featured laser-cut openwork
motifs. An exceptional tailor, Alexander McQueen
created an outfit made of green moiré ottoman
fabric with notched lapels that formed wide storm
flaps and a new kind of padded shoulder that
curved into a crescent moon shape (see right).

Many of the designs seemed to draw on styles
favoured by sex workers. McQueen presented
boots with stiletto heels, outfits with suggestive
cut-outs, and a number of skimpy figure-hugging
strapless dresses. He used python snakeskin belts
to accentuate the waist, while the pencil skirts
had splits at the thigh. One stretchy lace outfit
had an imitation leopard-skin pattern – a motif that
appeared throughout the collection, alongside real
furs: purple rabbit fur on a jacket with a belt at
the front and a cape-like back and black goatskin
on a loose jacket. Long coats, including one in
mauve python snakeskin, were paired with leather
miniskirts. Sometimes the models had caps perched
on top of their tall hairstyles. Design no. 69 saw the
scandalous French actress Béatrice Dalle take
to the catwalk in a strapless black patent-leather
dress, wearing matching cut-off gloves that
covered only her fingers (see p. 385, left).

The collection once again mystified onlookers,
giving off a sexual energy that was unheard of
for Givenchy.

A.S.

'ECLECT DISSECT'

A huge birdcage containing live crows was the centrepiece of a gothic set where walls were draped with red fabric and the floor was covered with Persian rugs. Drawing on the dark romanticism of Mary Shelley's tale *Frankenstein* (1818) and the horror of Robert Wiene's 1920 film *The Cabinet of Dr Caligari*, Alexander McQueen and his artistic director Simon Costin invented a tale of a serial killer surgeon. The story went that, throughout the 1890s, this surgeon travelled around the world and collected the bodies of different women, which he grafted onto animal skins, exotic objects and elements of historical or traditional dress. The cosmopolitan collection 'Eclect Dissect' brought together an impressive range of different historical and cultural references.

Exaggerated silhouettes created by bustles, as in the late Victorian era, were interspersed with heavily embellished bullfighter jackets, Scottish tartan from the McQueen clan, and tall platform shoes. One dress, with a bodice that extended to cover the head, was crowned with a cage that held a live bird. This was followed by a tribal coat made of horsehair with flecks of different colours, topped off with a fascinator of ostrich feathers made to look like porcupine quills (see opposite, bottom right). Some of the models wore blood-red contact lenses.

The animal forms that had become one of McQueen's signatures appeared again here in the shape of a black swan, its neck wound around the model's own (see p.389, bottom right), in the bird-of-prey heads worn as epaulettes, and in the sandals with straps that divided the toes into three. Following on from a series of kimonos and embroidered mandarin coats, the show closed with dresses inspired by Audrey Hepburn's costumes in King Vidor's 1956 film *War and Peace* (see, for example, p.389, left).

At the end of the show, McQueen appeared on the catwalk with a live falcon perched on his arm. He had decided not to look to the label's past for inspiration any longer, but instead to explore his own universe. The audience's reactions were mixed, some marvelled at his creativity while others were shocked.

A.S.

RHINESTONE COWGIRLS

The Givenchy 4G logo (see p.376) was projected onto large screens on the wall, which lit up the black-and-pink striped catwalk. As was clear from the invitation, which featured a photograph of a woman dressed in Native American costume, the collection was heavily influenced by Westerns. The hairstyles were inspired by the 1970s, especially Farrah Fawcett's iconic look with thick hair and flicked-out ends.

Dresses and suits made of dipped lambskin were covered with flame and star motifs created with insets of fabric or appliqué. The cowgirl outfits featured embossed leather corsets and short gloves adorned with extravagant fringing. The suits and jumpsuits were decorated with embroidered feathers or falcons, Alexander McQueen's favourite animal. His signature silver metal embellishments also appeared throughout the collection in the form of badges, harnesses, fake revolvers, chain-link muzzles, and belt buckles in the shape of buffalo heads.

While McQueen was inspired by the American West, he did not entirely abandon classic suits and traditional grey wool. One skirt suit had pleated, flared sleeves (see opposite, top right), while the Prince of Wales checked pattern on a jacket with dramatic padded shoulders was outlined in glitter (see opposite, top left). Jackets with notched lapels made of laminated lace or black satin were paired with flared trousers. Once again, Philip Treacy created stunning hats, this time inspired by men's trilbies, which stretched upwards like top hats. These appeared alongside American Stetsons.

The show closed with the hit song 'I Will Always Love You' by Dolly Parton, whose influence infused the entire collection.

A.S.

JAPANESE GARDEN

Alexander McQueen drew inspiration from
Japan, as seen through the filter of the Art Deco
movement. This influence was clear in the fringed
dresses embroidered with cherry blossoms (see
p.396, right) and designs that evoked Hokusai's
c.1831 woodblock print *The Great Wave off
Kanagawa* (see p.396, left). The influence of the
exhibition 'Japonisme and Fashion' at the Palais
Galliera, which also explored these themes, was
clearly felt in the Koi dress, which was embellished
with a fish-scale motif (see p.399) that referenced
an evening gown designed by Gustave Beer in 1919,
in the collection of the Kyoto Costume Institute.
The dress, with its hood made of delicate chains,
also evoked the sumptuous illustrations of Erté.
The influence of the kimono came through in both
the cut and motifs of a coat called Marakesh [*sic*],
which was decorated with orange and white stars
(see opposite, right). Traditional Japanese tattoos
were the inspiration for a bolero embroidered all
over with dragons (see p.397, top right), while
a gold circle on the back of a black raffia jacket
evoked the Japanese flag.

In a nod to the house of Givenchy's past, McQueen
presented a number of jumpsuits. Grey suiting
fabric reigned supreme. One outfit drew on a design
that had first featured in 'The Hunger' show (Spring/
Summer 1996) for McQueen's eponymous label; the
jacket was left open to reveal a flurry of preserved
exotic butterflies trapped inside a transparent PVC
dickey (see opposite, top left).

This collection also contained the seeds of
ideas that McQueen would later develop for
collections released under his own label. The
fans made of blond wood that formed the sleeves
of the Hiroshige bolero (see p.397, bottom right)
reappeared in heightened form on a bustier and
skirt in his collection 'No.13' (Spring/Summer 1999);
'Eye' (Spring/Summer 2000) reinterpreted the
chainmail hood, this time made of gold 5-yen coins;
while the headpieces featuring dioramas of the
Chinese countryside sculpted in cork by Philip
Treacy (see, for example, p.397, left) doubled
in size for the collection 'It's Only a Game'
(Spring/Summer 2005).

In order to pay tribute to his haute couture ateliers,
Alexander McQueen took to the catwalk at the
end of the show with the heads of the flou and
tailoring workshops.

A.S.

BLADE RUNNER

While on holiday in San Francisco, Alexander McQueen was captivated by the charming historic trams of the F line. Judith Watt wrote in her book *Alexander McQueen* (2013) that their red and chrome design reminded him of Ridley Scott's 1982 film *Blade Runner*. This collection was inspired by the character of Rachael, an android replicant. Her severe black suit with padded shoulders and a pencil skirt served as a template for the entire collection, while the models also wore wigs that emulated her sophisticated brown fringe.

The futuristic set was made up of two walkways on different levels and a catwalk with light-up panels. The collection featured new variations on the suits for which McQueen was famous. One design made of flecked wool had a large T-shaped inset made from bands of grey and black fabric (see right). These graphic inserts also appeared in dark red and blue dipped lambskin (see opposite, top right) and as multicoloured geometric shapes.

The wide collars and grey, blue or burgundy fur sleeves echoed the heroine's coat, as did the slim pinstriped woollen dresses, their high waists accentuated by leather belts in a contrasting colour. The dresses featured diamond motifs similar to those seen on argyle sweaters, sometimes in the form of openwork.

Apart from two evening gowns embroidered with cherry blossoms that evoked the Japanese themes of the previous collection (see p.394), most of the designs had a severe cut and graphic patterns, such as a distorted checked design that was reminiscent of Victor Vasarely's Op Art works (see p.403, bottom left).

When he took to the catwalk at the end of the show, McQueen adopted the same frozen, robotic stare as some of his models, wearing opaque metallic contact lenses.

A.S.

'ENDOGENOUS, RUSSIAN, AMAZONIAN'

'The idea is about Anastasia, when she goes away from the Revolution. I found her in the Amazon,' Alexander McQueen said in an interview for the television programme *Paris Mode*, shown on Paris Première. Before the show started, the designer explained the meaning behind his set. Twisting vines snaked across the floor, which was decorated with a mosaic of the 4G logo. 'It was like the idea of Anastasia bringing part of the palace with her and the jungle was growing in.'

The names of the designs, make-up looks and hairstyles sought to combine the old-world pomp of aristocratic Europe with the stunning diversity of cultures across South America. The frogging on a number of designs evoked military uniforms from imperial Russia. The Velikaja Katarina corset (see opposite, bottom right) was modelled on a historical ceremonial saddle embroidered in gold on red, while military uniforms were also the inspiration for the Baboushka dress, which was embellished with braid. Philip Treacy created huge headpieces with exotic bird feathers that trailed down or framed the models' faces.

There were numerous references to fashions from the 1930s, particularly in the bias-cut sheath dresses and the designs inspired by old fashion magazines. An ermine cape that had appeared in *Vogue* was the inspiration for the Alissa coat, made of mink with a black/lilac ombré effect (see p.406, right), while McQueen reinterpreted a design by Jean Patou to create the Faisa ('Pheasant') cape, which was covered with dark red feathers (see p.406, left).

The huge train on the Zmeia Koroleva ('Queen of Snakes') wedding dress, made from tiered flounces of laminated lace supported by underwiring (see p.407, top right and bottom), was inspired by Eiko Ishioka's costume for the character of Lucy, the flame-haired woman transformed into a vampire in the 1992 film *Bram Stoker's Dracula*.

Dressed in white, McQueen acknowledged the crowd at the end of the show, dedicating his collection 'to my sisters, with all my love'.

A.S.

SAINT-GERMAIN-DES-PRÉS, 1960S

Inspired by the smoke-filled jazz clubs of Saint-Germain-des-Prés in the 1960s, Alexander McQueen presented his collection on a black catwalk, the simplicity of the set drawing attention to the clothes and their cuts. 'It's kind of a new approach for me, trying to cut down the theatrical and trying to concentrate on people who buy the clothes,' he said in an episode of *Paris Mode* shown on Paris Première. Paying tribute to the beauty of Catherine Deneuve in Luis Buñuel's film *Belle de Jour* (1967), he proposed hairstyles with a natural look as well as discreet, barely-there make-up.

The first silhouette hung loose on the body and did not accentuate the shoulders, its relaxed look drawing on men's clothing. The tuxedo jackets were asymmetrical and unstructured. Sometimes the wool was adorned with sequins so that it looked as if it was covered with drops of dew. However, McQueen did not abandon the complex graphic patterns made from inset pieces of fabric, or the innovative cuts of his trousers, which took five distinct shapes. Shades of grey, black and white appeared alongside cold colours and variations on bright blue.

The second silhouette was highly feminine, with minidresses featuring cut-outs in the style of swimming costumes, embellished with black and white squares or draped with fabric covered in Swarovski crystals. Evoking the lightweight feel of summer dresses that wafted around the body in the slightest breeze, the dresses were held up by thin, almost invisible straps. Tiered ruffles of pleated satin served as a reminder that this ready-to-wear collection had been created entirely by the haute couture ateliers at Givenchy.

A disturbing photographic print of an oversized eye (see right) was the sole concession to McQueen's taste for the bizarre.

A.S.

'THE FRENCH VILLAGE'

Characters drawn entirely from Alexander McQueen's imagination appeared randomly from all four corners of a room made to look like a village square. Veiled in black lace, The Widow wore the portrait of her departed husband on the button of her jacket (see opposite, top left). She followed The Equestrian, whose outfit featured a pattern of inset squares in gradually increasing sizes (see opposite, top right), and The Jester, wearing a bodysuit embellished with beaded triangles (see right). The School Mistress, wearing an embroidered shantung suit, led out her four pupils, each sporting a blazer, while a line of choirgirls walked in the wake of The Biker Clergy, who wore black leather trousers and a corset dress that boasted a long train lined with white lace ruffles (see p.413).

Influences drawn from fashions of the 17th, 18th and late 19th centuries all blurred together, alongside tributes to contemporary figures, such as The 'Alaïa' Archer (see opposite, bottom left). This laminated wool suit, with mauve satin appliqué motifs around the edges, featured a corset made of lilac lambskin, with delicate openwork embellishments in the style of the wide hourglass belts created by Azzedine Alaïa. Inspired by *Young Farmers* (1914), a photograph by August Sander showing three men dressed in black and holding canes, McQueen created three outfits made of ivory lacquered satin (see p.412). The collection paid tribute to the traditional skills of artisans in designs such as The Ribbon Maker, a suit entirely covered with criss-crosses and loops of multicoloured satin ribbon (see opposite, bottom right).

This highly personal collection, dedicated to Alexander McQueen's aunt Patsy, allowed the designer's vulnerability and his tender side to show through. Not many of the guests would have known that the look called Mircea's 'Eddie' The Biker, featuring a leather jacket and a pink satin gilet, paid tribute to Mircea, a young cancer patient who was an admirer of McQueen's work. He had invited her to spend a day with him in his studio, and she was also in the audience to see the show.

A.S.

HALF-WOMAN, HALF-CYBORG

Against the backdrop of widespread panic about the Millennium Bug, Alexander McQueen presented his final ready-to-wear collection of the millennium, heavily inspired by Stanley Kubrick's film *2001: A Space Odyssey* (1968). McQueen described the show's aesthetic as 'a mixture of human and machine, like a baby that grew up inside a computer'.

The models wore pale make-up and walked along the mirrored catwalk in time to the beat of an electro music soundtrack. Half-woman, half-cyborg, their wigs were sculpted into a square shape that was referenced the titular character's helmet-like hair in Paul Wegener and Carl Boese's film *The Golem: How He Came into the World* (1920).

Strips of fur added a graphic feel, highlighting the seams and darts of suits and dresses that had been cut out with a scalpel (see right and opposite, top left), while strips of contrasting colours – red on grey, white on red, or white on black – accentuated the geometric cuts of figure-hugging designs (for example, p.416, left).

Embracing his love of silver metal adornments, McQueen presented a sculpted pectoral, like those worn by Egyptian pharaohs (see opposite, right). The anatomical design fitted snuggly around the neck and shoulders of the dress. A top made of moulded red leather with white edges accentuated the curves of the female torso (see p.416, right). Silver coatings and laminated wool appeared alongside corsets (see opposite, bottom left), jackets and coats made of transparent PVC.

Black-and-white prints created from photographs of a lake surrounded by snow-covered trees were followed by the main motifs of the collection: prints of computer circuits, which spread further and further with each design, until they completely covered skin-tight bodysuits (see p.418).

The two final looks of the collection appeared in total darkness (see p.419). Hundreds of bright red and yellow diodes illuminated the PVC bodices, which were threaded through with tin connecting cables. They were worn with trousers with integral shoes, which had circuit motifs printed in phosphorescent colours that matched the models' contact lenses.

A.S.

'THE EXECUTION OF LADY JANE GREY, PAUL DELAROCHE, OIL ON CANVAS, 1833'

Alexander McQueen was a teenager when he first saw Paul Delaroche's painting *The Execution of Lady Jane Grey* (1833), which depicted the heir to the English crown who was overthrown nine days after her coronation in 1554 and beheaded on the orders of Mary Tudor. 'Being a hopeless romantic,' the designer wrote in the collection's accompanying programme, 'the emotion evoked that day has never left me.'

Live human models were replaced by fibreglass shop-window mannequins with transparent illuminated plexiglass heads, which rose up from under the floor on rotating platforms. 'It was so you didn't focus on the models but on the clothes,' McQueen told Suzy Menkes of *The New York Times* backstage. 'And it should be like an art gallery – because it's the closest fashion gets to art.'

Almost all of the looks were inspired by great paintings, from the Middle Ages to the Renaissance. The outfit worn in *The Portrait of Doge Leonardo Loredan* by Giovanni Bellini (1501–2) was reproduced down to the smallest detail (see right). The cloqué pattern on a luxurious green velvet coat (see opposite, bottom left and right) was modelled on the dress in *The Arnolfini Portrait* by Jan van Eyck (1434), while McQueen reinterpreted the gold brocade tunic from the triptych *The Martyrdom of Saint Erasmus* by Dirk Bouts (1458) in silk organza brocade embellished with mink (see opposite, top left). Finally, the designer drew inspiration from the fish-scale pattern embroidered on an Yves Saint Laurent dress (Spring/Summer 1983) and the scooped neckline of the praying figure's robe in Hans Memling's *Moreel Triptych* (1484) to create a dress embellished with scales of grey wool (see p. 422, bottom right).

This collection was dedicated to the fashion historian Katell Le Bourhis. McQueen said, 'I designed that collection when I was going through quite an emotional turmoil in my life, both professionally and personally.' Drawing inspiration from the history of fashion, he said in an interview with Cathy Horyn of *The New York Times* that the richness of the fabrics and cuts was 'a good thing for the end of the century'.

A.S.

SPORTY CASUAL LOOKS

The set for this show reproduced the rectangular proportions of a basketball court – an appropriate setting for a collection inspired by sport. On the floor, a complex network of red, yellow, green and blue lines marked out the different paths taken by each model to reach the Olympic podium that was placed in front of the photographers' section. The models all stopped there and struck a pose, their ponytails blowing in the wind from the fans behind them.

Sportswear, sweatshirts and tracksuits, tiny shorts and cropped trousers dominated the collection. Lightweight wool, techno cotton, mesh fabric and netting – all in strong, acidic colours – appeared alongside an exclusive neon print, while motifs inspired by basketball courts also adorned minidresses in the form of sparkly embroidery (see, for example, opposite, top left).

Large, thick stitches like those traditionally seen on baseballs highlighted the cut-outs on a dress and the edges of a leather coat, while laces from basketball shoes were used as fastenings on an outfit made of coated satin (see opposite, bottom left). A long sleeveless coat was covered in leather hexagons in shades of yellow, orange and brown, inspired by the patterns on footballs (see p. 426, right). Sports equipment appeared in the form of harnesses on suit jackets and skirts. Fingerless leather gloves were a reference to motocross, while some models also sported padded headgear similar to that worn by wrestlers.

The response to the collection was mainly one of confusion, although Alexander McQueen had wanted to highlight how women had taken over sport, a discipline that had previously been dominated by men. He came on stage at the end of the show accompanied by Katy England, his right-hand woman.

A.S.

LYRICAL OPERA

The main theme from the score of *Princess Mononoke* (1997), an animated film by Hayao Miyazaki, provided the soundtrack for this show, which was inspired by the theme of memory.

The grey set called to mind the vast stage of an opera house, bathed in coloured light and decorated with large photographs of flowers. For the opening scene, a man came on stage wearing a valet's uniform. His height and carefully styled white hair were reminiscent of Hubert de Givenchy. He took pieces of clothing out of a large trunk, one by one, and dressed model Erin O'Connor in them to create the first look (see opposite, top and right).

Drawing on his talent as a tailor, Alexander McQueen once again presented a range of grey woollen suits. He also created a new jumpsuit with a low scooped neckline that revealed an organza blouse with a large houndstooth print (see right). In what was almost a first for haute couture, he presented a version of the 'bumster' trousers that he had been designing for his own label since 1993, with such a low waist that they revealed the model's hips and the top of the buttocks (see opposite, bottom left).

A moulded leather top, covered with handwritten words that evoked scrolls of parchment, was paired with a brown snakeskin skirt (see p.431, top right). Another top, made of silver-painted resin, was moulded into the shape of a female torso and featured slashes filled with sprays of roses (see p.431, bottom right).

Prints of white ferns on a black background (see p.430, left) had the feel of photograms. Feathers once again took centre stage in this collection, with a profusion of grey ostrich, pigeon and swan feathers covering capes and suits.

A.S.

BRITISH ROCK

The fashions of the English rock scene were the inspiration for this nightlife-themed collection, which had a soundtrack made up of songs by groups such as The Pretenders, The Rolling Stones, and Siouxsie and the Banshees. Ties and blazers, dog collars and studded bracelets, leather and straps, all evoked the clothes worn by late 1970s post-punk musicians and their fans.

The collection opened with a khaki blazer worn as a minidress, paired with a silver lamé tie (see right). This was followed by two short dresses with a zip down the side. The first was made of black leather, the second of khaki wool (see opposite, top left). They each had two straps running horizontally around the shoulders and the dropped waist, echoing the straps on Vivienne Westwood and Malcolm McLaren's punk designs of the mid-1970s. Suit jackets were paired with leather accessories: belts in a contrasting colour, often white, and cut-off gloves that covered only the fingers, a common sight in Alexander McQueen's collections since his first ready-to-wear show (see p.382).

Silver moiré lamé fabric appeared throughout the show, in a pair of trousers worn with a green leather top, then in a trouser suit with lapels edged with black lamé (see opposite, bottom left). Scottish tartan, first in shades of brown and blue, then in blue and black with red stripes, was used to create jackets and daring tops that were draped diagonally across the body, revealing the stomach. These were accessorized with dog collars and wide silver bracelets worn around the upper arm. Purple and blue dominated the latter stages of the show, with designs such as a draped top with purple and black stripes, and a minidress that had inset stripes of black and blue leather and straps all down the back (see opposite, bottom right).

At the end of the show, Alexander McQueen made his way down the huge catwalk on a scooter.

A.S.

'HOT COUTURE'

Two women dressed in trouser suits (see right) walked around a huge box, its brick walls tagged with graffiti of the Givenchy logo. They found a door and rang the bell. A man answered. Techno music exploded from inside the box, which split open, the walls falling gently to the ground to reveal the interior of an apartment where a wild party was taking place. 'Fashion is supposed to be fun and dressing up is for parties,' Alexander McQueen wrote in his press release. 'This collection is for a woman who wants to stand out. She wants to look completely different from the rest of the guests at the party. This fall-winter Haute Couture is meant to give this woman the dress she needs to celebrate the true start of the millennium.'

The result was 51 looks for night-time revellers. The models took it in turn to step forward from the crush of dancers and present their outfits to the audience. The designs were a frenzied mix of fabrics, cuts, colours, patterns and embellishments, drawing on references as eclectic as the outfits themselves. A photograph of a sequinned dress worn by singer and actress Sylvie Vartan in 1981 was the inspiration for a jumpsuit made of transparent tulle embellished with shimmering crystals (see opposite, left), while a sheath dress worn by the actress Lilian Harvey in the 1930s, with a dangerously low plunging back, was reinterpreted in red panne velvet. The motifs on a Pucci cape, photographed by Henry Clarke in 1965, were recreated in the form of starburst embellishments on a draped cellophane dress that required 200 hours of work. Finally, the crosses of the Union Jack appeared in satin on a coat worn with a 'bearskin' hat, associated with the British Grenadier Guards, that had a chin strap featuring a ball gag (see opposite, top right), then again on a sheath dress made of red, white and blue lace, with an integrated flagpole at the back (see opposite, bottom right).

A.S.

1950S ICONS AND EAST END BANKERS

This collection was the first time that Alexander McQueen's designs looked back to the 1950s and the early days of Hubert de Givenchy. 'I want to accentuate the waist,' he explained. With this in mind, he added impressive corset-like leather belts that cinched the wearer in and emphasized the bust. This hourglass silhouette was accentuated by short, generous skirts, some of which were made from layered flounces of organza and evoked the lavish feel of Mexican traditional dress. The small briefcase-like bags were reminiscent of post-war vanity cases, while some of the organza blouses carried vague echoes of the separates that Hubert de Givenchy had presented in 1952 (see p.26).

Black dominated the opening designs in the collection, its starkness enhancing the silhouettes. It was followed by bright colours, mainly red and green. Little by little, motifs began to appear: stripes, houndstooth, floral prints taken from 1950s upholstery fabric and reproduced in jacquard or patterned velvet. The cocktail dresses featured swathes of fabric draped diagonally across the body, revealing boned corsets made of tulle, created by expert corset-makers, whose craftsmanship was also displayed in the suspender belts, stockings and daring basques.

In contrast to this highly feminine silhouette, McQueen was also inspired by the classic suits worn by East End bankers. His suits were embellished with an array of details, from shoulder darts, pick stitching and basting stitch to stiff collars and trousers with buttoned flies. Even the shoes were like the brogues traditionally worn by City workers in London. However, McQueen reinterpreted these classic looks in his own style, adding a revealing diamond-shaped cut-out to the back of a jacket or creating a pattern with insets of fabric.

A.S.

WORLD TOUR

The official show was cancelled at the last minute, and designs were presented only to 170 clients of the *maison*.

The 34 looks drew on a wide range of cultural references. Alexander McQueen's passion for Scottish and British culture, and his admiration for Japan (see p.394) and the tribes of the Amazon (see p.404), were well known, but this time he looked to Africa for inspiration. The backing music for his show mixed melancholy classical concertos with African songs. This influence could also be seen in the veils wrapped around some models' faces, which were reminiscent of those worn by the Tuareg people, and the red-dust make-up and sculptural braided hairstyles sometimes daubed with red clay.

While this collection featured McQueen's first trench-coat dress (see opposite, bottom left), with a beige tartan lining, he mostly remained faithful to his signature looks, once again presenting leather designs with laser-cut embellishments like those seen on fans, sheath dresses with diagonal patterns that evoked 1930s fashions, and luxurious finishes on all the grey suiting fabrics. He also drew on 18th-century French designs, emulating their delicate floral embroidery around the collars and wrists of his garments (see, for example, right).

McQueen presented a jumpsuit made of lacquered houndstooth fabric, one of the few pieces that drew on Hubert de Givenchy's designs. It had a V-shaped neckline at the back with two lengths of fabric trailing down past the waist, like an obi bow (see p.440, top left and right). The model also wore one of the many corsets in the collection that were inspired by human anatomy, made of moulded leather in the shape of abdominal muscles and protruding spinal columns. This restrictive feel was taken to the extreme in a bodice made from bands of silver metal (see opposite, right), which built on an idea that had featured in the Autumn/Winter 1999–2000 show (see p.416, right). McQueen preferred silver to gold, and used it to create a pectoral made of rhinestone-encrusted rings adorned with falcon talons gripping a pearl (see p.440, bottom left), a reminder of the designer's passion for birds of prey.

A.S.

'SEESHORE AT THE SEASHORE SEESHORE AT THE SEASHORE SEESHORE AT THE SEASHORE'

Transformed into a beach hut, the salons of the Givenchy townhouse headquarters were covered with blond wooden cladding that looked as if it had been weathered by the light, wind and salt of the sea. The sound of rolling waves covered the sharp clicking of the models' heels as they walked. Wearing natural-looking make-up, their faces were bathed in soft daylight that filtered through net curtains.

This intimate collection, presented as two shows of 90 people, played around with layering coats, jackets, blouses and mesh knitwear in natural colours: shades of green, camel and grey, with hints of gold and pink.

McQueen built on the impressive anatomical corsets made of moulded leather that had first appeared in his previous haute couture show (see p. 438), as well as the glittering silkscreen-printed Prince of Wales checks (see p. 444, left) and the tulle bustiers. One of these, worn with a pair of sand-coloured leather trousers, was partly hidden under a half-blouse made of organza with a print of black roses, which draped across the body and extended to form a frothy train on one side (see opposite, left).

Alongside suits with wide stripes, which evoked British cricket club blazers, the ever-present grey tweed and Prince of Wales checks were embellished with printed or embroidered flowers. Floaty fabrics and structured tailoring were combined to create trouser suits with trains made of materials including ostrich feathers and antique lace. This dichotomy dominated the entire collection, also coming through in outfits that paired shirts and ties with flared skirts that had flounces made of leather or crepe georgette.

A smiling Alexander McQueen appeared at the end of the show with his nose painted red, holding his young godson in his arms. He dedicated this final show to 'all those who have worked with [me] at Givenchy over the last four and a half years'.

A.S.

JULIEN MACDONALD

A SHORT BIOGRAPHY

When Julien Macdonald was appointed artistic director of Givenchy in 2001, the designer, then 28, was already known as the 'King of Bling' of London Fashion Week. After a period of minimalism, the late 1990s had been driven by a newfound desire for opulence amid the economic boom. As a consequence, the market for occasion-wear began to flourish. With his perfectly timed talent for glitz and disco dresses, Macdonald became synonymous with the high-octane glamour and skimpy clubwear favoured by a fresh shopping mentality. He had founded his eponymous line, Julien Macdonald, in 1997, thrilling the fashion industry with an unapologetic approach to sexiness and excess that quickly caught the eye of showbusiness. Soon, he was dressing local celebrities like television presenter Kelly Brook and *Big Brother* contestant Anna Nolan, and drawing in international names like Kylie Minogue.

Macdonald was born in 1972 in Merthyr Tydfil, a small town in Wales. His father worked in a washing machine factory, and his mother in a lightbulb factory. In the evenings, his mother turned into a profuse knitter, creating pieces for friends and family in the town, and instilling in the young Julien – whose name she spelled with an 'e' in homage to a French ancestor – an early talent for knitting. It led him to the Faculty of Arts and Architecture at the University of Brighton, and ultimately to the Royal College of Art in London. He side-lined his studies with knitwear jobs for Koji Tatsuno and Alexander McQueen, whom he would later succeed as artistic director at Givenchy. Upon his graduation in 1996, he gained the attention of Karl Lagerfeld, who recruited him as a knitwear designer for Chanel and stated that 'Julien plays with his machine like Horowitz plays on his piano'.

As the new knitwear prodigy on the fashion scene, Macdonald showcased his talent in the sexy and glamorous treatment of a material which wasn't traditionally seen through that lens. Working with luminous and lightweight yarns, he invented a seductive netting technique, which lent itself to cocktail-wear and earned him the nickname 'King of the Cobweb'. It was followed by monikers like 'the Welsh Donatella Versace' and, indeed, the 'King of Bling'. In 1997, he designed Chanel's best-selling outfit that year.

Soon after, he launched his eponymous line and took to the London Fashion Week runway, where gimmicks like a dress encrusted with De Beers diamonds worth £650,000 and a Michael Jackson lookalike in the front row became part of his brand of frivolous fun and fancy – supported by rave reviews.

In 2001, shortly after winning an award for British Glamour Designer of the Year, Macdonald was appointed at Givenchy. On the phone from a holiday in Bali, he told press it was 'a dream come true' and that his vision for the house was 'sex on legs'. His tenure, however, received its share of criticism from the fashion press, who detected a season-to-season incoherence in his collections, founded in the balance between juggling the genetics of the Givenchy legacy and his personal design identity. 'Paris is bourgeois; in London, it's more fun,' he told reporters at one of his eponymous shows in London in 2002, adding: 'I can be cheeky and sexy and take risks here.' After Macdonald parted ways with Givenchy in 2004, he designed a homeware line, a successful affordable label with Debenhams department store, and costumes for the likes of Beyoncé Knowles and Lady Gaga. Today, he continues to create eponymous collections and gowns for the red carpet.

Anders Christian Madsen

GIVENCHY CODES

Referring to his radical predecessors, Julien
Macdonald told press that his debut show for
Givenchy was 'not about Alexander McQueen
and John Galliano', but about Hubert de Givenchy.
As a 29-year-old London designer, who was
largely celebrated for party dresses and vibrant
knitwear, Macdonald created a collection that was
characterized by a desire to assert his reverence
for the founder's codes, which had little in common
with his own.

He presented the show – which also marked
his haute couture debut – in a ritzy Belle Époque
apartment on Avenue Foch as the definitive symbol
of the Parisian fashion establishment embodied by
Givenchy. Macdonald painted the founder's archive
tropes – the Bettina blouse, the tulip skirt, the little
black dress – in a muted colour palette exercised in
austere and often body-covering silhouettes, which
relegated his own signature sexiness to more subtle
expressions like tightness and transparency.

'It's about putting the customers back where they
belong – not about costume drama and theatrics,'
Macdonald said. He modernized the tulip skirt in
all-black ensembles styled with trousers, sexed
up the sober Givenchy spirit with touches of black
leather and silk, and interpreted his own brand of
evening glamour in lashings of fur, feathers and
crystal embellishment.

Ultimately, critics found his display of veneration
too far-removed from the Macdonald they knew
from the London runway. The collection would
become the first in a line of challenges for the
new Givenchy designer.

A.C.M.

BLACK AND WHITE

Through a business lens, Julien Macdonald's
first ready-to-wear collection for Givenchy was
his most important. Tasked with re-engaging the
clientele after the brief and much more theatrical
residencies of John Galliano (see p.352) and
Alexander McQueen (see p.374), he put his money
on a reconnection with the subtlety and purity of
Hubert de Givenchy's original propositions. And so,
Macdonald continued to go against the clubby grain
of his eponymous work and stuck to the sober guns
first loaded at his haute couture show some months
before (see p.448).

His debut ready-to-wear collection for the
house riffed on classics like the Bettina blouse,
transforming it into somewhat deconstructed ruffle
tops, frilly 'boho chic' dresses, and tunics styled
over trousers. His loosely Victorian tailoring first
proposed in the haute couture show evolved into
cutaway frock coats – likewise worn over trousers –
and materialized as riding jackets with leather
front panels.

Perhaps conscious of injecting his take on Givenchy
with the identity associated with him prior to joining
the house, Macdonald flexed his knitwear muscle
in sensual sheer dresses, fishnet tops, and natural
macramé bags and belts. While some critics thought
the designer's surface decoration 'heavy-handed'
and his takes on archive classics contrived, the
collection's commercial potential did not go
unnoticed – a fact backed up by Macdonald's
continued preference for a muted colour palette
founded in black and white.

A.C.M.

'ANGE'

The show notes for Julien Macdonald's second
haute couture show for Givenchy rhapsodized
about dreamy angels (*anges*, in French) 'falling
to earth' in 'rich fabrics'.

After a debut season of playing it safe (see p.448),
the designer tried out intellectual deconstructivism –
an arena previously unfamiliar to him – while
introducing more signs of his own style into the
sober and subdued premise that had characterized
his take on the house thus far.

He smothered his fallen angels in the intricate
knitwear that had given him his London nickname,
'King of the Cobweb', producing an ethereal and
ghostly collection of ruched and tiered volumes
realized in gothic lace, tattered chiffon and netting.
The unravelling Miss Havisham-like deconstruction
increased Macdonald's stakes in the showmanship
department, and, while some critics remained hard
to please, the sophomore couturier continued to find
consolation in favourable reviews of his tailoring.

Here, generously cut tuxedos in black and
white and a peplum trouser suit demonstrated
Macdonald's knack for bringing a contemporary
point of view to Givenchy's codes, while a cutaway
ruffled blazer revealing a decaying sheer white
underlayer (see right) earned nods of approval
on the drama front.

A.C.M.

SPORTY GLAMOUR

Nearly a year into his tenure at Givenchy, Julien Macdonald turned his back on the formality that had embodied his first collections and set his sights on a direction more in tune with the sporty glamour embodied by the winds blowing through the Y2K fashion landscape.

His second ready-to-wear show opened with a casual parka in patchwork leather, matching trousers and stacked leather boots (see right). Rendered in greens, browns and black, it set the tone for a decidedly outdoorsy collection that revisited eras beyond the classic annals of Givenchy in Renaissance hooded outerwear, Elizabethan bloomers, and brocade and tapestry fabrication exercised in scaled-up shoulder bags. Those elements contributed to a look that defied time and geography, freely jumping between eras and cultural dress codes.

Macdonald continued to insert his own trademarks into his Givenchy practice, presenting oversized knitted sweaters, unravelling knitted cardigans, and enormous scarves. Reviewers highlighted his takes on motorcycle uniforms interpreted in classic leather manifestations as well as in the lines of soft overcoats with high collars. Less popular were Macdonald's harem pants and 1980s sensibility, which some critics felt contributed to a lack of direction.

A.C.M.

NEON CLUBWEAR

In what would become his most memorable show for Givenchy, Julien Macdonald took out the old Paris stock exchange for a fashion experience that stunned his wealthy clients and delighted the press. 'This is the first time people have seen the real Julien Macdonald – fun, flamboyant, colourful, youthful,' he told reporters. 'I am young and I am learning. I haven't perfected anything, but I am working with the couture atelier.'

Casting aside previous forays into sophistication and deconstruction, the designer embraced the flashy sex appeal at the core of his eponymous brand and created his most personal collection for Givenchy. With overtones of bondage, he forged leather into military jackets, miniskirts, and a trouser suit cut up and manipulated into bows. Coats were dripping in mink tails, fringes were bursting from epaulettes, feathers cascaded from the necklines of cocktail dresses, and crystals and sequins assumed the spotlight.

The contrasts to Macdonald's previous collections for the house couldn't have been more pronounced. Gone was the muted, monotonous colour scale. In its place came the bright neons and glistening metallics of clubwear, with all the bareback dresses of Macdonald's signature dreams. Backdropped by a pink, gold and blue neon sign that spelled out 'Hotel Givenchy' like something out of a red-light district, the show was an exercise in what the time defined as 'shock value couture': anti-sophisticated, anti-conservative and anti-'good taste'. It was Macdonald's first season of rave reviews, and a silver lining in his tenure at Givenchy.

A.C.M.

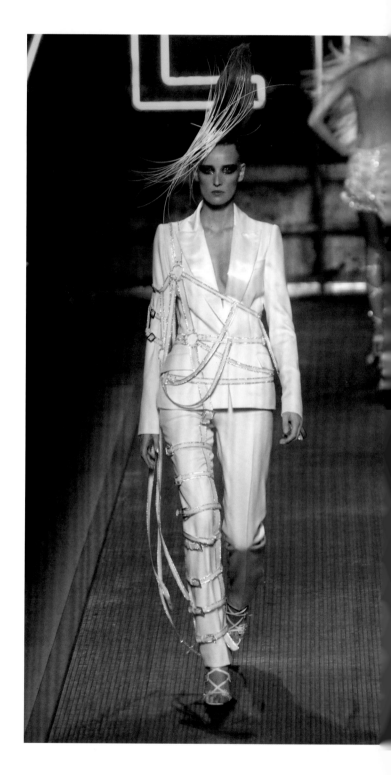

RESORT STYLE

Hot off the heels of his applauded haute couture
show (see p.456), Julien Macdonald presented a
ready-to-wear collection so characteristic of its
time, it could have been an MTV music video. From
little white suits with ultra-short skirts and shorts
to combat-like red and orange mesh jackets and
shorts, and elaborate 'couture jeans', it ticked all
the boxes of early 2000s glam.

Macdonald worked his trademark fishnet and
macramé into barely-there minidress constructions
in solar colours, echoed in knotted Flintstones
dresses and beaded eveningwear more native
to beachwear than anything else. On his runway,
actual swimwear appeared like daywear, presented
alongside floaty resort print dresses that may
not have served as an olive branch to Givenchy's
traditional clientele but certainly reached out to
a new one.

After surrendering to his self-referential haute
couture collection a few months before, the press
came down hard on Macdonald for what they saw
as his abandonment of the sophisticated soul of
Givenchy. In hindsight, however, the show was –
more than anything else – a product of its time; a
memorable page in the Y2K fashion history books.

A.C.M.

SOPHISTICATED PURITY

By the fall of 2002, Paris was buzzing with rumours of Julien Macdonald's exit from Givenchy. Amid unfavourable reviews, his fourth stab at haute couture was widely billed as a make-or-break collection.

No doubt aware of the challenge at hand, he returned to the point of departure that had fuelled his initial approach for the house: Hubert de Givenchy. Attempting to reconnect with the classic purity and sophistication of the founder's legacy, Macdonald opened his show in a Parisian mansion with riffs on Givenchy's little black dress immortalized by Audrey Hepburn in *Breakfast at Tiffany's*. The choice may have been obvious, but it wasn't ignorant. At its foundation, Givenchy stands for a timeless appeal that's also universal, and rehashing it could be Macdonald's saving grace. The little black dresses – reworked with cut-outs, lace and plume – were followed by demonstrations of the atelier's masterful tailoring, adapted with rigid hardware, plunging décolletés, and exposed midriffs for added sex appeal.

The show concluded in a cascade of red-carpet dresses, each of which illustrated a different technique central to haute couture, and – by proxy – Macdonald's growing understanding of his role. If it was a tactic on his part, it worked. Critics were kind, and the designer would soon be back with another ready-to-wear collection.

A.C.M.

SECRET AGENTS

Newly reverted to archival mode following an haute couture collection that returned to Givenchy's roots (see p.460), Julien Macdonald presented a ready-to-wear collection founded in a classic approach to the job of a designer working under someone else's name: stick to the codes and change up the spirit.

Inspired by a trip to Russia, he came up with a narrative about a KGB spy living undercover in Paris – and let it unfold through the tropes of Hubert de Givenchy. Macdonald's secret agent wore tweed coats or classic belted trench coats with high collars over turtlenecks and pencil skirts, with strict leather gloves. He brought back the motorcycle cap recalling a Vespa-riding Audrey Hepburn in *Roman Holiday* and matched it to his spy's outfits. When she morphed into her evening persona, so did the garments in her wardrobe: trench coats became little black dresses, some trimmed in gold mesh or rhinestone embroidery, and pencil skirts were covered in sequins.

His collection touched on the same chords as the debut show that had originally sparked criticism for being too safe (see p.448), but at this stage Macdonald – for all the persistent rumours of his exit – had gained a confidence when it came to the codes of Givenchy. That learning curve manifested in a well-received show.

A.C.M.

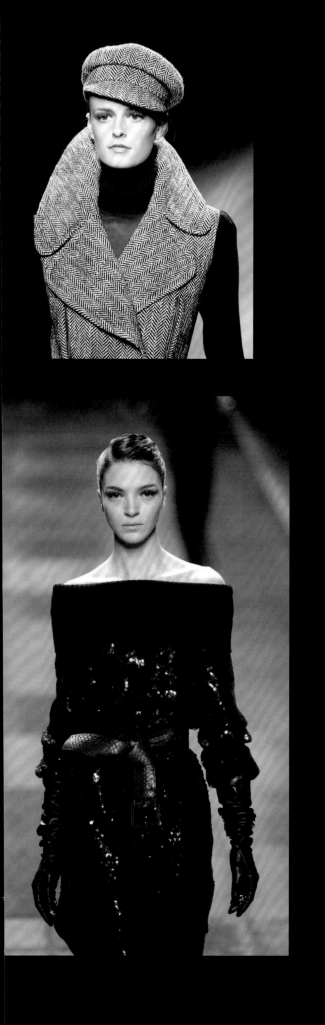

HOMAGE TO
AUDREY HEPBURN

For Julien Macdonald, sticking to the classics had
become both an audience-pleaser and a way to
calm critics. Hitting two birds with one stone, the
haute couture collection he showed at the Grand
Hôtel in the summer of 2003 had reporters quoting
clients on the front row gushing about his creations.

Once again, Macdonald turned to the house's
poster girl Audrey Hepburn for a collection that
took its point of departure in the Givenchy outfits
worn by the actress in two of her signature films.
He interpreted the skirt suit and cocktail dress from
Sabrina in a series of black and navy looks, adding
his own high collars dramatically framing the face.
Then, he set his sights on the floor-length dress
seen on Hepburn in *Breakfast at Tiffany's*, riffing on
the classic in silhouettes that gradually expanded
and increased in surface decoration. In between,
he presented a show-stopping leopard-print
fur coat (see opposite, left), which he named
'L'Interdit' after the house's fragrance.

Macdonald's take on Hubert de Givenchy's
tropes was sexier – more body-conscious – and
consequently more 1980s than 1950s, as more than
one critic observed. His demure and ultimately chic
homage to the founder continued to hit a vein of
relative timelessness which was hard to fault. But,
bar the massive multicoloured cellophane ballgown
that appeared towards the end (see opposite, right),
Macdonald's personal aesthetic remained hard
to detect.

A.C.M.

EASY, BREEZY

By the fall of 2003, Julien Macdonald was ready
for a new proposition at Givenchy. His last three
collections had reverted to archive reverence
and shown his audience that he was well-versed
in the house's history. Since joining, Macdonald
had infrequently juggled that type of proposal with
directions truer to his eponymous clubwear style,
as well as ideas that were entirely new to both the
house and his own disposition. This collection fell
into the latter category.

With The Carpenters on the sound system and not
a single black dress in sight, the mood was easy
and breezy: cream or lilac cheesecloth dresses and
skirts with pretty macramé inserts, shift dresses
in peach or fawn so light they slid off the body, and
drapey holiday dresses in ruffles and tiers in all the
colours of the sunset. American *Vogue* noted that
the collection 'included the sort of luxury details
French women like when summering around the
Mediterranean'. Tailoring played with shrunken
volumes for a cute and almost childlike effect,
a sentiment echoed in leathers which – contrary
to previous manifestations – had been softened
and rendered in the dusty cream colours of
the collection.

In tune with the Y2K 'boho chic' moment that
reached its zenith around the time of the show,
Macdonald adorned his collection with flirty tassels
and lace. Airy and sweet, the show cut a decided
contrast to his previous offerings at Givenchy,
but summed up the spirit of the time.

A.C.M.

ETHEREAL ELEGANCE

For his final haute couture collection for Givenchy, Julien Macdonald chose to focus on the clientele who had served as his biggest support system throughout his time at the house. With just 80 seated guests made up predominantly of couture clients – alongside Liv Tyler and a few members of the press – it was an intimate and publicly played-down affair.

The collection paid homage to the core codes of Givenchy in delicate lace dresses imbued with the ruffles of the Bettina blouse and sheathed in ethereal sheer overlays. Little black dresses and skirt suits were dramatized with dense ruching, elaborately beaded décolletés and transparent flounces in millefeuille. The *Guardian* wrote of the 'show-stopping, flesh-revealing gowns' that closed the show, highlighting how Macdonald's personal touch had always been a success with the couture clientele he had cultivated at the house.

The day before the show, Givenchy had announced the departure of Macdonald, who took a gracious bow following the finale, smiling at the audience who had accompanied him on his rollercoaster ride in Paris. The next day, the press was already busy taking guesses as to which designer could take over from him at the house.

A.C.M.

LADYLIKE CHIC

In January 2004, Julien Macdonald had already announced he would be departing Givenchy when his contract was up in April. His final show for the house was bittersweet. Speaking to the press, he was candid about the challenges he had experienced during his three-year stint in Paris: 'Let's face it, I haven't had the greatest success there,' he said, admitting he felt 'so much more Marilyn Monroe than Audrey Hepburn'.

If his final show was fuelled by the relief of his departure, Macdonald only expressed it in a deep-rooted respect for the house. The collection was full of tributes to the genetics of Givenchy, from voluminous pouf skirts to below-the-knee little black cocktail dresses, strapless evening silhouettes, and belted ladylike coats with sculptural collars informed by the language of haute couture. Lingerie dresses played on some of the deconstruction Macdonald had introduced early on in his tenure but to a more successful degree, in gem-coloured silk cocktail dresses with grey chiffon overlays that disintegrated around the bustier and slipped into a cloudy filter over the skirt.

It was a fitting farewell for Macdonald, who returned to London to focus on his eponymous line. Following his departure, the next three Givenchy collections – A/W 2004–2005 haute couture, S/S 2005 ready-to-wear (no haute couture collection was presented for S/S 2005) and A/W 2005–2006 ready-to-wear – were designed by the in-house studio, while the fashion world eagerly awaited the announcement of Macdonald's successor.

A.C.M.

RICCARDO TISCI

A SHORT BIOGRAPHY

In his 12 years as artistic director – from 2005 to 2017 – Riccardo Tisci transformed the house of Givenchy into one of the most agenda-setting brands in fashion. He radicalized its haute couture, modernized its ready-to-wear, and spearheaded a luxury streetwear culture that would come to define a new approach to dressing. Rooted in the emotional impressions of his childhood, Tisci's creative vision at Givenchy was founded in dark romanticism, religious and mythical motifs, and a collaging of global references. With his diverse casting and celebrity associations, his tenure contributed to creating a more inclusive fashion industry, putting at the forefront of his runways and campaigns the equal representation of colour, culture, subculture and sexual identity. 'Impressions from the street made me different to other couturiers,' Tisci has said.

He was born in the Apulian seaside town of Taranto in 1974. Tisci's father, a fruit importer, died when Tisci was young, leaving his mother to take care of him and his eight older sisters. She relocated the family north, to a small town near Como. Tisci's 1970s upbringing was defined by poverty and the divisions between Italy's polar geographic identities. As a southerner in the north, he recognized in his sisters – whom he credits as his greatest inspirations – a tough and sexual self-confidence dressed up in the dark Roman Catholic aesthetic of the family's cultural heritage. Along with musical interests that turned Tisci into a teenage goth – and an instinct for escape that would take him out of Como and around the world – these elements formed the visual and emotional underpinnings of his work. He has described his Givenchy collections as deeply personal: 'You can see the phases of my life through my collections: the security, the insecurity, the happiness, the darkness.'

At 17, following studies at the Istituto d'Arte Applicata e Design in Cantù, Tisci moved to London, where he immersed himself in the self-expression of a 1990s British fashion scene defined by John Galliano and Alexander McQueen. An extraordinary talent for illustration landed him a full scholarship at Central Saint Martins, where he side-lined his studies with a passion for techno and rave. Tisci graduated in 1999 and worked for Puma and Ruffo Research before relocating to India for a few months to create his own fashion line. In 2004, he presented two eponymous collections in Milan, unveiling an early design identity founded by the dark Catholic dress codes of his upbringing. The shows gained attention and in 2005, aged 30, Tisci was appointed artistic director at Givenchy, taking over from Julien Macdonald. 'I promised myself that when I left this house, it would be at the top, the way it deserved to be,' Tisci has said.

The first two years of his tenure garnered mixed receptions for the designer, who the press largely wrote off as 'goth'. But the haute couture ateliers of Givenchy became an education for Tisci. He grew with the job and steadily expanded the dark elegance and romance he shared with Hubert de Givenchy into a radical, sexual and street-smart proposition, applauded by critics and contemporary fashion audiences alike. Tisci shook up the conventional rules of fashion, switching and revising archaic dress codes. Through intersected haute couture, ready-to-wear and menswear, traversing the traditional borders of purpose, gender and environment, his progressive approach was mirrored in diverse celebrity and model associations, including his muse Mariacarla Boscono and the likes of Lea T, Beyoncé Knowles, Jay-Z, Madonna, Rihanna, Bella Hadid and Kim Kardashian, whose 2014 bridal gown he created. In 2017, Tisci left Givenchy and joined Burberry, where he served as chief creative officer until 2022.

Anders Christian Madsen

DARK ROMANCE

Few guests knew what to expect from Riccardo Tisci's first collection for Givenchy, which also marked his haute couture debut. But one thing was certain: this designer could pull a crowd. Outside the Givenchy *maison* on avenue George V, onlookers had amassed to catch a glimpse of the house's new designer and his work.

The season before, at Tisci's second runway show for his eponymous brand in Milan, a similar scene had unfolded. There, the 30-year-old designer had erected a cross and presented enough gloomy monastic robes and nun-like cornettes to be labelled 'goth'. For his Givenchy debut, he mirrored that vision in the black-clad elegance at the heart of the house. Lined up in a tableau vivant in the different salons of the *maison*, his collection was largely floor-length: lanky, draped, drifty, and darkly romantic. He adorned his dramatic silhouettes with pieces of fur, knots and crochet lace, achieving a luxurious primitivity that felt part gothic and part post-apocalyptic.

Bar the first look's Bettina blouse – modernized in poplin with petal pleats – paired with a slick black patent-leather pencil skirt (see right), Tisci omitted any obvious house references, prompting kudos from critics, who deemed the affair 'promising'.

A.C.M.

OPTICAL WHITES

If parts of his audience already had him down as
'goth', Riccardo Tisci wasn't about to play to their
presumptions. For his second show for Givenchy –
and first ready-to-wear proposal – the designer let
in the light, illuminating a bright white space for a
collection that opened with a series of looks that
inverted the house's signature black silhouette
into optical white manifestations.

He lightened and romanticized the Bettina blouse
in sheer white chiffon with delicate ruffles and
paired it with a high-waist, tiered, super-tight pencil
skirt that cut a strict and constricting silhouette for
the show (see right). As white became two-tone –
contrasted with black – Tisci's romanticism
sharpened in architectural tailored jackets and
skirts sculpturally flounced at the hem. Throughout,
one could have attributed his references to archival
nods, until, that was, distinctly foreign elements like
wrestling belts and tapered trousers with stirrups
worn under skirts appeared from out of the blue,
foreshadowing the very personal propositions
this designer would eventually bring to the ball.

Tisci's early change of direction confused critics,
who didn't hold back. Little did they know what
was coming.

A.C.M.

BLACK, WHITE AND RED

If Riccardo Tisci's first ready-to-wear collection for Givenchy (see p.478) had felt like an objection to the gothic pigeonhole in which the fashion press was quick to place him, it seemed he felt comfortable returning to that dark romance for his second turn. But unlike his haute couture debut show (see p.474) – much heavier on the monastic styles of the eponymous line he had now put on hiatus – this collection presented Tisci's gothic glamour through the grammar of Hubert de Givenchy.

Tisci opened the show with a series of little black dresses, each of which demonstrated his own technical language: some were draped, some were adorned with tabs, others were folded like origami or wrapped around the body in volumes that felt part haute couture and part sci-fi. Blood-red leather gloves introduced a new colour to Tisci's universe, repeated in shirt prints featuring the first appearance of the mirrored motifs that would become a recurring element in his design vocabulary.

But, more than anything, two other occurrences indicated this designer's connection with the future image of fashion. One was to be found in the glossy puffer jackets that infiltrated the collection (see opposite, top left) as an early sign of streetwear's influence on both Tisci's career and his surrounding industry. The other: the procession of women of colour who opened the show in a time when diversity on the runway was still a work in progress.

A.C.M.

'MAPPEMONDE'

No doubt uplifted by reactions to his ready-to-wear
collection the season before (see p.480), when
it came to his second haute couture collection
for Givenchy, Riccardo Tisci delved into the
contemporary gothic glamour vision that
was still under construction on his runway.

Presented in a blackened-out room with a
black lacquered runway, the show exercised
the possibilities of the house's master ateliers
in a collection that explored classic tropes of
elegance – the black suit, the little black dress,
the belted coat – by splicing them with folkloric
dress elements from around the world. Bosnian,
Indian, Indonesian, Myanmarese and pan-African
inspirations manifested in exploding feather-like
headpieces, coats and skirts with tiered fringing
that resembled raffia, gems and beads rustically
encrusted on coats and dresses, and a nature-
centric and ferocious use of fur, which resonated
in lashings of crocodile leather. At Givenchy, it was
Tisci's first foray into the travel-focused, ritualistic
and mythical aspects that would paint a more
exotic side to his work.

The presentation concluded with a show-stopping
finale of the gloomy, clerical, black gowns that
always filled his dreams: these were raised to
haute couture level.

A.C.M.

GEOMETRIC EXPLORATIONS

By March 2007, reviewers were reporting increasing sales at Givenchy. Riccardo Tisci was on to new territory for the house, and his third ready-to-wear show was set on further exploration.

It materialized in a continuation of the folklore of his haute couture collection (see p.482) fused with modernist geometry that paid tribute to the dress codes of the Indigenous Maori people of New Zealand. It was a meeting of contrasts expressed in passementerie adornments, batik prints on bubble suits and draped silk jersey dresses, and collage dresses with circular cut-outs.

At Givenchy, Tisci seemed to be making notes along the way, developing the elements that delighted his audiences while pushing those that challenged them. It made for an irreverent approach to the house backed up by a point of view that – in the case of a collection like this – felt both courageous and cheeky. Tisci proved that point by buckling his models up in the confections of an erotic wardrobe, from strict black bustiers and brassieres to prettified codpieces and dog collars, and striped stockings.

A.C.M.

'THE MERMAID'

Two years into his tenure at Givenchy, audiences had a clearer understanding of Riccardo Tisci's vision. Whether he was 'goth' or 'geometrist' or 'deconstructivist' was slowly but steadily fading in the light of the work he was producing, and it paved the way for an haute couture collection that was both poetic and personal.

Reminiscing about his birth town of Taranto by the Apulian seaside, he imagined a childlike – though slightly horror-infused – narrative of the metamorphosis of sailors into mermaids. Walking through a dense mist, models in deconstructed naval coats dragged trailing silk skirts on a wet stone floor. Similarly deconstructed suits seemed to morph with the gills of fish, while some took on metallic water-like surfaces. Romantic gowns were melancholically netted in translucent layers, trapped in marine ropes, or overgrown with appliqué resembling the sea life that reclaims a sunken ship. But no look received as many accolades from reviewers as a navy suede coat rippling down the front and fading into a long train like that of a mermaid's tail (see opposite, bottom left). 'Witness the gloomy brilliance,' wrote Cathy Horyn in *The New York Times*.

For Tisci, the show was a turning point not just in his exploration of haute couture, but in his approach to Givenchy. Now, his personality was showing in a big way, and it was paying off.

A.C.M.

PUNK MARINE

With his feet firmly planted on the right path at Givenchy, Riccardo Tisci used his next ready-to-wear collection to demonstrate the organization that comes with a decisive sense of direction. Rather than putting his haute couture collection behind him (see p.486), he filtered its experimental and poetic ideas into a real-life wardrobe of tailoring and flou.

The deconstructed naval coats of the previous show transformed into wearable tailoring with an unmistakable point of view – an approach echoed in sculptural fur jackets – while its trailing mermaid skirts mutated into slinky everyday skirts and dramatically flared trousers. Inspired by a Japanese marine jacket from the 1920s, Tisci sent out one terrific peacoat and blazer after the other, styled over cool white shirts with deconstructed ribbon collars and high-waist sailor flares.

It was a viable and distinctly contemporary line, which fused the characters of Givenchy and Tisci with a realistic idea of the sober elegance that attracted women to the house in the first place. And while some questioned the more ostentatious addition of Art Deco stud adornment on dresses and jackets, those garments became some of the most photographed of the season.

A.C.M.

MYTHICAL CREATURES

By now, Riccardo Tisci had managed to establish
an early fanbase at Givenchy, not just in terms
of audiences, but real-life customers who were
beginning to swear to the flattering cuts of his
modern tailoring and draped dresses. This was
clear in an haute couture collection that confidently
continued to explore the fantastical, this time
by way of Greek mythology with all the sirens
and medusas that come with the territory. He
presented it confidently, too, in a stripped-back
production exposing every seam and pleat of
his artisanal merit.

It opened with a silhouette to remember:
a deconstructed peplum jacket caressing the
volume of a plumed orb skirt from which mile-
long legs clad in thigh-high lace-up boots protruded,
every inch rendered in blush cream (see opposite,
top left). Tisci exercised his hyper-luxurious side in
a fur-lined crocodile jacket with scales individually
deconstructed to heighten its natural opulence
(see opposite, top right), and in head-to-toe
or dégradé leopard-print looks fusing furs
and skins with intarsia and embroideries.

Technically, it was his most impressive haute
couture collection to date: a display of the
knowledge Tisci had gained during his time at
the house, and the territory he still wanted to
charter. Visually, it cemented the distinct look
he had created for Givenchy – an impact that
had only just begun.

A.C.M.

WARRIOR WOMEN

By the fall of 2007, the glitz and glamour that had ruled fashion since the millennium were starting to fade. Customers were tuning in to a new minimalism imbued with the same sense of luxury to which they'd grown accustomed, but more subdued.

Riccardo Tisci played to that mentality with a collection that walked the tightrope between opulence and restraint. He essentially showed a collection of little black dresses and black tailoring heightened by surface decoration, which was simple but impactful. Cases in point were the black dresses and suits that opened the show covered in vastly oversized polka dots – a motif that prevailed throughout the collection – and the large grommets that adorned everything from elegant blazers to chiffon dresses.

Taking his point of departure in the mythical warrior women that still filled his dreams after the last haute couture show (see p.490), Tisci introduced the gladiator boots that would become an early signifier for him at Givenchy, matched them with leather belt bags, and dyed his models' eyebrows a signature bleach blonde.

A.C.M.

'BALLERINA'

In an haute couture show that could have inspired
the film *Black Swan* two years ahead of its time,
Riccardo Tisci tackled the ballet motif through the
label of Gothicism. It had followed him since the
beginning of his Givenchy tenure – now, he was
running with it.

An exploration of the 'gothic ballerina', as his
show notes explained, the collection reinforced
the delicate, romantic lines of ballet through the
sharp hand of Tisci's graphic expression. Slender
and elongated military jackets were styled over full
flouncy skirts underpinned with frilly white tutus,
elegantly evoking Hubert de Givenchy's dance
skirt silhouette through two – very contrasting –
references that weren't archival at all.

It was an intelligent approach to honouring
the house codes, which demonstrated the
understanding Tisci had gained for the brand
he was evolving, and the confidence with which
he now considered it. The ballet reference proved
the perfect way for the designer to evolve his own
codes, too: the gladiator boots that were becoming
something of a trademark were mirrored in ankle-
and knee-high sandals with criss-crossing straps
borrowed from the ballerina wardrobe.

As the show progressed, Tisci overlaid his dance
skirts with floor-length translucent overskirts,
creating the dramatic and quite medieval line
he had brought to Givenchy in the first place.

A.C.M.

LATIN GOTHICISM

In March 2008, Riccardo Tisci presented a Givenchy show that would become one of his most memorable – and impactful. The product of the travels he was starting to undertake in South America, where he felt an affinity with the Catholic aesthetics of his own Italian upbringing, the collection hit the fashion industry with tone-setting force. Style.com critic Sarah Mower noted, '[T]his collection finally shifted Tisci out of the "promising" category into a place where he deserves to be seen as a designer who has come of age.'

Tisci had already established the strict and modern tailoring that created the foundation for his looks, but the faint influence of Latin codes and sportswear that permeated these looks was a game-changer. Gradually introducing an idea of sporty to the formality that defined Givenchy, he paired his crisp and graphic takes on the Bettina blouse with tight, stretchy leggings – some in leather – and filtered in the hyper-elevated glossy puffer jacket that had already infiltrated one of his early Givenchy collections (see p.480). In the fashion establishment, the sportswear influences that the world eventually came to know as streetwear were in their infant stage, and Tisci was only starting to surf a wave that would grow to tsunami-like heights.

He expressed his South American theme in cropped toreador jackets, hints to flamenco, and black lace dresses that bordered his familiar line between eveningwear and monastery dress. But before the collection's impact was truly felt, it was Tisci's multi-chain gold necklaces that became the instant topic of desire.

A.C.M.

'A TRIP IN MACHU PICCHU'

In between this collection and the momentous ready-to-wear show he had put on the season before (see p.492), Riccardo Tisci presented a Givenchy menswear proposal that had the rapidly growing and progressive menswear appetites of the late 2000s salivating. Drawing on his new-found South American motif, it formalized a shorts-over-leggings sportswear silhouette in leather and lace manifestations that didn't just play with gender codes but spliced every genre of dressing, from formal masculinity to boyish sportiness and girly romanticism. His subsequent women's collection followed suit.

Going against the grain of how haute couture was often represented – eveningwear, ballroom dresses, lavish surface decoration – Tisci largely focused on daywear, continuing his empowered noncompliance with wardrobe genres and codes on a runway covered in something as un-couture as wood chips.

A modernized vision of the Inca citadel of Machu Picchu – which he planned to visit later that year – the collection proposed waxed leather jackets lined in alpaca fur, sculptural utilitarian shorts styled over cropped leggings, geometrically embossed leather coats, striped ponchos transformed into little dresses, and cocoon knitwear with Peruvian motifs. When a series of draped or lace evening dresses made their arrival, Tisci broke down their formality with sturdy bombers, leather jackets and peacoats, cementing his uncompromising sense of modernity and new taste for sportswear. The crowning moment: the debut of the spat-covered leather boot that would become a mainstay of Tisci's practice.

A.C.M.

'WESTERN BONDAGE'

During the fall fashion weeks of 2008, as Riccardo Tisci found himself going from one critically acclaimed collection to the next, dressing Madonna for her *Sticky & Sweet Tour*, and killing it in the sales department, the Great Recession decided to rear its ugly head. Not one to surrender his decidedly luxurious disposition without a fight, he put on a proposal for anti-recessionary perseverance.

Tisci's South American travels (see pp.496 and 498) brought him north, to the cowboy country of Mexico and the American West, which added a certain rodeo quality to his sporty modernism. He dubbed the show 'Western bondage' and opened it with a puff-sleeved pioneer dress deconstructed into a midriff-baring bustier laced in bondage straps attached to a miniskirt (see top right). As the silhouette transitioned into tailoring and workwear, he exercised his reference in sporty suits and utilitarian jumpsuits. But it was those thigh-high cowboy boots, jeans morphed with leather chaps, leggings with white rodeo appliqué, and dresses slashed open at the shoulder and adorned in Western diamanté studs that really set hearts racing.

A.C.M.

ETHEREAL EROTICISM

With the fashion industry now in recession
mode, Riccardo Tisci used his first show of 2009
as a moment of calm reflection. Foregoing the
sombre, he created a collection of feather-light
and translucent fabrics retained in a largely
white and ecru colour scheme and staged it on
a runway strewn with rose petals in the style
of the 1888 Lawrence Alma-Tadema painting
The Roses of Heliogabalus.

Likewise, his airy, angelic dresses were inspired
by erotic turn-of-the-century paintings of ancient
rituals, a motif that manifested in the underpinnings
of fetishy chains and Lycra bondage straps, some
of which were encrusted with pearls and crystals.
Those effects nodded at the dance costumes
of Pina Bausch, a reference that built on Tisci's
previous investigations of the properties of the
ballet wardrobe (see p.494).

In many ways, the collection was an exercise in
the layering and filtrage he had been exploring since
his early beginnings at Givenchy. Now, his shrouded
religious silhouettes emerged as elegant, delicate,
sensitive brides in togas that veiled their faces in
draped cowls. Tisci was discovering a different side
to his melancholic, celestial romanticism, and this
softer touch was in tune with the zeitgeist.

A.C.M.

SUBVERSIVE DECONSTRUCTION

The impact of Riccardo Tisci's continuous successes at Givenchy had hit his surrounding industry with such force that his peers were starting to take a leaf out of his book. Around the runways of the fashion capitals, the gothic melancholia that Tisci had been trading since day one was popping up in many manifestations.

So, for his next collection, perhaps it wasn't so strange that he chose to go all-out in his most well-versed language. He applied his gothic grammar to asymmetric silhouettes founded in the modernist tailoring he was now accomplishing with his eyes closed. He morphed little black suits into dresses, pulled out the shoulders of tailored tops and turned them into pagodas implanted with sparkly or furry pads, and sliced and diced his way through tailored dresses that took his deconstruction to new levels.

White evening dresses and tops angelically plumed in ostrich cemented his way with feathers, but it was a series of black dresses, tops and sandals swathed in silky black goat hair that really got fashion critics out of their seats. The self-assured experimentation with which Tisci was evolving Givenchy's identity had become as subversive as it was covetable.

A.C.M.

MOROCCO

After seasons of South American influences
(see pp.496 and 498), Riccardo Tisci turned
to North Africa. In June 2009, he had shown a
menswear collection covered in keffiyeh patterns,
and for the haute couture proposal the following
month, the trip went to Morocco.

With models' heads veiled in translucent scarves,
Tisci took his point of departure in Givenchy's black
hourglass outline, opening the show with tailored
velvet and leather looks with cinched waists and
raised shoulders. Gradually, the shape morphed
into a body-covering harem silhouette: headscarves
draped into cascading tops styled with sarouel
trousers, models' faces and wrists bedecked with
Berber gold. Metallic skirts mimicked the patterns
of Moroccan metalwork and tile, and harem
trousers and full-length dresses were sequinned
so intricately that the rigid shapes took on an
air of sci-fi.

Then Tisci departed any literal referencing and
went freestyle, exercising his distinct sense of
draping and asymmetric deconstruction in a series
of white and blush dresses with his trademark
passementerie and oversized stud adornments,
expanding the sci-fi feeling into pure ballroom
futurism. Mariacarla Boscono closed the show
in a translucent gown with magnified keffiyeh
embroideries (see p.511), bringing Tisci's season
reference full circle.

A.C.M.

OPTICAL LINES

'Riccardo Tisci has moved up to the elite group
of designers who matter most in Paris,' declared
critic Sarah Mower, reporting on his next Givenchy
collection for Style.com. In five years at the house,
the designer had gone from 'who?' to 'here he is
again!', commanding a hype fuelled by a social
media culture that was evolving alongside him.
His show had become one of the hottest tickets
in Paris, and it was as visible outside the venues
as it was on his crammed runway benches.

The press couldn't find enough superlatives
for his next collection, which fused his ongoing
explorations of Middle Eastern motifs (see p.508)
with studies of the Roman couture of his homeland.
The graphic modernism of that reference took
shape in geometrically striped monochrome
tailoring cut with corresponding linearity, and in
advanced transformations of the keffiyeh patterns –
which had already become a Tisci staple – into
digitalized psychedelic zigzag patterns. Developing
his harem silhouette, he raised the waistline to
elongate the impact of its dropped crotch, creating
a long, lean stature elevated on platform wedges.

If tailoring had been seen as Tisci's forte,
he now used the collection to amp up his flou,
presenting complex tiered blouses and dresses
with handkerchief hems woven, twisted and
draped with a kind of geometric precision that
projected his haute couture experience onto
the everyday wardrobe.

A.C.M.

OSCAR NIGHT

Having turned Givenchy into one of fashion's most coveted brands by early 2010, Riccardo Tisci had become a celebrity magnet. His haute couture show had the likes of Ciara and Paz Vega on the front row, and the highly glamorous collection showed clear signs of a strategic Hollywood courtship. Tisci had conquered the catwalk; now the time had come for him to take over the red carpet.

The show – inspired by the erotic Parisian spirit of photographer, art director and make-up artist Serge Lutens – was decidedly evening-centric: tuxedos and tailcoats worn over feathered dégradé tops with sequinned gloves were followed by cocktail dresses sensually wrapped in organza, and stripped-down column dresses styled with minimal sheer capes or little boleros. Sure, there were more avant-garde concepts on Tisci's runway – wildly sculptural takes on the Bettina blouse, plumed Bermuda shorts, orbital hats – but the bottom line of this haute couture exercise was to be found in the consolidated effortlessness of looks targeted at the red carpet.

After a series of mosaic-embellished jumpsuits in emerald, amethyst and sapphire – making a play for the rock 'n' roll segment as well as the silver screen – the show closed with a gown constructed from a crystal bodice with a cascading hand-pleated and ruched lilac and purple silk organza skirt (see opposite, right). A few weeks after the show, Zoe Saldaña wore it to the Oscars. Tisci would go on to dress dozens of celebrities during his tenure at Givenchy, from Natalie Portman and Rooney Mara to Laetitia Casta and Jessica Chastain. In 2017, Emma Stone would pick up her Academy Award in head-to-toe Givenchy couture.

A.C.M.

MAXI-MINIMALISM

In the ready-to-wear reality of 2010, inescapably changed by the recession, a new appetite for minimalism was on the agenda. At Givenchy, Riccardo Tisci embraced it by reducing his signature sense for drama and glamour into a restrained collection that still had the seduction and kink that came with his territory.

Next to the religious and ceremonious influences audiences associated with him, Tisci's work had gradually increased its appropriation of sportswear elements, and for his most pragmatic women's collection to date, that was where he went. Filtering in looks from his men's collection – the ongoing riffs on hoodies, leggings and shorts, which were contributing to a new market of luxury streetwear – Tisci showed a collection founded in diving and skiwear.

Rendered mainly in black, white and red – a tricolour he had relied on since his early Givenchy days – the collection proposed sharply tailored blazers, razor-cut trousers, and double-breasted coats created in performance fabrics like neoprene and rooted in a decidedly viable no-fuss approach to everyday dressing. The feeling was mutual when it came to tailored day dresses and bodysuits with simplified adornments, and eveningwear proposals that counted feathered tops styled with black trousers. This was post-2000s maxi-minimalism in its purest form.

A.C.M.

MEMENTO MORI

Show-goers couldn't believe it when Givenchy announced that Riccardo Tisci was replacing his haute couture runway show with an intimate static presentation. The momentum that comes with the catwalk experience had epitomized his career at the house, but for this collection Tisci had a different point to make.

In various rooms of a salon on Place Vendôme, guests were met by just ten looks presented on mannequins suspended from a metal structure, each of them intricately embroidered for thousands of hours by his expert atelier. While Tisci had proven himself a commercial success at Givenchy, with a celebrity following to back it up, his journey at the house had also been the formative story of the designer who became a couturier.

Based on Mexican traditions such as the Day of the Dead, as well as what the show notes described as 'the strength and seductive ambiguity of surreal Mexican painter Frida Kahlo and her three great passions: religion, anatomy and sensuality', this collection showcased how Tisci had come to master haute couture from a design perspective, and above all as a dressmaker and a craftsman.

Dresses in duchess silks, Chantilly lace and tulle were embellished with ostrich feathers, gold crystals, bone-white beads, and industrial hardware like chains and zips foreign to the domain of haute couture. On a sheer tulle column dress, Tisci mapped out the anatomy of the human body with appliqué in the shapes of bones (see fourth from right), while a lace bodysuit was encrusted with crystals in the image of a skeleton (see fifth from right). His most artisanally ambitious and radical haute couture outing to date, the collection's memento mori motif would become a recurring theme in proposals to come.

In the final room of the presentation, guests were met with a huge photograph by Willy Vanderperre of Tisci's models wearing the dresses, seen from the back. Walking around the portrait, the same shot was visible from the front.

A.C.M.

LEOPARD PRINT AND ZIPS

Throughout his era at Givenchy, maintaining
the balance between Riccardo Tisci the showman
and Riccardo Tisci the salesman had been key.
In many ways, the ready-to-wear proposal he
presented after his most technically ambitious
haute couture staging for the house (see p.518)
felt like a reaction to both the artisanal and
thematic weight of that collection.

The latest of his menswear offerings, which
always had a fly-off-the-shelves quality about them,
had made investigations into the leopard pattern,
a perhaps clichéd but also timelessly appealing
trope in the old treasure trove of fashion. Its
reappearance in his next ready-to-wear collection
cemented the market-savvy side of Tisci's practice.
Filtered into shirts, gilets, skirts and dresses, and
as details on the lapels and panels on jackets, his
leopard elements had the instant shopability that
had come to justify his fantastical forays into
haute couture.

It set a back-to-business tone for a collection
founded in slightly twisted but polite modernist
tailoring, utilitarian tops and skirts embellished with
something as industrial as zips and pushbuttons,
and just a handful of Tisci's more adventurous
experiments with ruffles in the shape of tops and
miniskirts that transformed combat-wear into
cocktail-wear.

A.C.M.

JAPAN

While the nature of haute couture was always experimental to some extent, the irreverence with which Riccardo Tisci approached this most revered tier of fashion was shaking up the gilded chambers of Paris. One such scene took place at the historic Hôtel d'Évreux on Place Vendôme, where he presented a Givenchy haute couture collection inspired by an alternative side to the Japan typically portrayed in Western fashion.

Tisci's way in was his idol Kazuo Ohno, a master Butoh dancer whose passionate and highly artistic practice informed an extreme take on haute couture. Chiffon and tulle dresses constructed in the form-language of kimonos were hand-appliquéd with crane motifs, some nestled among plume embroidery, crystal encrustation and beading. As guests proceeded through the tableau vivant, the silhouettes grew increasingly three-dimensional: the feathers of cranes began to burst out of the surfaces of the garments; plumage increased in volume; and on the backs of dresses, laser-cut organza materialized as bright red, yellow and green wings.

It was a tech element which, at the time, still felt decidedly new in haute couture, and one that Tisci took all the way in giant samurai helmets partly inspired by Japanese robots, created by the milliner Philip Treacy.

A.C.M.

VARSITY BAROQUE

In a collection that reflected a turning point in fashion, not only for Givenchy but for audiences' approach to dressing, Riccardo Tisci definitively embraced the sports- and casualwear influences which had slowly infiltrated his work.

The month before his ready-to-wear show, he presented a men's collection defined by playful, almost teen-spirited prints of Rottweilers and graphic stars sprawled across a wardrobe that mixed sporty shorts and sweatshirts with formal tailoring. That collection would become a best-seller and eventually inspire the term 'trophy jumper', a phenomenon that took fashion by storm in the early days of the luxury streetwear influx. At his women's show, Liv Tyler was wearing such a men's Rottweiler T-shirt in the front row, illustrating the genderless power of Tisci's approach to print. She looked on as the women's version of his new fashion methodology unfolded.

Shirts, sweatshirts and varsity jackets adorned with prints of panthers or purple lilies worked into baroque motifs had an easy, attractive, instantly wearable quality about them. Paired with strict pencil skirts and elegant blouses inspired by 1950s pin-ups, they were dressy but casual, ripping up the conventional dress codes that had long been questioned by new generations and social segments of fashion fans, who were breaking with traditional attitudes towards design and dressing. As the *Los Angeles Times* concluded: 'the real message of this collection was that Tisci is capable of producing a bonanza of saleable merchandise'.

A.C.M.

ANGELIC BRIDES

Perhaps as an ironic nod to the impact of his previous ready-to-wear collection (see p.526), Riccardo Tisci dressed the first look of his haute couture show in what one might define as a sweater. Beaded angelically in clusters of ivory pearls that resembled coral or moss (see opposite, third from left), it was styled with a floor-length white tulle skirt speckled with the same pearls.

The collection followed the template Tisci had now established at Givenchy: his haute couture collections – presented statically in salons on Place Vendôme – were devoted to a sensory overload of craftsmanship exemplified by surface decoration, while his ready-to-wear and men's collections were getting increasingly sportier in nature and employing seasonal signature prints. This time, Tisci exercised a premise of purity, lightness and fragility in tulle dresses that evoked natural patterns – ostrich skin, fish scales, botanic foliage – through intricate beading, pluming, appliqué, and embroidery including sequin-work.

In many ways, it evoked the core references Tisci had drawn on since his early days at the house. It may have been far from his trademark dark Gothicism, but it had all the myth and magic of his romantic touch. In that sense, the all-white collection also made a play for the bridal market. Four months before the presentation, Tisci had designed model Natasha Poly's wedding dress, and a gown with a heart-shaped bustier (see opposite, fifth from left) echoed the design he would create for Kim Kardashian's nuptials in 2014. In 2017, with perfect synergy, the star wore the opening look of this collection to an award ceremony.

A.C.M.

SEQUINNED SURFERS

Hard on the heels of his all-white haute couture collection (see p.528), Riccardo Tisci served up a ready-to-wear proposal that took its point of departure in a similarly bright palette, with maritime additions. Like his previous collection for S/S 2007 haute couture (see p.486), it explored the motif of the mermaid which was eternally entrenched in the mythologic mind of the Givenchy designer. True to his taste for sportswear, which was gaining much traction in the fashion landscape, he side-lined it with the idea of a surfer's wardrobe. The collection materialized in a romantic meeting between the two.

Worthy of Hans Christian Andersen, the marriage unfolded through Tisci's go-to language of tailoring: ivory suits with coattails and peplums were deconstructed to evoke the fishtails, fins and gills of mermaids and sharks; lapels – dropped and cropped – were trimmed in the exotic skins of stingray, shark and eel. Tisci styled his aquatic jackets with tight trousers and leggings as a nod to the wetsuits of surfers, elevating his long, lean silhouettes on heels evoking the teeth of sharks. Taking a leaf out of his haute couture practice, he covered entire looks in blue-silver sequins mimicking the underwater metallic reflection of fish scales.

In a demonstration of the duality Tisci's work had come to embody, three weeks after the show he dressed Jay-Z and Kanye West for their *Watch the Throne Tour*.

A.C.M.

ART DECO TEXTURES

In January 2012, Riccardo Tisci had hit his seven-
year mark at Givenchy. In the tradition of fairy tales,
the milestone number – whether consciously or
not – triggered a sense of reflection in the designer.
For the first time at the house, he was looking back
at his track record, self-referencing, consolidating
and expanding on the idiosyncrasies that defined
his creative identity. It paved the way for an haute
couture collection founded in the meeting between
the high and the low: dressy versus sporty, ballroom
versus street, and – indeed – reality versus fantasy.

At the static presentation on Place Vendôme,
now an haute couture tradition for the house, Tisci
showed studded leather jackets worn over nubuck
crocodile-skin dresses, jewel-encrusted sheer robes
over cashmere tank tops, and delicate organza
evening gowns adorned with industrial studs, stars
and zips. As a counterpart to the latter element, he
street-ified crocodile skins by deconstructing each
scale, only to bleach and dye them individually,
then reconstruct them in their natural pattern onto
a tulle body and jacket. Inspired by the Fritz Lang
film *Metropolis* from 1927 and the score from
the Russian film *Aelita: Queen of Mars* from
1924, the collection explored Art Deco themes
in oversized crystal earrings and metal
embellishments on dresses.

Emphasizing the contrasting spirit of his proposal,
Tisci photographed his haute couture collection
against the wooden wall-bars of a gym, with a
basketball placed decoratively at the models' feet.

A.C.M.

EQUESTRIAN SEDUCTION

The 1970s photography of Guy Bourdin informed a Givenchy ready-to-wear collection that rekindled the kink, goth and glamour of Riccardo Tisci's early work.

Taking his point of departure in the equestrian wardrobe – with a fanfare of galloping horses on the soundtrack – he fetishized the riding jacket with razor-sharp shoulders, tightening its nipped-in waist, and repeating it all in glossy, lascivious leather. From the back, his silhouette took on more ladylike manners in sculptural peplums and tails, injecting the collection with a constant balance of hard and soft, which Tisci had come to master. Trousers took the shape of jodhpurs, some tucked into matching leather boots that reinterpreted his by-now classic spat-covered leather manifestations.

As the show progressed, Tisci evoked his riding silhouette in black and red leather dresses and silk coats, which gradually morphed into the kimono lines native to a geisha's wardrobe, drawing parallels between different cultural codes of eroticism retained in a 1970s lens.

Tisci closed his show with embellished patterns on strap dresses, echoing the mirrored motifs he had introduced way back in his third collection for the house (see p.480). At this stage, his work had become as much about reinventing his own oeuvre and reminding his audiences of his path to success.

A.C.M.

NOMADIC GLAMOUR

At the Met Gala in May 2012, Riccardo Tisci had dressed Beyoncé Knowles in a custom-made second-skin sheer black tulle gown with strategically placed opulent embellishments and a skirt hem that cascaded into effervescent purple plume. It was a meeting between two artists at the height of their careers, and one of the most photographed fashion moments of 2012.

Three months later, Tisci rolled out an haute couture proposal in Paris to cement an of-the-moment impact on the fashion industry, which had more than extended to showbiz. He illustrated his universal desirability in a collection that mastered the balance between 'haute and low', as the fashion press would have it, juxtaposing Hubert de Givenchy's 1960s simplicity with his childhood admiration for the opulence of the traveller communities in southern Italy.

Tisci opened the line-up with a sweater – a couture take on his best-selling garment – covered in hand-beaded fringing with hand-embroidered passementerie shoulder guards, worn over matching tapered trousers (see fourth from left). From that point on, the collection ascended into eveningwear: Roman cloak silhouettes – harking back to Tisci's clerical beginnings – in strings of nappa leather, or beaded fringes layered over dresses fully embroidered in the same materials or shingled in sequins. The *Guardian* reported that with 'haute couture week drawing to a close in Paris, it takes something truly bold to stand out amid the eye-poppingly gorgeous gowns. But Givenchy have done just that…'

A.C.M.

RELIGIOUS RITES

On an elevated plateau at the vast Lycée Carnot, where Riccardo Tisci staged many of his ready-to-wear shows for Givenchy, the young French organist Mathias Lecomte played up a storm as the designer's newest collection hit the runway. He was joined by the Italian house DJs Discodromo, who appeared inside a cube structured from plastic film. In musical tandem, the artists perfectly illustrated the dialogue at the root of Tisci's practice: the ceremonious, romantic and mythical counterpoised by the industrial, sexy and cool.

His recent men's show had hailed the Madonna of his Catholic heritage as Givenchy's newest print. Now, Tisci took his religious rites to a new stage. Scored by the duality of the live performance, he showcased a collection of contemporary dresses and tailoring which evoked the codes of clerical garb and Catholic iconography.

Trouser suits and shift dresses appeared with white priest collars; sculptural blazers and draped cocktail dresses evoked the volumes of bishops' robes; and minimalist pinafore and apron dresses in black and white felt unmistakably like cassocks. But eight years into his Givenchy tenure, Tisci was approaching the religious iconography that inspired his early work with a lighter touch: it was less literal and more instinctive. Cathy Horyn at *The New York Times* summed up the collection as 'superb and satisfying'.

A.C.M.

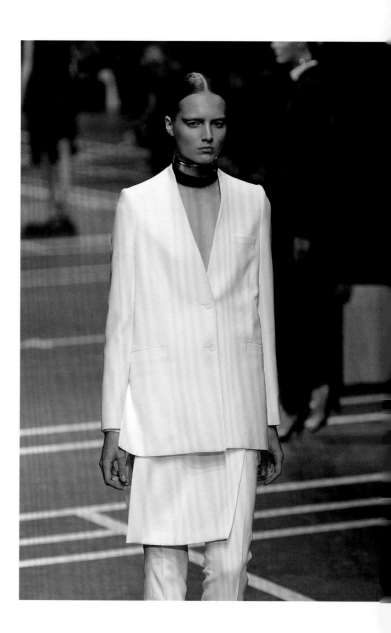

'FUTURE FEMINISM'

It wasn't an anniversary but there was plenty to celebrate: by early 2013, the impact of Riccardo Tisci's work had become fashion history. While he had started to forego haute couture shows, he was about to dress Beyoncé Knowles for a second Met Gala (see also p.536) in a corseted black gown trimmed with golden baroque edgings that looked like flames, as well as a pregnant Kim Kardashian in a body-covering pink-floral gown that would go on to break the internet. With perfect timing, two of the ready-to-wear collection's prints (see opposite, bottom and top right) matched the ones Knowles and Kardashian would wear down the Gala's red carpet.

Tisci opened his ready-to-wear show with the sweater-and-skirt silhouette that, largely owing to him, had transitioned into public property (see right). He debuted his newest sweatshirt motif in the shape of Bambi juxtaposed with an outline of the female form. Admitting he had been mining his own archives, Tisci – who grew up with eight older sisters – dedicated the collection to a 'future feminism' and brought in his friend Anohni (then Antony Hegarty) to perform songs, including 'You are My Sister'.

Centred around the casual-cum-elegant silhouette key to his Givenchy, the collection doled out biker and bomber jackets, shift dresses, and skirts in all the furs, leathers and graphics that had gained Tisci one of fashion's most trusty followings – styled with zippy peplum belts nodding at another of his shapely trademarks. Reporting for Style.com, Nicole Phelps gushed: 'Just beautiful. Riccardo Tisci's Givenchy show tonight was one of those fashion moments that true believers slog through four weeks of shows for. It gave you goose bumps.' Three months later, Tisci won the prestigious CFDA award for best international designer.

A.C.M.

EARTHY ELEGANCE

If the smoking pile of crashed cars on the
Givenchy runway – situated in the super-sized
Halle Freyssinet, on Paris's Left Bank – had
guests thinking they were in for the Riccardo Tisci
treatment to which they'd grown accustomed, the
designer had something very different up his sleeve.

Gone were the graphic prints, the 'trophy jumpers'
and the multi-layered styling. In their place, an
understated earthy elegance took over in a new
take on the sophistication that had traditionally
rhymed with Givenchy. With Ciara, Isabelle Huppert,
Lily Collins and Noomi Rapace taking their seats
on the front row, live drummers set the beat to an
equatorial setting in which draped, wrapped and
roped stretch-jersey dresses unfolded in a sandy
palette alongside bronze-sequinned silhouettes and
warrior face masks. Speaking to American *Vogue*,
Tisci cited the 'the fragility of Japan and the draping
of Africa' as his cross-cultural sources of inspiration,
with the former manifesting in the kimono-like
construction of suits.

Following the previous season's self-referential
show (see p.540), Kim Kardashian's subsequent turn
on the Met Gala's red carpet – which became the
subject of many an Instagram meme – and a men's
collection that brought Tisci's print culture into
overdrive, the much-applauded ready-to-wear show
was largely seen as an effort on the designer's part
to change things up and turn a new leaf in his
Givenchy narrative.

A.C.M.

'THE FREEDOM OF CLASSICISM'

If the previous season (see p.542) had signified Riccardo Tisci's departure from the 'trophy jumpers' and street-style fixings that had characterized his commercial output at Givenchy, this collection brought his audience a step further into his new chapter of 'bon ton', as he put it.

Tisci embraced the ladylike, transforming the earthy elements of his last outing into a dainty but fierce wardrobe of sheer ruffled chiffon dresses in animal and insect motifs, neatly styled with black stockings and heels. Coats in blush fox fur or leopard-printed astrakhan and beaver carved out a hyper-feminine sense of power-dressing that made for an anti-street and more grown-up Givenchy. Garments adorned with Bauhaus-inspired bands at the hips of trousers and between the shoulders of jackets revisited Tisci's early deconstruction in a fresh way.

With Rihanna and Beth Ditto in the audience – and Kendall Jenner on the runway – the show was testament to a time when Tisci and his surrounding industry were breaking out of the loaded boxes fashion had created for itself (formalwear, streetwear, sportswear) and inventing a new democratic look. It was a point no better illustrated than in a sweater – the symbol of Tisci's former success – now worn curiously as an accessory suspended from an elastic band on the back of an outfit like some figurative reinvention of the status quo.

A.C.M.

CORSETS AND LACE

By 2014, Riccardo Tisci had cultivated a close rapport with Kim Kardashian. That summer, he dressed the star for her Florentine wedding to Kanye West in a pure white figure-hugging bridal gown with a mermaid skirt, a heart bodice, long lace sleeves and a dramatic veil. It sealed Tisci's place in pop culture history, and when the wildly famous couple attended his ready-to-wear show that September – their toddler daughter wearing a Givenchy infanta gown – on what the *Guardian* called their 'quasi-state visit to Paris', it created the synergy of publicity dreams. In the absence of the house's haute couture presentations, which were still on hiatus, Kardashian's much-publicized wedding dress had reinjected Givenchy's image with associations to romanticism and Parisian confection, and for his ready-to-wear show, Tisci amplified his savoir-faire.

Inspired by traditional Tyrolean costume, the designer sexed up the founder's little black dresses with corset lacing and layered them with coats constructed from painstaking whip-stitching and filigree. He put the same degree of artisanal merit into gladiator dresses, corseted jackets, and little suits and dresses realized in fine, delicate lace. Cementing a return to the core values of Givenchy, Tisci reintroduced the Bettina blouse, interpreting it with graphic stripes and elegant drapery (see opposite, top left). American *Vogue* deemed the show 'sensational'.

A.C.M.

LATIN VICTORIANA

Ten years into his residency at Givenchy, Riccardo Tisci had become as unafraid of referencing his own archives as he was of going places he had never gone before. As a gothically inclined boy in southern Italy, he had grown up with a British obsession he had never had the courage to explore through his work. Now was the time for Victoriana.

Presenting the show against the stylized backdrop of an antiques yard scattered with ramps and electronic bric-à-brac, he morphed his Victorian widows with cholas, the Latin American urban goddesses known for their slicked kiss curls, graphic make-up and piercings galore. Tisci adorned his models' faces with exquisite chola jewelry – septum rings, tear-drop gems, glued-on cheek piercings – and clad them in Victorian velvet dresses, corseted tops and equestrian jackets. In a fusion of Latin spirit and 19th-century British dress with his own trademarks developed through a decade at Givenchy, he flounced and ruffled his dresses, stitched Catholic crosses into their bodices, and layered skirts over trousers. Jackets native to streetwear manifested in opulent fur, while little Victorian riding jackets were fully bejewelled with beads and embroideries.

For Tisci, who had been called 'goth' since his first collection for Givenchy, his critically applauded show illustrated just how authentic and promising those early proposals had been.

A.C.M.

UNITY IN MONOCHROME

In September 2015, Riccardo Tisci relocated his show to New York. The one-off excursion – which celebrated his tenth anniversary at Givenchy, marked with the opening of a new store in the city – took place on a set featuring recycled wooden pallets and steel, where the artist Marina Abramović staged a performance art piece founded in 'the cycle of love and life'. Coinciding with the fourteenth anniversary of 9/11, and with the newly erected One World Trade Center glistening in the sunset behind Pier 26, the presentation featured live musicians, as well as statuesque dancers in white shirts and black trousers carrying out simple human rituals in slow motion as a symbol of healing.

The show, one of his most elaborate, epitomized Tisci's decade-long impact at Givenchy in a black-and-white collection – nodding at his debut for the house (see p.474) – which evolved the tropes of his tenure for a future mentality. In tune with the emotive frame of the show, he softened his modernist tailoring and paired it with quietly erotic slip dresses and lace camisoles. He reintroduced haute couture, exercising his trademark dégradé plumage and leatherwork on sheer gowns that memorialized his most unforgettable creations in purified manifestations.

Guests including Nicki Minaj, Julia Roberts, Courtney Love, Debbie Harry, Erykah Badu, Pedro Almodóvar, Kanye West and Kim Kardashian, as well as one thousand members of the public, served as a testament to Tisci's inclusive pulling-power. '[H]is commitment to diversity has helped propel him to the top of his game not just with the usual crowd of (mostly) white editors and fashionistas, but also with a strikingly multicultural fan base,' wrote *The New York Times*. Tisci likened his collection to the universal image of a bride and groom, and told press he wanted to strip it of classifications: 'No colour, no sex, no religion.'

A.C.M.

MONASTIC MAJESTY

In January 2015, Julianne Moore had accepted a
Golden Globe in a chilly metallic Givenchy gown
with a plumed mermaid skirt typical of Riccardo
Tisci, reminding audiences of the impactful haute
couture collections he had created before the
line was put on hiatus. In September, he had
reintroduced couture to the Givenchy agenda,
showing it alongside his ready-to-wear (see p.550)
and menswear in New York.

Throughout his practice at the house, stupendous
craftmanship had always married with more
grounded propositions in a constant code-switch
between the genres of formal- and streetwear.
And so, for Tisci's next haute couture collection,
it seemed only natural to continue that marriage.
He presented it as part of his cobra-themed
men's show in Paris, nonchalantly slipping
in majestic, monastic couture silhouettes
between the cross-culturally inspired casual
tailoring and elevated sportswear that defined
the season's menswear.

All dramatically floor-length, the 12 looks exercised
the artisanal grammar of Tisci in a priestly cloak
covered in hexagonal adornments (see opposite,
left), erotic lace dresses sheathed in black chiffon
overlays, and midriff-bearing plissé gowns draped
organically around the body. As the epitome of his
core aesthetic, he closed his Parisian couture
comeback with a black lace dress styled with a
sheer coat with black fox fur lapels and crocodile
cuffs with folkloric embellishment (see opposite,
right).

A.C.M.

MYSTICAL GRAPHICS

If recent Givenchy women's collections had seen
a change in direction from an approach to fashion
which had made Riccardo Tisci more associated
with sweatshirts and power prints than haute
couture and gothic romanticism, this collection
served as a momentary reversion. While those
on fashion's frontlines had hailed his departure
from those things, there was still a booming
demand among mainstream audiences for graphic
merch-like luxury fashion (a fact only intensified
by streetwear-oriented newcomers on the
designer scene).

Within the Carreau du Temple, Tisci erected a
wooden maze worthy of a pyramid interior and
rolled out a print-based collection in the name
of ancient Egypt. Iconography native to the era's
mythology was sprawled across dresses and tops,
and clashed with military coats, cabans and furs in
all the animal prints one might have found roaming
the palaces of the pharaohs. Along the way, Tisci –
ever the traveller – picked up symbols from other
ancient tribal cultures, creating an extravagant
sensory overload of Art Deco Egyptology,
psychedelia and mysticism; all retained within
the frames of the gladiatorial glamour-puss
silhouette so familiar to his work.

A.C.M.

EMBELLISHED ARMOUR

By the time Riccardo Tisci had reintroduced his haute couture proposals as part of his men's shows (see p.554), the formats of fashion were rapidly changing. Around the landscape, designers were beginning to merge their collections – main, pre, men's, women's, couture – and at fashion weeks, critics were complaining that they never knew what they were looking at. It created an anything-goes sensibility, which often did a disservice to the work. As a result, Tisci decided to stage a static presentation of his haute couture collection – like in the old days – after initially filtering its looks into his men's collection in June 2016. He also photographed the garments in isolated look-book pictures released to the press.

Presented on the runway side-by-side with menswear founded in survival and combat codes, Tisci's 13 haute couture looks came off as protective – even martial: column dresses intricately pleated and adorned with metallic sequins, plastic embellishments, and strands of mini grommets. Black evening suits were armoured in pieces of mirror, which, in the midst of things, evoked shattered glass.

The month before, Tisci had dressed Beyoncé Knowles for the Met Gala for the third time, in a medieval peach-coloured beaded rubber dress – a contrast to the direction of the haute couture collection, which fuelled the anything-goes feeling of the time and confirmed Tisci's virtuosic versatility.

A.C.M.

NATURE

Free your mind and the rest will follow: Riccardo Tisci's work had always been spiritual, but the path he chose for his next ready-to-wear collection wasn't rooted in holy books or mysticism. It was the therapeutic power of nature.

He presented it outside, in the courtyard of the Jardin des Plantes, its surroundings echoed in a collection of mineralogy motifs on velvet, supersized quartzite pendants on imitation tortoiseshell chains, an organic sense of plumage, and botanic prints. The healing natural elements appeared on slip dresses layered over long tank tops, black suits adorned with Tisci's recurring zips, and dresses in millefeuilles of polka dots and stripes prettified with strands of chiffon. As a nod to the house's little black dress, Tisci had emblazoned one with theme-appropriate mandalas (see opposite, left).

While the collection generated positive reviews for its functional and effortless proposals, there was a feeling that its Mother Earth theme somehow felt like too much of a kumbaya for Tisci's darkly romantic, more severe and sexualized nature. In its light and airy approach, some critics grumbled, the show lacked the devotion they had come to expect from this master of ceremonies. They didn't yet know it, but it would be his last women's ready-to-wear collection at Givenchy.

A.C.M.

WESTERN VICTORIANA

In one way, you could say Riccardo Tisci's
final collection for Givenchy closed the
circle he had started drawing 12 years before.
Late 19th-century portraits of Native American
women wearing Victorian dresses inspired
body-covering ceremonious silhouettes in black
and white, faintly echoing the gothic, clerical
grammar of his first Givenchy collection in
2005 (see p.474).

But more than a wrap-up, these haute couture
looks represented a formative process which
had seen Tisci through an expansive investigation
of his childhood influences and obsessions, from
Catholicism and mysticism to South America, the
American West and Victorian England. He had come
out of that evolution an accomplished and changed
designer – or rather, as the intricate techniques
and volumes of these looks illustrated, *couturier*.

Now, as he told American *Vogue* backstage at the
men's show during which his haute couture looks
were presented, he felt a serenity: 'For nine years
as a designer, I did darkness. I've just come out of
that.' It was clear in the checked pioneer dresses
and sheer gowns with surface decoration that
conjured the spiritual body-adornment of a
culturally obscure tribe, which, most of all, felt
like the cultural signifiers Tisci had created for
his Givenchy community through a long career
at the house. The week after the show, he
announced his departure.

A.C.M.

CLARE WAIGHT KELLER

A SHORT BIOGRAPHY

The first female designer to take the helm at Givenchy, Clare Waight Keller's three-year tenure at the house made a strong impact. When she dressed Meghan, the Duchess of Sussex, for her wedding to Prince Harry in 2018, the bridal gown – made in complete secrecy before being unveiled to 1.9 billion viewers worldwide – encapsulated the simplified but rigorous elegance Waight Keller had re-instilled in Givenchy. Through a succinctly modern approach to design, her mission was to reconnect with the founding values of Hubert de Givenchy and reintroduce his brand of elegance to a post-digital fashion industry largely ruled by streetwear. With the exuberant haute couture shows she brought back to Givenchy – which now included both women's- and menswear – Waight Keller set the tone for a sophisticated dialogue between the dramatic and the understated. It filtered into cinematic ready-to-wear expressed in architectural but delicate lines both in tailoring and flou, and menswear embodied by a retro dandyism.

Born in Birmingham, England, in 1970, Waight Keller was raised by an engineer father and a legal secretary mother, whose passion for knitting and sewing she inherited at a young age. In the early 1990s, she completed a BA in fashion design at London's Ravensbourne College of Art and an MA in fashion knitwear at the Royal College of Art. Upon moving to New York, she joined the womenswear team of Calvin Klein – one of the most influential designers of the decade – and was soon headhunted by Ralph Lauren, who made her senior menswear designer of his Purple Label. Here, Waight Keller established an appreciation for tailoring that would become a defining factor of her practice at Givenchy. In 2000, at the height of Gucci's fashion dominance under the vision of Tom Ford, the designer brought her on board his women's ready-to-wear team. The move would catapult her into her first artistic director position at Pringle of Scotland in 2005.

Having attracted the attention of Paris, Waight Keller ascended to Chloé as artistic director in 2011. During her six years at the house, she modernized and simplified the Parisian brand's breezy, boho-chic romanticism, infusing its female-driven spirit with a sporty and glamorous energy that proved a great commercial success. Waight Keller was appointed artistic director of

Givenchy in March 2017. Her first ready-to-wear collection, for Spring/ Summer 2018, was met with lukewarm reviews by critics. The haute couture collection that followed struck back, igniting an inspired exploration of savoir-faire that would define Waight Keller's time at Givenchy and land her the most famous bridal gown commission of the decade.

Soon, Waight Keller's ensembles were gracing red carpets around the world, from Rihanna and Rooney Mara to Meryl Streep and Rami Malek: Julianne Moore wore Givenchy haute couture to the Cannes Film Festival in 2018, as did Gal Gadot when she attended the 2019 Met Gala in New York alongside Waight Keller. The designer re-established Givenchy's image as a house assuredly founded in haute couture, and did so with the blessing of Hubert de Givenchy, who received her at his home in Paris before his death in 2018. While her haute couture and menswear largely drew accolades, Waight Keller's ready-to-wear wrestled with finding an authoritative voice. Upon her exit from Givenchy in April 2020, amid the rise of the Covid-19 pandemic, the press nonetheless praised her tenure for its at once respectful but history-making dedication. 'Focusing on a world based on haute couture has been one of the highlights of my professional journey,' she said in a parting statement. Waight Keller lives in London and Cornwall with her husband and their three children.

Anders Christian Madsen

'TRANSFORMATION SEDUCTION'

As a valued name on the fashion scene, Clare Waight Keller was met with high hopes and goodwill upon her arrival at Givenchy. Preceded by an A/W 2017–2018 ready-to-wear collection designed by the in-house team in homage to the newly departed Riccardo Tisci, now, Waight Keller was poised for her debut. Set in the imposing Palais de Justice, her first show merged the women's and men's collections in one slick, dramatically lit set that looked like a *film noir* alley.

In advance of the show, Waight Keller had visited Hubert de Givenchy, then 90, at his Parisian apartment, and quizzed him on his core design beliefs. Based on what she had learned, her debut collection manifested in a minimal but cut-glass silhouette with the super-sharp shoulders she had seen in the founder's sketches, bossy knife-pleat skirts and sharp ruffle dresses. Feline motifs found in the very early stages of the house's heritage (see p.34) were interpreted in claw marks tufted on garments in velvet, and in snow-leopard prints.

If Waight Keller carried over some of the boho chic of Chloé, it materialized in the flou: a little black dress transformed into a mini with transparent Bettina cape sleeves tufted with leopard spots and a front ruffle panel (see opposite, top right); and sweet glamour, like her black asymmetric plissé cocktail dress with a cascading mega-ruffle down the sleeve (see opposite, bottom left).

It was, at heart, a reverential affair, all the way to the founder's lucky-charm four-leaf clover motif from 1954.

A.C.M.

'MYSTERIES OF A NIGHT GARDEN'

At Clare Waight Keller's first haute couture show, the wintry violins of Max Richter's 'November' filled a palatial Parisian salon dimmed and bathed in stripes of white light cast through blinds. As a pristine ivory coat swayed from a model's shoulders while she paced ceremoniously through the room, lusciously lined in pure white plume that faded dramatically into scarlet red at the hem (see opposite, left), it quickly became clear that Waight Keller had haute couture blood in her veins. As accessible as her ready-to-wear had felt (see p.568), this was savoir-faire at full throttle: linear tailoring cut like crystal, fantastical fabrics so fluid they bounced like waves, embroidery as delicate as magic dust.

'I was working in the best laboratory in the world,' she enthused. Referencing pieces from the 1950s corners of the founder's archive, Waight Keller approached her couture with equal parts exuberance and restraint. A sleekly structured, almost triangular black top faded into the spectacular cascading ruffles of a skirt in sunrise hues (see right), a look that Cate Blanchett would go on to wear at two red-carpet events. A dress with a rigid full skirt in black erupted in sunset-coloured plume from the bustier. Throughout, she walked an elegant tightrope between purity and abundance, demonstrating a much stronger confidence than in her ready-to-wear collection. For the first time, men walked the Givenchy couture show dressed like rock 'n' roll princelings (a major departure from the red-blooded muscle men of Riccardo Tisci's era). The *Financial Times* hailed it as a 'ravishing, relevant show'.

A.C.M.

'NIGHT NOIR'

With her searchlights and clubby salons divided by suggestive velvet curtains inside the Palais de Justice, Clare Waight Keller seemed like a British outlaw bringing her sexy grit to Givenchy's French grail of glamour. Weeks before the show, fan-favourite Phoebe Philo had left Céline, orphaning hordes of women who were now hoping Waight Keller would answer their prayers for the refined modern tailoring Philo had mastered.

Devoted to sass and sleaze, Waight Keller's second ready-to-wear collection married Berlin in the early 1980s with New York in the early 1990s. You could see her long-line tailoring, sharp leather coats and slithering lingerie dresses roaming Berlin's arid metallic streets by night, while little party dresses structured rigidly with stiff cascading ruffles, sexy fringes and big bows inspired by the archives lent themselves well to the New York reference. She added to them voluminous sculptural faux fur coats, contrasting the sleek lines of her tailoring with the exuberance reflected in her couture debut (see p.570).

Because Waight Keller's arrival at Givenchy had coincided with the wake of the 2017 Women's March against Donald Trump, the rise of the Time's Up and #MeToo campaigns, and indeed Philo's exit from fashion, audiences were judging her work through the lens of neo-feminism. As a response, she amped up a pure sense of femininity, retaining an elegant sense of sex appeal and romanticism – both for women and men – which many felt was more relevant than fashion's typical view of strength as a broad masculine shoulder or an armour-like bustier. The critics were pleased.

A.C.M.

'CARAMAN'

One year into Givenchy, Clare Waight Keller's tenure
was already reading like a Hero's Journey: in March
2018, less than a year after he had received her at
his Parisian apartment, Hubert de Givenchy passed
away at 91. Two months later, Waight Keller dressed
Meghan, the Duchess of Sussex, for her wedding to
Prince Harry in a purist white gown with a boatneck
and a veil embroidered with the flowers of the
Commonwealth.

This solemn series of events inspired the pathos
of a sophomore haute couture show in the garden
of the Archives Nationales, which saw Waight Keller
take a grand and emotive bow, surrounded by
members of her atelier, as Audrey Hepburn's
'Moon River' crescendoed on the sound system.
From lukewarm reviews of her first ready-to-wear
collection (see p.568) to unanimous praise for the
debut couture show that preceded this one (see
p. 570), Waight Keller had now placed herself firmly
on the fashion map. The *Financial Times* was quick
to praise her 'accomplished study in the "purity of
the line"', and paid tribute to her 'sublime synthesis
of the *tailleur* and *flou*'.

Waight Keller named her collection after the Hôtel
de Caraman, Givenchy's townhouse headquarters
at 3 avenue George V. She dedicated her show to
Hubert de Givenchy by interpreting elements from
his creations. This materialized in abundant
plumage, Space Age gladiator elements, capes and
peekaboos, and made for some larger-than-life
numbers: a birdcage shingled in white feathers,
a floor-length tailcoat lined in sparkly hand-beading,
and a bird-peck leather dress. On social media,
a new generation was discovering the grandeur of
haute couture, and Waight Keller was happy to give
these followers what they wanted.

A.C.M.

'I AM YOUR MIRROR'

Possessed by the spirit of haute couture,
Clare Waight Keller's ready-to-wear at Givenchy
was beginning to show signs of the same
accomplishment. For her third such collection –
inspired by Annemarie Schwarzenbach, the
androgynous cross-dressing writer from the
Weimar Republic era – she approached her tailoring
with new determination. Petite in proportion, its
shoulder line sent strict creases down the front of
sleeves of jackets and created sculptural gestures
around the waist. When worn with voluminous
high-waist trousers structured with a small basque,
it made for a decidedly architectural silhouette.

Along with the strict construction of geometrical
gowns with rigid fans of plissé cutting out from the
bust, and icy silver lace dresses lacquered in more
silver and applied with even more silver resin for
a foil effect, the result was a collection high in
technical effort but somewhat restrained in impact.
At Givenchy, Waight Keller said, she wanted to
convey a spirit of modesty. It was a new word for
sophistication – a term that had always been tied
to the house – and a brave move in a digital-age
run on the opposite desire.

Her androgynous theme fed into another corner
of the zeitgeist. Referencing the 1960s wardrobes
of Lou Reed and Nico, she staged a marriage
between gender codes that corresponded with
the gender-nonbinary waves that were becoming
key to a new dawn of fashion.

A.C.M.

'BLEACHED CANVAS'

Over the course of 2018, Clare Waight Keller's haute couture dresses had graced the backs of everyone from Rihanna and Lady Gaga to Cate Blanchett and – continuously – Meghan, the Duchess of Sussex, who rang out Givenchy's *annus mirabilis* by presenting her new dressmaker with the British Designer of the Year Award at the Fashion Awards.

Now, Waight Keller wanted a clean slate. At her third haute couture show, a bleached-white runway room at the Musée d'Art Moderne de la Ville de Paris provided a stark contrast to the saturated primary paint-box colours that daubed the slick and shiny surfaces of garments and shoes as if they had been dipped in silicone. She exercised latex in a collection that rarely felt fetishy, but instead conjured a sense of futurism. A floor-length scarlet dress with a latex cape was cinched in at the waist and covered in hand-dipped red paillettes like something out of an Italian arthouse horror (see opposite, left). Multicoloured fringe dresses – the fringes hand-made separately and painstakingly like tubes in organza – looked like party streamers and lifted the collection out of its strict overtones and into more surreal and playful territory. The opening look saw Adut Akech in a rigorously tailored black evening jacket with a cut-glass white lapel (see right) – lines echoed in Waight Keller's menswear created from fabrics that looked native to the women's ballgown closet but found new identities in masculine shapes.

At this stage, Waight Keller's appetite for savoir-faire was infectious. 'I kind of almost live for couture now,' she told the press.

A.C.M.

'THE WINTER OF EDEN'

By 2019, Clare Waight Keller had made her objective at Givenchy clear: she was re-establishing its essential elegance.

On the image front, she was succeeding in her mission thanks to the grand gestures of her haute couture collections and the red carpets she had placed them on. In ready-to-wear, it didn't necessarily lend itself to the clear-cut points of view that made her predecessor's collections so market-savvy. The search for such a direction seemed to spawn an increase of proposals on Waight Keller's part.

Presented on a mile-long runway in the Jardin des Plantes, its windy tree tops visible through a clear roof in the blackened-out pavilion, her next collection took inspiration from the genesis of the Garden of Eden: an Adam/Eve duality was reflected in masculine tailoring and feminine flou, and sometimes both in a single outfit. Waight Keller also took inspiration from the moment in the early 1990s when young British and Irish aristocrats like Honor Fraser, Jasmine Guinness, Iris Palmer and Dan Macmillan 'wore haute couture on the pages of *Vogue* with an insouciant attitude', as the *Guardian* put it.

Waight Keller packed her collection with new tailoring silhouettes and sculptural flou. Nearly every look seemed part of a new story: shoulder proposals covered everything from the hyper-curved and exaggerated to the super-snug and reduced; flou and knitwear drew on some of the silhouettes from January's couture collection (see p.578). But it was the micro-pleated print dresses inspired by Japanese vases that eventually epitomized the collection, a blue variety of which was immortalized by Meryl Streep at the Venice Film Festival that autumn.

A.C.M.

'NOBLESSE RADICALE'

At Givenchy, Clare Waight Keller continued to expand her presence on the fashion scene. In June 2019, she had headlined the Pitti Uomo fashion fair in Florence with a menswear spectacular in the gardens of Queen Victoria's favourite Tuscan residence, Villa Palmieri. Titled 'Noblesse Radicale', the haute couture collection she presented in Paris in July was founded in a type of narrative she hadn't previously explored at Givenchy.

Dreaming up an idea of a French château possessed by an anarchic spirit, Waight Keller imagined a world in which, as her press notes said, 'the threads of a gilded past weave a radical future'. Her 'bird woman trapped in the house' embodied eccentric glamour, in 'heirloom finery' inspired by 'flowering wallpapers and rich upholstery'. The theme transpired in silhouettes with skirts shaped like lampshades, in dresses made from drawstring, and gowns that had curtains coming out of angular back structures. There were interwoven hotchpotch textures like the inside of a sofa or a wall, dishevelled tweed pieces informed by graphic flooring, and many looks with surface embellishment that resembled interior decoration. The birds were in the hair, with several models sporting gravity-defying flicks that recalled the wings of raptors.

The collection followed an haute couture tradition in which each look is imbued with its own individual character, rather than a collection which interprets and evolves a particular motif as the line-up progresses. Within her refined but radical premise, it made for an unpredictable collection, which fed into the pre-pandemic fashion appetite for bold, theatrical displays of haute couture.

A.C.M.

'NY PARIS 1993'

While Clare Waight Keller's eveningwear had become a fixture on red carpets, two years into her tenure at Givenchy she was yet to carve out a clear identity for her daywear. That wasn't reflective of her talents as a designer. In another era, it had taken designers seasons to define their directions. But, along with demands, fashion's attention span had changed.

She based her next collection on the contrasts she observed living in New York in the early 1990s, when raw minimalism was at its height, and visiting Paris, where opulence and extravagance were still the practice. This inspired looks that jumped from the poles of sexy minimalism to romantic maximalism – from sleek leather tops and skirts to monastic mega-volumes daubed in florals – evading any concise direction in silhouette and fabrication.

It resulted in a runway packed with everything from contemporary streetwear and sportswear to ladylike and red-carpet dressing. 'So here there were long dresses, super-flou from top to toe. But there was also Kaia Gerber in a satin bra and black leather pencil skirt [see opposite, top left]. And here were more pencil skirts, with leather bandeau tops. Colour me confused,' wrote Tim Blanks of *The Business of Fashion*. It was symptomatic of an increasingly digital fashion forum saturated by individual and often contrasting trends and desires. As a result, audiences were now looking for very specific product to buy into: a clear point of view.

A.C.M.

'A LOVE LETTER'

In what would become her last haute couture
collection for the house, Clare Waight Keller went
back to the archives of Hubert de Givenchy. Here,
wide-brimmed hats inspired her to make enveloping
headpieces and what she called 'cloche-shaped'
skirts, denoting the silhouette of a bell.

Against the backdrop of an orchestra playing
along to the soundtrack of *The Hours* – each
member individually perched on columns that
lined the runway – the show was crafted for a social
media moment. The collection dug into the soil
of English gardens with all the flowery and fluffy
manifestations that reference conjures. Waight
Keller's starting point was the letters Virginia Woolf
and Vita Sackville-West would send one another,
and the gardens at Sissinghurst where the latter
lived. The poet and fervent gardener's landscaping
influenced colours and petal shapes that turned
the line-up into a study in traditional flora couture.

'Upon entering Givenchy's show space,
showgoers were hit with a floral scent that
instantly transported the weariest among us to
memories of balmy summer nights,' reported
British *Vogue*. The collection read like the
illustrations of a botany book, one flower shape
after another, interpreted in painstaking pleats,
sculptural necklines or dramatic Watteau backs;
some dresses doubling up on flowers in thousand-
fold by way of expansive floral embellishment.
It cemented Waight Keller's knack for haute
couture, and the chance it gave her at Givenchy
to explore the archives and delve into focused
points of reference.

A.C.M.

'ARTHOUSE BEAUTY'

Symbolically, Clare Waight Keller's final collection
for Givenchy featured the comma as a key motif.
While it was the grammatical symbol of separation,
it was also an indication of continuation: a sentence
half-phrased. Five weeks later, she would announce
her departure from the house, but in the final days
of the March 2020 shows during which Givenchy's
took place, fashion was more concerned with the
rapid rise of Covid-19, which would change the
industry for years to come.

The collection – inspired by *nouvelle vague*
heroines and the work of artists Ketty La Rocca
and Helena Almeida – was a collage of classic
garments clashed together into new renditions.
It materialized in mismatched scarf dresses that
took form somewhere between evening- and
daywear, or unusual silhouettes that looked as
if they were composed from several traditional
ones, like an oversized grey wool dress that slightly
wrapped, slightly hourglassed, and suddenly burst
into a puff-shouldered matching cape (see opposite,
top left). Halfway through the show, a masterfully
cut black trouser styled with a sculptural white
blouse with a black comma abstracted over it
(see opposite, top right) spoke volumes of the
bold simplicity embodied by Waight Keller's work
at Givenchy at its best. 'I wear the clothes myself so
I know a sense of what my story is here at Givenchy.
I'm living it every day,' she told the press.

A.C.M.

MATTHEW M. WILLIAMS

A SHORT BIOGRAPHY

While all the designers who have followed in the footsteps of Hubert de Givenchy have been vastly different, none has been more atypical than Matthew M. Williams. A product of a new era in fashion, his post at Givenchy is a sign of the times. Where his predecessors were all classically trained, Williams was not. Where they nearly always approached design through narrative or theme, Williams does not. For this designer, fashion is a call-and-response to the zeitgeist: 'It's just about today. My work is really instinctual,' he has said. Williams – who joined the house in 2020 – goes with the flow. At Givenchy, his work embraces social media culture's desire for statement fashion of the graphic, sexy and subversive kind. As he told *Le Figaro*, 'Of course I'm not going to re-do what's already been done. I'm going to give my own vision.'

Born in Evanston, Illinois, on 17 October 1985, Williams was raised in Pismo Beach, California, by parents who both worked in the medical industry. Growing up, he split his time between hanging out with the West Coast's skateboarding community and immersing himself in fashion magazines that showed the latest collections from Paris. After completing a semester of art classes at the University of California, Santa Barbara, he eventually applied to Parsons School of Design in New York but was not admitted. In 2008, Williams met Lady Gaga – who hadn't yet had her breakthrough – and started creating costumes for her performances under her Haus of Gaga workshop, and teaming up on projects with photographers like Nick Knight. When their collaboration ended in 2010, Williams – now a fixture in music circles – started working as a creative director.

At age 27, Williams launched 1017 Alyx 9SM, named after his birthday, his daughter, and the address of his first studio at St Mark's Place in New York. The brand established his glamorously industrial and highly textural approach to fashion, a design methodology that evades inspirational references in favour of an all-in focus on fabric treatments and hardware applied to silhouettes informed by the dressing mentalities of a social media-era youth. Since joining Givenchy as artistic director, he has put product at the forefront, proposing a wardrobe for statement dressing in line with a contemporary fashion culture. As he announced to the press on the launch of his Spring/Summer 2021 collection: 'To me, fashion expresses a point of view where formality and informality, construction and comfort co-exist. My ethos is about the luxury of infusing clothes with your own personality, not being worn by them.'

Heralded by a series of moody portraits of himself taken by photographer Paolo Roversi and released on social media, he entered the house in June 2020 at the height of Covid-19 and had to present his first two collections in digital formats. If the pandemic influenced his work, it was in the heightened power of social media. After his first collection, an online campaign featuring the likes of Kim Kardashian and Kylie Jenner photographing themselves in Givenchy reached 500 million people. In 2021, Williams dressed The Weeknd for his Super Bowl Halftime Show. He also dressed celebrities for the Met Gala: Kendall Jenner in 2021, Rosalia in 2022, and Gigi Hadid in 2023. The exposure cemented the aesthetic with which Williams has approached the Givenchy genetics: a hard-edged, sexy boldness loosely founded in the codes of the utility and combat wardrobes, embodied in strict, boxy tailoring, intricately treated workwear, and flou embellished with the industrial hardware adornments echoed in every sector of his design practice, from robust metal padlocks on garment fastenings and shoes to cold, shiny 'G' logos on handbags. Williams, a father of three, divides his time between Paris, London, New York, Ferrara and Los Angeles.

Anders Christian Madsen

INDUSTRIAL HARDWARE

In March 2020, three months before Matthew M. Williams was announced as Givenchy's new artistic director, the fashion industry had gone into lockdown. While October offered a brief window of freedom, the house's new custodian had to replace his debut runway show with a look book presented to press in showroom appointments and video calls.

Williams described his stream-of-consciousness design process in a press statement: 'I start building textures that I want to feel, then there'll be something from a material, something from a silhouette of a prototype, an image, a kind of scale I want to see on the body and it's just this machine where I keep just mixing things… At the end of the day I want that hit in your heart like when you just see something and you know it's good, but you don't understand why.'

The collection crystallized the house's choice of Williams: fashion's obsession with sports-influenced urbanwear showed no signs of slowing down. As a designer entrenched in the music scenes that spawned that culture, maybe Williams could re-establish the audience of Riccardo Tisci's streetwise heyday. He tackled those expectations in a women's- and menswear collection that twisted and elevated everyday wardrobe tropes: a denim jacket adorned with reflective embroideries, tank tops transformed into draped blouses, or black column dresses embellished all over with the industrial hardware that already served as Williams's signature.

He doubled down on the latter statement in accessories ornamented with padlocks, telling the press, 'The connecting thread of this first season is the padlock, inspired by the ones that lovers hook all over bridges in Paris. I've turned it into jewelry, bag clasps, or applications on garments. To me, it's a symbol of love, of kinship, and a sign of my commitment to Givenchy.' Williams's padlocks were inscribed with the Givenchy 'G', which, he noted, also 'becomes a chainlink, a ring, an earring'.

The spirit of Hubert de Givenchy was present in the black rigour that defined the collection's tailoring, and in the high level of artisanship, but, as a 34-year-old designer engrained in social media culture, Williams's take on Givenchy was about sexy statement dressing. 'It is a sign of Williams' Californian sensibility transplanted to Europe', reported *Numéro*, 'that he approaches the two sides with equal aplomb and rigour, both classicism and subversion, with a sense of ease and respect for the humanity of the wearer infusing all.'

A.C.M.

'BETWEEN MONUMENTS AND MUSIC'

By Matthew M. Williams's second ready-to-wear collection for Givenchy in March 2021, fashion found itself in an even harder lockdown, with physical activities suspended. Defying the limitations cramping his ambitions, Williams took out Paris La Défense Arena and staged a pre-recorded runway show with all the sleek post-apocalyptic sci-fi trimmings of a music video. In it, he clashed his own industrial language with the haute couture grammar of Givenchy.

'In many ways, this collection is about a constant tension between two worlds,' Williams noted in his press release. 'It's about finding personal meaning in difficult circumstances; it's about sincerity in what we do rather than strategy. We wanted to bring a sense of lived reality alongside precision, elegance and extravagance in the clothing and looks. Ultimately, fashion for us is a way of being, feeling and connecting rather than a game to be played. It's almost like monumentalising the everyday, filling it with emotion – like music you can wear.'

The focus was on tailoring: sharp, black and slightly exaggerated at the shoulder, it interpreted the house for a new age of women's and men's power-dressing, with all the silvery padlock closures, bar buttons and chunky chains native to Williams's trademark. He refined the oversized volumes of the skateboarding wardrobe – hoodies, puffer jackets, utilitarian gilets – through the tricks of tailoring, and realized his garments in rigid materials that added a hard and intensely luxurious sensibility. Big furry outerwear supplied the statement dressing called for by the new-generational audience Williams's work seemed to be aimed at. It was echoed in subversive accessories practically made for social media brags: giant furry mittens, horned balaclavas and hoofed platform shoes. Reporting for *The New York Times*, Vanessa Friedman concurred that this 'luxury hard-core, haute-street territory' was 'high in aggression and attitude, rife with extreme accessories that will probably become viral hits'.

Contrary to his predecessors, Williams explained that his methodology wasn't informed by themes but simply by an instinct for the zeitgeist: what felt right in the moment. After his first collection, some of the most-followed stars on Instagram posted pictures of themselves in his clothes and accessories as part of a social media campaign. With names like Kaia Gerber and Bella Hadid on his roster, Williams's target audience was unmistakable.

A.C.M.

BETWEEN EXTRAVAGANCE AND DISCIPLINE

With the pandemic at bay, Matthew M. Williams could finally invite an audience to his first live runway show for Givenchy. In Paris La Défense Arena, he erected an imposing oval light structure inside which models walked in circles to an original soundtrack by Young Thug. Orchestrated like a pumping, no-budget-spared stadium concert experience, it served as a suitable frame to a women's and men's collection that intensified Williams's feeling for statement dressing.

Now, every garment was worked and styled to new dimensions: tight neoprene tailored jackets were layered tonally with deconstructed corsetry or imbued with rigid peplums bursting out from the hips; shoulders expanded in sculpting, waists became extra nipped-in, and bloomers worn over thigh-high leather space-walk boots flared out in stiff ruffles. Williams turned up the volume on his industrial surface decoration, covering column dresses in dense over-dimensional sequins and crafting armour-like boleros in thick micro-pleating. One critic enjoyed the 'grand concert spirit', concluding: 'The collection is a whiplashing mix between the decadent and the utilitarian.'

Playing to the streetwear scene's love of an arty collaboration, the designer adapted imagery by the contemporary artist Josh Smith – written words, clowns, the Grim Reaper – into denim, leather and knitwear, veiling the latter in transparent overlays that added a new dimension to Williams's textural expression. In all their colour and vibrancy, those looks were testament to a post-pandemic approach to design where everything had to be graphic enough to pop through a screen.

'For the Spring–Summer 22 collection,' Williams stated in his press release, 'I wanted to build on the tradition of Givenchy's history while also really looking towards the future. To do this, I worked with people I admire across different disciplines who have truly unique perspectives… The collaboration and this collection offer people a remarkably immersive and special experience.' With this, Givenchy had entered a new era.

A.C.M.

ARCHETYPAL ELEVATION

For his second live runway show, Matthew M. Williams continued to cement the visual language he envisioned for the house – in a big way. Elevated above the ground of the vast Paris La Défense Arena, his models made their way down an industrial glass-floored metal structure lit up from every corner by four gigantic football field lights and lined with a front row that counted the likes of Paris Jackson and Kim Jones.

His press release noted: 'I really wanted to create a synthesis of powerful, sophisticated femininity, with an interplay of multiple American and Parisian influences, sports and craftsmanship. Next to her stands a contemporary man with an instinct for chic nonchalance. On the runway, both are grounded by a sense of reality.'

The collection honed the study of urban wardrobe archetypes that Williams had now firmly established at the core of his Givenchy practice: sweatshirts cropped and layered with graphics evocative of metal bands, cargo trousers and jackets constructed in leather, and floor-sweeping greatcoats developed from the codes of the formal tailoring found in Hubert de Givenchy's archives. In the same spirit, pearl embroideries on streetwear and cocktail dresses paid homage to the signature necklace of Audrey Hepburn in *Breakfast at Tiffany's*.

Williams was paying reverence to the archives, but the grungy and gothy sensibilities of the collection didn't beat around the bush: his eyes were firmly fixated on the dress sense of a young, contemporary clientele. As Jessica Testa reported for *The New York Times*, 'The overall effect was cool and tough, heightened by the models' faux face piercings and, occasionally, bleached eyebrows. As the brand noted about the collection, "nothing is overly precious" – not even the memory of Holly Golightly.'

A.C.M.

CULTURAL EXCHANGE

For his first dedicated womenswear show –
departing from the co-ed format he had been
practising – Matthew M. Williams shifted focus.
'In creating the collection,' he noted in his press
release, 'I wanted each silhouette to embody
the exchange between traditionally French
and American ways of dressing in the urban
environment. It's a study of the elements we
associate with "Parisian chic" and "Californian
cool", and how those contrasts have integrated
in the digital borderless world.' He continued:
'Everything begins with Hubert [de Givenchy].
I looked at his archives with my adopted Parisian
eye but also with my instinctive American eye.'

Presented in the Jardin des Plantes with Olivia
Rodrigo, Doja Cat and K-pop girl band Aespa on
the front row, the collection served as a purification
of what Williams set out to do from day one: fuse
the storied elegance of Givenchy with the workwear
he had grown up with in California. 'I wanted to
communicate this interaction with a new clarity
and strip the final expression of any complexities,'
he noted. For the American part, Williams zoned
in on perfecting the archetypes of cargo-wear,
while the French genetics seeped through in
dresses, blouses and box jackets adapted
from the Givenchy archives.

This simplified cultural exchange manifested
in a fresher take on the codes of Givenchy: an
invitation for a younger audience to partake not
only in the workwear that defined Williams's own
creative disposition but also the sophisticated
evening culture at the heart of the house. In
amplifying his Parisian proposal – and unpacking,
through rationalized styling, his vision for Givenchy –
Williams also won the attention of a new, less
streetwear-focused audience, as illustrated
by Helen Seamons and Jo Jones writing for the
Guardian: 'A finale of slinky evening dresses in
Givenchy's signature black had awards season
written all over them.'

A.C.M.

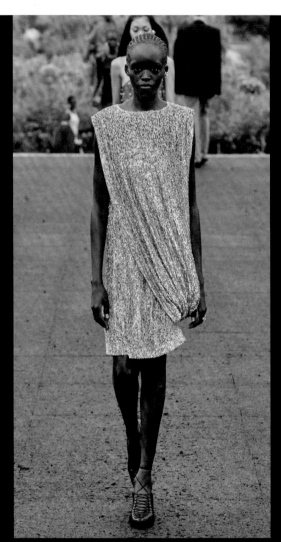

'NEW ELEGANCE'

What does Givenchy mean in the 2020s? It was the question with which Matthew M. Williams had been faced since taking the helm at the house at the cusp of the decade, and a challenge that remained under investigation. '[T]he founder's patrician aspect and perceived conservatism … means the house's DNA is harder to glibly categorize,' Luke Leitch wrote in March 2023, reporting for *Vogue* Runway. Six weeks earlier, Williams had presented a men's show that studied how fresh dressing mentalities were conjuring a new sense of elegance through generational uniforms that freely sampled tailoring, workwear and sportswear.

Applying the same methodology to his successive women's show – staged in a white box erected within the École Militaire – he moved a significant step further towards cracking the contemporary code of Givenchy. Williams consolidated his proposal into simplified sharp broad-shouldered tailoring with nipped-in waists (some created in the haute couture ateliers) and purified double-face cashmere coats and separates, and injected the proposition with his own workwear genetics in looks composed from sweats, bondage trousers and cargo garments, but layered as a proposal for how to make that category of clothing elegant. He titled the collection 'New Elegance'.

'I looked at the women who surround me and the silhouettes that empower them; that make them stand a little taller and feel confident. Today, those silhouettes are made up of everything from tailoring to workwear. My approach was to elevate those pieces and enhance the elegance they reflect,' Williams told British *Vogue*. The collection – which climaxed in a series of evening dresses inspired by the archives of Hubert de Givenchy, one of which was worn by Elizabeth Olsen at the Academy Awards the week after – generated optimism from the press. '[H]e seems to have struck upon an effective recipe through which to appetizingly blend himself with the house that Hubert built,' deemed American *Vogue*.

A.C.M.

BIBLIOGRAPHIC NOTE

In order not to disrupt the flow of reading, we have decided not to include references or footnotes in the main body of the text. Sources for the quotations in the biographies and collection texts can be found below.

L'Album du Figaro, no.39, December 1952

Brigitte Amalvy, 'Givenchy retrouvé', *La Nation*, 28 January 1971

L'Aurore, 'Premiers pronostics sur la mode nouvelle', 17 January 1955

Jacob Bernstein, 'Givenchy's Riccardo Tisci is the King of Fashion Week', *The New York Times*, 16 September 2015

Tim Blanks, 'Raw Meets Polished at Givenchy', *The Business of Fashion*, 30 September 2019

Andrew Bolton, Tim Blanks, Susannah Frankel and Sølve Sundsbø, *Alexander McQueen: Savage Beauty* exhibition catalogue, The Metropolitan Museum of Art / Yale University Press: New Haven, CT, 2011

Françoise Bougon-Colin, 'Que nous apporte la nouvelle mode automne-hiver 55', *Maroc*, 19 August 1955; 'Haro sur la robe-sac', *L'Aurore*, 23 January 1958

Jess Cartner-Morley, 'Macdonald on way out as Givenchy plays down his latest collection', *The Guardian*, 22 January 2004; 'Kim Kardashian sets the scene for Givenchy at Paris fashion week', *The Guardian*, 28 September 2014; 'Meghan effect on full display in Paris at Givenchy's show', *The Guardian*, 3 March 2019

Jacqueline Claude, Agence France-Presse, 27 January 1971

La Dépêche Tunisienne, May 1953

Dernière Heure (Algiers), 21 August 1954

Elle, no.319, 7 January 1952; 'Coup de foudre: Paris s'enflamme pour un nouveau genre', 3 March 1952; 'Paris s'enflamme pour une blouse', 14 July 1952

Jo Ellison, 'Fantasy dressing in a feminist age', *Financial Times*, 26 January 2018; 'The pursuit of perfection: Couture AW18 review', *Financial Times*, 6 July 2018

Gloria Emerson, 'New line and new boutique make Givenchy feel frisky', *The New York Times*, 2 February 1968

Emilie Faure, 'Rencontre avec Matthew Williams, le "cool kid" de Californie à la tête de Givenchy', *Le Figaro*, 5 October 2020

France-Soir, 'Chez H. de Givenchy, le jersey ramène la nouvelle "Belle Époque" et les imprimés font signe à la chance', 6 February 1954

Vanessa Friedman, 'The Party is Coming. Here's What to Wear', *The New York Times*, 8 March 2021

The Guardian, 'Look of the day: Givenchy gives good couture', 4 July 2012

Phyllis Heathcote, 'Givenchy, the odd man out', *Manchester Guardian*, 25 February 1959

Cathy Horyn, 'The Cult of Personality, Wrapped Up in Couture', *The New York Times*, 20 July 1999; 'Far From Hollywood', *The New York Times*, 25 January 2007; 'Givenchy Looks Back, but Not Too Far', *The New York Times*, 1 October 2012

Le Journal du Dimanche, 'L'année prochaine, les femmes auront un corps fluide et sans os', 31 August 1955

Boris Kochno, *Christian Bérard*, Herscher: Paris, 1987

Luke Leitch, 'Givenchy: Fall 2023 Ready-to-Wear', Vogue Runway, 2 March 2023

Jiawa Liu, 'Review of Givenchy Spring/Summer 2022', *Harper's Bazaar* (Singapore), 12 October 2021

Los Angeles Times, 'Givenchy Top Man in French Couture', 3 August 1959; 'Givenchy', 13 March 2011

Anders Christian Madsen, 'Post-Givenchy, What Will Clare Waight Keller Do Next?', Vogue.co.uk, 15 April 2020; '5 Things To Know About Givenchy's "New Elegance" AW23 Show', Vogue.co.uk, 3 March 2023

Suzy Menkes, 'Givenchy's Automated Models: Museum Drama From McQueen', *The New York Times*, 20 July 1999

Le Monde, 'Hubert de Givenchy a choisi la liberté', 30 August 1955

Midi Libre, 15 August 1954

Jeanne Molli, 'Balenciaga and Givenchy Styles Offer Last Word on Spring', *The New York Times*, 1 March 1963

Nathalie Mont-Servan, 'Vers une mode signée Boldini?', *Le Monde*, 29 August 1963; 'Arrière-saison des collections d'automne', *Le Monde*, 23 September 1965; 'Deux couturiers pilotes', *Le Monde*, 22 September 1966; 'Haute Couture 79: Madame le cadre', *Le Monde*, 28 July 1978; 'Court, court, court', *Le Monde*, 31 July 1981

Bernadine Morris, 'Paris Shows: A 40's Mood', *The New York Times*, 1 February 1979; 'Saint Laurent: Shorter Skirts, Bubble Shapes', *The New York Times*, 30 July 1981; 'Saint Laurent, Givenchy Shine', *The New York Times*, 28 January 1982; 'Givenchy's Elegance Closes Paris Show on a High Note', *The New York Times*, 31 January 1986; 'Givenchy Blossoms', *The New York Times*, 29 January 1988; 'From de la Renta, Sensible Chic', *The New York Times*, 29 January 1993

Sarah Mower, 'Givenchy Spring 2004 Ready-to-Wear', Style.com, 10 October 2003; 'Givenchy Fall 2008 Ready-to-Wear', Style.com, 26 February 2008; 'Givenchy Spring 2010 Ready-to-Wear', Style.com, 3 October 2009; 'Givenchy Spring 2015 Ready-to-Wear', Style.com, 28 September 2014 'Givenchy Fall 2017 Menswear', Vogue Runway, 20 January 2017

Sarah Mower and Ellie Pithers, '5 Things To Know About Givenchy's Flower-Filled SS20 Couture Show', Vogue.com, 21 January 2020

Lucie Noel, 'Fashion News', *Herald Tribune*, October 1952

Numéro (Netherlands), 'Givenchy for Spring & Summer 2021', 5 October 2020

Paris-Presse, 'Imprimé roi', 5 February 1953

Patricia Peterson, 'Report on Fashion Trend Abroad', *The New York Times*, 1 August 1959

Nicole Phelps, 'Givenchy Fall 2013 Ready-to-Wear', Style.com, 2 March 2013; 'Givenchy Spring 2014 Ready-to-Wear', Style.com, 28 September 2013; 'Givenchy Spring 2015 Ready-to-Wear', Style.com, 28 September 2014; 'Givenchy Spring 2018 Ready-to-Wear', Vogue Runway, 1 October 2017

Virginia Pope, 'Designer, at 25, Has Big Success in Exacting World of Paris Fashion', *The New York Times*, 21 April 1952

Régine, 'Printemps-été 1972, une mode en plis', *La Nouvelle République du Centre-Ouest*, 29 January 1972

Helen Seamons and Jo Jones, 'Paris fashion week, spring/summer 2023: the highlights – in pictures', *The Guardian*, 5 October 2022

Semaine du monde, 'La cloche de Givenchy sonne le glas de la mode classique', 14 September 1955

Eugenia Sheppard, 'Givenchy', *New York Herald Tribune*, 28 August 1958; 'Paris fashion shows wind up in great finale', *The Daily Gleaner* (Fredericton), 19 August 1959; 'Givenchy's Smash Hit', *New York Herald Tribune*, 1 February 1962; 'Givenchy's great collection', *International Herald Tribune*, 24 January 1973

Faith Shipway, 'Now Givenchy gives women the tube look to make them glide', *Evening Standard*, 21 February 1957

Carmel Snow, 'The French Accent', *New York Journal*, 29 August 1954

Amy M. Spindler, 'Investing in Haute Couture's Lower-Brow Future', *The New York Times*, 22 January 1996

Y.T., *L'Écho d'Oran*, March 1953

Jessica Testa, 'Holly Golightly, Hypebeast', *The New York Times*, 8 March 2022

Vogue (USA), 1 March 1952

Vogue Voices (online), 'Riccardo Tisci', 16 May 2013

Nadeane Walker, 'De Givenchy lets down his hemlines', *News Dispatch*, 1 August 1953

Judith Watt, *Alexander McQueen* (preface by Daphne Guinness), Eyrolles: Paris, 2013

Women's Wear Daily, 29 August 1955; 1 July 1976

COLLECTION CREDITS

HUBERT DE GIVENCHY

S/S 1952 Haute Couture
1 February 1952; 8 rue Alfred
de Vigny, Paris
A/W 1952–1953 Haute Couture
1 August 1952; 8 rue Alfred
de Vigny, Paris
S/S 1953 Haute Couture
3 February 1953; 8 rue Alfred
de Vigny, Paris
A/W 1953–1954 Haute Couture
31 July 1953; 8 rue Alfred
de Vigny, Paris
S/S 1954 Haute Couture
4 February 1954; 8 rue Alfred
de Vigny, Paris
A/W 1954–1955 Haute Couture
28 July 1954; 8 rue Alfred
de Vigny, Paris
S/S 1955 Haute Couture
1 February 1955; 8 rue Alfred
de Vigny, Paris
A/W 1955–1956 Haute Couture
28 July 1955; 8 rue Alfred
de Vigny, Paris
S/S 1956 Haute Couture
2 February (buyers) and 27 February
1956 (press); 8 rue Alfred de Vigny,
Paris
A/W 1956–1957 Haute Couture
27 August 1956; 8 rue Alfred
de Vigny, Paris
S/S 1957 Haute Couture
21 February 1957; 8 rue Alfred
de Vigny, Paris
A/W 1957–1958 Haute Couture
31 July (buyers) and 26 August 1957
(press); 8 rue Alfred de Vigny, Paris
S/S 1958 Haute Couture
2 February (buyers) and 26 February
1958 (press); 8 rue Alfred de Vigny,
Paris
A/W 1958–1959 Haute Couture
1 August (buyers) and 26 August 1958
(press); 8 rue Alfred de Vigny, Paris
S/S 1959 Haute Couture
2 February (buyers) and 26 February
1959 (press); 3 avenue George V, Paris
A/W 1959–1960 Haute Couture
2 August (buyers) and 29 August 1959
(press); 3 avenue George V, Paris
S/S 1960 Haute Couture
1 February (buyers) and 26 February
1960 (press); 3 avenue George V, Paris
A/W 1960–1961 Haute Couture
30 July (buyers) and 26 August 1960
(press); 3 avenue George V, Paris
S/S 1961 Haute Couture
1 February (buyers) and 23 February 1961
(press); 3 avenue George V, Paris
A/W 1961–1962 Haute Couture
31 July (buyers) and 24 August 1961
(press); 3 avenue George V, Paris
S/S 1962 Haute Couture
31 January (buyers) and 22 February
1962 (press); 3 avenue George V, Paris
A/W 1962–1963 Haute Couture
31 July (buyers) and 27 August 1962
(press); 3 avenue George V, Paris
S/S 1963 Haute Couture
2 February 1963 (buyers; press date
unknown); 3 avenue George V, Paris
A/W 1963–1964 Haute Couture
31 July 1963 (buyers; press date
unknown); 3 avenue George V, Paris
S/S 1964 Haute Couture
3 February (buyers) and 26 February
1964 (press); 3 avenue George V, Paris
A/W 1964–1965 Haute Couture
3 August 1964 (buyers; press date
unknown); 3 avenue George V, Paris

S/S 1965 Haute Couture
3 February 1965 (buyers; press date
unknown); 3 avenue George V, Paris
A/W 1965–1966 Haute Couture
2 August 1965 (buyers; press date
unknown); 3 avenue George V, Paris
S/S 1966 Haute Couture
2 February 1966 (buyers; press date
unknown); 3 avenue George V, Paris
A/W 1966–1967 Haute Couture
31 July (buyers) and 29 August 1966
(press); 3 avenue George V, Paris
S/S 1967 Haute Couture
31 January (buyers) and 24 February 1967
(press); 3 avenue George V, Paris
A/W 1967–1968 Haute Couture
3 August 1967 (buyers and press);
3 avenue George V, Paris
S/S 1968 Haute Couture
28 January 1968; 3 avenue George V,
Paris
A/W 1968–1969 Haute Couture
31 July 1968; 3 avenue George V, Paris
S/S 1969 Haute Couture
31 January 1969; 3 avenue George V,
Paris
A/W 1969–1970 Haute Couture
1 August 1968; 3 avenue George V, Paris
Hair: Alexandre de Paris
Make-up: Givenchy
Shoes: Mancini for Givenchy
S/S 1970 Haute Couture
30 January 1970; 3 avenue George V,
Paris
A/W 1970–1971 Haute Couture
30 August 1970; 3 avenue George V, Paris
Hair: Alexandre de Paris
Make-up: Givenchy
Shoes: Mancini for Givenchy
S/S 1970 Haute Couture
27 January 1971; 3 avenue George V,
Paris
A/W 1971–1972 Haute Couture
29 July 1971; 3 avenue George V, Paris
Hair: Alexandre de Paris
Make-up: Dominique Bertola
for Givenchy
Shoes: Mancini for Givenchy
S/S 1972 Haute Couture
26 January 1972; 3 avenue George V,
Paris
Hair: Alexandre de Paris
Make-up: Dominique Bertola for
Givenchy
Shoes: Mancini for Givenchy
Hosiery: Givenchy
A/W 1972–1973 Haute Couture
26 July 1972; 3 avenue George V, Paris
Hair: Alexandre de Paris
Make-up: 'Snowbird' by Givenchy
Shoes: Mancini for Givenchy
Scarves, hosiery, sunglasses: Givenchy
S/S 1973 Haute Couture
23 January 1973; 3 avenue George V,
Paris
Hair: Alexandre de Paris
Shoes: Mancini for Givenchy
Perfumes, scarves, hosiery,
sunglasses: Givenchy
A/W 1973–1974 Haute Couture
24 July 1973; 3 avenue George V, Paris
Hair: Alexandre de Paris
Shoes: Mancini for Givenchy
Perfumes, scarves, hosiery,
glasses: Givenchy
S/S 1974 Haute Couture
29 January 1974; 3 avenue George V,
Paris
A/W 1974–1975 Haute Couture
23 July 1974; 3 avenue George V, Paris
Hair: Alexandre de Paris

Make-up: 'Angora' by
Olivier Echaudemaison for
Harriet Hubbard Ayer
Shoes: Mancini for Givenchy
Jewelry, perfumes, scarves, hosiery,
sunglasses: Givenchy
S/S 1975 Haute Couture
28 January 1975; 3 avenue George V,
Paris
A/W 1975–1976 Haute Couture
29 July 1975; 3 avenue George V, Paris
Hair: 'New Angel' by Alexandre
de Paris
Make-up: 'Brume' by
Olivier Echaudemaison for
Harriet Hubbard Ayer
Shoes: Mancini for Givenchy
Jewelry, perfumes, scarves, hosiery,
sunglasses: Givenchy
S/S 1976 Haute Couture
27 January 1976; 3 avenue George V,
Paris
Hair: Alexandre de Paris
Make-up: 'Candeur' by
Olivier Echaudemaison for
Harriet Hubbard Ayer
Shoes: Mancini for Givenchy
Jewelry, perfumes, scarves, hosiery,
glasses: Givenchy
A/W 1976–1977 Haute Couture
27 July 1976; 3 avenue George V, Paris
Hair: Alexandre de Paris
Make-up: 'Fortissimo' by
Olivier Echaudemaison for
Harriet Hubbard Ayer
Shoes: Mancini for Givenchy
Jewelry, perfumes, scarves,
sunglasses: Givenchy
S/S 1977 Haute Couture
27 January 1977; 3 avenue George V,
Paris
A/W 1977–1978 Haute Couture
26 July 1977; 3 avenue George V, Paris
Hair: 'Amazone' by Alexandre
de Paris
Make-up: 'Intense' by
Olivier Echaudemaison for
Harriet Hubbard Ayer
Shoes: Mancini for Givenchy
Jewelry, perfumes, scarves,
glasses: Givenchy
S/S 1978 Haute Couture
25 January 1978; 3 avenue George V,
Paris
Hair: 'Ligne Eventail' by Alexandre
de Paris
Make-up: 'Aquarelle' by
Olivier Echaudemaison for
Harriet Hubbard Ayer
Shoes: Mancini for Givenchy
Jewelry, perfumes, scarves,
glasses: Givenchy
A/W 1978–1979 Haute Couture
26 July 1978; 3 avenue George V, Paris
Hair: 'Glamour' by Alexandre de Paris
Make-up: 'Smoking' by
Olivier Echaudemaison for
Harriet Hubbard Ayer
Shoes: Mancini for Givenchy
Jewelry, perfumes, scarves,
glasses: Givenchy
S/S 1979 Haute Couture
31 January 1979; 3 avenue George V,
Paris
Hair: 'Vahine' by Alexandre de Paris
Make-up: 'Tobago' by Olivier
Echaudemaison for Harriet
Hubbard Ayer
Shoes: Mancini for Givenchy
Accessories, glasses: Givenchy

A/W 1979–1980 Haute Couture
  25 July 1979; 3 avenue George V, Paris
S/S 1980 Haute Couture
  30 January 1980; 3 avenue George V, Paris
  Hair: 'Papillon' by Alexandre de Paris
  Make-up: 'Pastel soleil' by Olivier Echaudemaison for Harriet Hubbard Ayer
  Shoes: Mancini for Givenchy
  Hosiery: Givenchy Bodygleamers by Round the Clock (USA)
  Accessories: Givenchy
A/W 1980–1981 Haute Couture
  28 July 1980; 3 avenue George V, Paris
  Hair: Alexandre de Paris
  Make-up: Olivier Echaudemaison for Harriet Hubbard Ayer
  Shoes: Mancini for Givenchy
  Accessories: Givenchy
S/S 1981 Haute Couture
  27 January 1981; 3 avenue George V, Paris
  Hair: 'Ligne poupée' by Alexandre de Paris
  Make-up: 'Lumières du Nil' by Olivier Echaudemaison for Harriet Hubbard Ayer
  Shoes: Mancini for Givenchy
  Accessories, perfumes: Givenchy
A/W 1981–1982 Haute Couture
  29 July 1981; Grand Hôtel, Salon Opéra, 1 rue Auber, Paris
  Hair: 'Metamorphose' by Alexandre de Paris
  Make-up: 'Roses des Vents' by Olivier Echaudemaison for Harriet Hubbard Ayer
  Shoes: Mancini for Givenchy; Daimaru Sensuous (Japan) for Givenchy
  Hats, jewelry, scarves, hosiery: Givenchy
  Perfume: Givenchy III
S/S 1982 Haute Couture
  27 January 1982; Grand Hôtel, Salon Opéra, 1 rue Auber, Paris
A/W 1982–1983 Haute Couture
  28 July 1982; Grand Hôtel, Salon Opéra, 1 rue Auber, Paris
  Hair and ornaments: 'Ballets russes' by Alexandre de Paris
  Make-up: 'Les Nymphéas' by Olivier Echaudemaison for Harriet Hubbard Ayer
  Shoes: Mancini for Givenchy; Sidonie Larizzi for Givenchy; Daimaru Sensuous (Japan) for Givenchy
  Hats, jewelry, perfumes, scarves, hosiery, lingerie: Givenchy
S/S 1983 Haute Couture
  26 January 1983; Grand Hôtel, Salon Opéra, 1 rue Auber, Paris
  Hair and ornaments: Alexandre de Paris
  Make-up: 'The chic and the look' by Olivier Echaudemaison for Harriet Hubbard Ayer
  Shoes: Mancini for Givenchy
  Hats, jewelry, perfumes, accessories: Givenchy
A/W 1983–1984 Haute Couture
  27 July 1983; Grand Hôtel, Salon Opéra, 1 rue Auber, Paris
S/S 1984 Haute Couture
  25 January 1984; Grand Hôtel, Salon Opéra, 1 rue Auber, Paris
A/W 1984–1985 Haute Couture
  25 July 1984; Grand Hôtel, Salon Opéra, 1 rue Auber, Paris
  Hair and ornaments: Alexandre de Paris
  Make-up: Olivier Echaudemaison for Harriet Hubbard Ayer
  Shoes: Mancini for Givenchy
  Furs: Revillon for Givenchy

Hats, jewelry, perfumes, scarves: Givenchy
  Hosiery: Le Bourget for Givenchy
S/S 1985 Haute Couture
  30 January 1985; Grand Hôtel, Salon Opéra, 1 rue Auber, Paris
  Hair: Alexandre de Paris
  Make-up: Olivier Echaudemaison for Harriet Hubbard Ayer
  Shoes: Mancini for Givenchy
  Hats, jewelry, scarves: Givenchy
  Perfume: Ysatis by Givenchy
A/W 1985–1986 Haute Couture
  25 July 1985; Grand Hôtel, Salon Opéra, 1 rue Auber, Paris
  Hair: Alexandre de Paris
  Make-up: Olivier Echaudemaison for Estée Lauder
  Shoes: Mancini for Givenchy
  Furs: Revillon for Givenchy
  Hats, jewelry, scarves: Givenchy Paris and Givenchy New York
  Hosiery: Le Bourget and Pennaco (USA) for Givenchy
  Perfumes: Givenchy III and Ysatis by Givenchy
S/S 1986 Haute Couture
  30 January 1986; Grand Hôtel, Salon Opéra, 1 rue Auber, Paris
  Hair: Alexandre de Paris
  Make-up: Olivier Echaudemaison for Monteil
  Shoes: Mancini for Givenchy
  Jewelry: Givenchy Paris and Givenchy New York
  Hosiery: Le Bourget and Pennaco (USA) for Givenchy
  Perfume: Ysatis by Givenchy
  Floral arrangements: Monsieur Bedat
A/W 1986–1987 Haute Couture
  31 July 1986; Grand Hôtel, Salon Opéra, 1 rue Auber, Paris
  Hair: Alexandre de Paris
  Make-up: Olivier Echaudemaison for Monteil
  Shoes: Mancini for Givenchy
  Jewelry: Givenchy Paris and Givenchy New York
  Hosiery: Le Bourget and Pennaco (USA) for Givenchy
  Perfume: Ysatis by Givenchy
  Floral arrangements: Monsieur Bedat
S/S 1987 Haute Couture
  29 January 1987; Grand Hôtel, Salon Opéra, 1 rue Auber, Paris
  Hair: Alexandre de Paris
  Make-up: Olivier Echaudemaison for Monteil
  Shoes: Mancini for Givenchy
  Jewelry: Givenchy Paris and Givenchy New York
  Hats, scarves: Givenchy
  Hosiery: Le Bourget for Givenchy
  Perfume: Ysatis by Givenchy
A/W 1987–1988 Haute Couture
  30 July 1987; Grand Hôtel, Salon Opéra, 1 rue Auber, Paris
S/S 1988 Haute Couture
  28 January 1988; Grand Hôtel, Salon Opéra, 1 rue Auber, Paris
  Hair: Alexandre de Paris
  Make-up: Olivier Echaudemaison for Monteil
  Shoes: Mancini for Givenchy
  Jewelry: Givenchy Paris and Givenchy New York
  Hosiery: Esmark (Paris / New York) for Givenchy
  Perfumes: Ysatis and Xeryus by Givenchy
A/W 1988–1989 Haute Couture
  28 July 1988; Grand Hôtel, Salon Opéra, 1 rue Auber, Paris

S/S 1989 Haute Couture
  26 January 1989; Grand Hôtel, Salon Opéra, 1 rue Auber, Paris
  Hair: Alexandre de Paris
  Make-up: Olivier Echaudemaison for Givenchy Beauty
  Shoes: Mancini for Givenchy
  Jewelry: Givenchy New York
  Hosiery: Esmark (Paris / New York) for Givenchy
  Perfume: Ysatis by Givenchy
A/W 1989–1990 Haute Couture
  27 July 1989; Grand Hôtel, Salon Opéra, 1 rue Auber, Paris
  Hair: Alexandre de Paris
  Make-up: Olivier Echaudemaison for Givenchy Beauty
  Shoes: Mancini for Givenchy
  Jewelry: Givenchy New York
  Hosiery: Esmark (Paris / New York) for Givenchy
  Perfume: Ysatis by Givenchy
S/S 1990 Haute Couture
  25 January 1990; Grand Hôtel, Salon Opéra, 2 rue Scribe, Paris
  Hair: Alexandre de Paris
  Make-up: 'Rose Toccata' by Olivier Echaudemaison for Givenchy Bea
  Shoes: Mancini for Givenchy
  Jewelry: Givenchy Paris and Givenchy New York
  Hosiery: Esmark (New York) for Givenchy
  Perfume: Ysatis by Givenchy
  Coordinator: Bernard Trux
  Music: Antoine Odier
A/W 1990–1991 Haute Couture
  26 July 1990; Beaux-Arts de Paris, 14 rue Bonaparte, Paris
  Hair: Alexandre de Paris
  Make-up: 'Dorabella' by Olivier Echaudemaison for Givenchy Bea
  Shoes: Mancini for Givenchy
  Jewelry: Givenchy Paris
  Hosiery: Esmark (New York) for Givenchy
  Perfume: Ysatis by Givenchy
S/S 1991 Haute Couture
  28 January 1991; Beaux-Arts de Paris, 14 rue Bonaparte, Paris
  Hair: Alexandre de Paris
  Make-up: 'Fantasia' by Olivier Echaudemaison for Givenchy Bea
  Shoes: Mancini for Givenchy
  Jewelry: Givenchy Paris
  Hosiery: Esmark (New York) for Givenchy
  Perfume: Ysatis by Givenchy
A/W 1991–1992 Haute Couture
  25 July 1991; Grand Hôtel, Salon Opéra, 2 rue Scribe, Paris
  Hair: Alexandre de Paris
  Make-up: Olivier Echaudemaison for Givenchy Beauty
  Shoes: Mancini for Givenchy
  Jewelry: Givenchy Paris
  Hosiery: Esmark (New York) for Givenchy
  Perfumes: Ysatis and Amarige by Givenchy
S/S 1992 Haute Couture
  30 January 1992; Grand Hôtel, Salon Opéra, 2 rue Scribe, Paris
  Hair: Alexandre de Paris
  Make-up: 'Nomade' by Olivier Echaudemaison for Givenchy Be
  Shoes: Mancini for Givenchy
  Jewelry: Givenchy Paris
  Hosiery: Pennaco (New York) for Givenchy
  Perfume: Amarige by Givenchy
  Music: Antoine Odier

A/W 1992–1993 Haute Couture
30 July 1992; Grand Hôtel,
Salon Opéra, 2 rue Scribe, Paris
Hair: Alexandre de Paris
Make-up: 'Boréale' by Olivier
Echaudemaison for Givenchy Beauty
Shoes: Mancini for Givenchy
Jewelry: Givenchy Paris
Hosiery: Pennaco (New York)
for Givenchy
Perfume: Amarige by Givenchy
Music: Antoine Odier
S/S 1993 Haute Couture
28 January 1993; Grand Hôtel,
Salon Opéra, 2 rue Scribe, Paris
Hair: Alexandre de Paris
Make-up: 'Régate' by Olivier
Echaudemaison for Givenchy Beauty
Shoes: Mancini for Givenchy
Jewelry: Givenchy Paris
Hosiery: Pennaco (New York)
for Givenchy
Music: Antoine Odier
A/W 1993–1994 Haute Couture
20 July 1993; Grand Hôtel,
Salon Opéra, 2 rue Scribe, Paris
S/S 1994 Haute Couture
18 January 1994; Grand Hôtel,
Salon Opéra, 2 rue Scribe, Paris
Hair: Alexandre de Paris
Make-up: 'Kendari' by Olivier
Echaudemaison for Givenchy Beauty
Shoes: Mancini for Givenchy
Hosiery: Pennaco (New York)
for Givenchy
Perfume: Amarige by Givenchy
Music: Antoine Odier
A/W 1994–1995 Haute Couture
19 July 1994; Grand Hôtel,
Salon Opéra, 2 rue Scribe, Paris
Hair: Alexandre de Paris
Make-up: 'Inspiration' by Olivier
Echaudemaison for Givenchy Beauty
Shoes: Mancini for Givenchy
Hosiery: Pennaco (New York)
for Givenchy
Perfume: Amarige by Givenchy
Music: Antoine Odier
S/S 1995 Haute Couture
24 January 1995; Grand Hôtel,
Salon Opéra, 2 rue Scribe, Paris
Hair: Alexandre de Paris
Make-up: Olivier Echaudemaison
for Givenchy Beauty
Shoes: Mancini for Givenchy
Hosiery: Pennaco (New York)
for Givenchy
Perfume: Amarige by Givenchy
Music: Antoine Odier
A/W 1995–1996 Haute Couture
11 July 1995; Grand Hôtel,
Salon Opéra, 2 rue Scribe, Paris
Hair: Alexandre de Paris
Make-up: Olivier Echaudemaison
for Givenchy Beauty
Shoes: Mancini for Givenchy
Hosiery: Pennaco (New York)
for Givenchy
Perfume: Amarige by Givenchy
Music: Antoine Odier

JOHN GALLIANO
S/S 1996 Haute Couture
21 January 1996; Stade Français,
2 rue du Commandant Guilbaud, Paris
Headpieces: Stephen Jones with
Atelier Givenchy
Hair: Odile Gilbert
Make-up: Stéphane Marais;
products Olivier Echaudemaison
for Givenchy Beauty
Shoes: Mancini for Givenchy
Set: Jean-Luc Ardouin
Lighting: Gaelle de Malglaive

Production and video: La Mode
en Images
Music: Jeremy Healy
A/W 1996–1997 Ready-to-Wear
16 March 1996; 50 avenue du Président
Wilson, Porte de la Chapelle, Paris
Production and video: La Mode
en Images
A/W 1996–1997 Haute Couture
7 July 1996; Stade Français,
2 rue du Commandant Guilbaud, Paris
Headpieces: Stephen Jones with
Atelier Givenchy
Hair: Odile Gilbert
Make-up: Stéphane Marais;
products Olivier Echaudemaison
for Givenchy Beauty
Shoes: Manolo Blahnik for Givenchy
Hosiery: Fogal for Givenchy
Set: Jean-Luc Ardouin
Lighting: Gaelle de Malglaive
Production and video: La Mode
en Images
Music: Jeremy Healy
S/S 1997 Ready-to-Wear
13 October 1996; Espace Auteuil, Paris
Headpieces: Stephen Jones with
Atelier Givenchy
Hair: Odile Gilbert
Make-up: Stéphane Marais;
products Givenchy Beauty
Shoes: Manolo Blahnik for Givenchy
Jewelry: Gripoix and Jacques Hurel
for Givenchy
Bags: Renaud for Givenchy
Production and video: La Mode
en Images
Music: Jeremy Healy

ALEXANDER McQUEEN
S/S 1997 Haute Couture
19 January 1997; École des Beaux-Arts,
14 rue Bonaparte, Paris
Headpieces: Philip Treacy
with Atelier Givenchy
Hair: Nicolas Jurnjack for Givenchy
Make-up: Topolino for Givenchy;
products Olivier Echaudemaison
for Givenchy Beauty
Make-up, men: Mira for Givenchy; Aveda
Shoes: Alexandre Narcy for Givenchy
Leather corsets: Whitaker Malem
for Givenchy
Jewelry: Erickson Beamon, Erik Halley,
Jacques Hurfi, Hervé Van Der
Straeten, Shaun Leane for Givenchy,
Fred Joaillier
Set: Simon Costin
Lighting: Simon Chaudoir
Production and video: La Mode
en Images
Music: Dom T
Harp: Sandrine Longuet performing
Brocéliande by Annie Challan
A/W 1997–1998 Ready-to-Wear
12 March 1997; Halle aux Chevaux,
Parc Georges Brassens, Paris
A/W 1997–1998 Haute Couture
7 July 1997; Université René Descartes,
45 rue des Saints Pères, Paris
Hair: Nicolas Jurnjack for Givenchy
Make-up: Val Garland and
Sharon Dowsett for Givenchy
Manicure: Marian Newman and
Kay Dodd for Givenchy
Shoes: Alexandre Narcy for Givenchy
Jewelry: Erickson Beamon, Shaun Leane,
Sarah Harmarnee, Gripoix
for Givenchy
Set: Simon Costin
Lighting: Chahine Yavroyan
Production and video: La Mode
en Images
Music: Dom T

S/S 1998 Ready-to-Wear
15 October 1997; Stade Français,
2 rue du Commandant Guilbaud,
Paris
Hats: Philip Treacy
S/S 1998 Haute Couture
18 January 1998; La Grande Arche
de La Défense, Puteaux
Headpieces: Philip Treacy for Givenchy
Hair: Guido for Nikki Clarke
Make-up: Val Garland for Givenchy;
products Olivier Echaudemaison
for Givenchy Beauty
Manicure: The Untouchables
for Givenchy
Shoes: Givenchy
Jewelry: Erickson Beamon,
Shaun Leane, Sarah Harmarnee
Lighting: François Austerlitz
Production and video: La Mode
en Images
Music: John Gosling
A/W 1998–1999 Ready-to-Wear
10 March 1998; Salle Equinoxe,
20 rue du Colonel Pierre Avia, Paris
A/W 1998–1999 Haute Couture
19 July 1998; Cirque d'Hiver,
110 rue Amelot, Paris
Headpieces: Philip Treacy for Givenchy
Hair: Guido for Nicky Clake
Make-up: Val Garland; products
Olivier Echaudemaison for
Givenchy Beauty
Furs: Saga Furs of Scandinavia; La
Fédération National de la Fourrure
Shoes: Givenchy
Jewelry: Erickson Beamon,
Lydia Courteille
Hosiery: Fogal
Silver bows and arrows: Sarah
Harmarnee
Production and video: La Mode
en Images
Music: John Gosling
S/S 1999 Ready-to-Wear
14 October 1998; Palais des Sports,
34 boulevard Victor, Paris
S/S 1999 Haute Couture
17 January 1999; Grande Halle de la
Villette, 211 avenue Jean Jaurès,
Paris
Headpieces: Atelier Givenchy and
Philip Treacy for Givenchy
Hair: Guido for Nicky Clarke
Make-up: Val Garland; products
Givenchy Beauty
Shoes: Givenchy
Pearl jewelry: Erickson Beamon
Jewelry: Lydia Courteille
Metalwork: Sarah Harmarnee
Production and video: La Mode
en Images
Music: John Gosling
A/W 1999–2000 Ready-to-Wear
10 March 1999; Le Carrousel
du Louvre, Salle Le Nôtre, Paris
Hair: Guido for Nicky Clarke
Make-up: Val Garland; products
Givenchy Beauty
Shoes: Givenchy
Hosiery: Fogal
Metalwork: Sarah Harmarnee
Lighting: François Austerlitz
Production and video: La Mode
en Images
Music: John Gosling
A/W 1999–2000 Haute Couture
18 July 1999; Studios de Boulogne,
4 rue de Silly, Boulogne
Headpieces: Atelier Givenchy
and Philip Treacy for Givenchy
Beaded mesh balaclava:
Atelier Safrané Cortambert
Shoes: Givenchy
Hosiery: Fogal

Lighting: Steve Chivers
Production and video: La Mode
    en Images
Music: John Gosling
S/S 2000 Ready-to-Wear
    6 October 1999; Le Carrousel
        du Louvre, Salle Le Nôtre, Paris
    Leather swimsuits: Société Industrielle
        de Lingerie
    Shoes: Givenchy
    Hosiery: Fogal
    Production and video: La Mode
        en Images
    Music: John Gosling
S/S 2000 Haute Couture
    16 January 2000; Studios de Boulogne,
        4 rue de Silly, Boulogne
    Hair: Guido Paulo
    Metal corsets: Shaun Leane
    Shoes: Christian Louboutin
        for Givenchy
    Hosiery: Fogal
    Set: Michael Howells
    Production and video: La Mode
        en Images
    Music: Frédéric Sanchez
A/W 2000–2001 Ready-to-Wear
    1 March 2000; Musée du Cinéma, Paris
    Hair: Guido Paulo
    Make-up: Linda Cantello
    Shoes: Givenchy
    Jewelry: Sarah Harmarnee and
        Shaun Leane
    Hosiery: Fogal
    Lighting: François Austerlitz
    Production and video: La Mode
        en Images
    Music: Frédéric Sanchez
A/W 2000–2001 Haute Couture
    9 July 2000; La Grande Arche
        de la Défense, Puteaux
    Headpieces: Ateliers Givenchy
        and Philip Treacy for Givenchy
    Beaded hair ornaments: Erickson
        Beamon
    Metal and leather hair ornaments:
        Sarah Harmarnee
    Furs: Saga Furs of Scandinavia
    Shoes: Givenchy
    Skin jewels: J. Maskrey
    Gloves: Daniel Sorto
    Hosiery: Fogal
    Set: Raymond Sarti
    Lighting: Xavier Lazarini
    Production and video: La Mode
        en Images
    Music: Geoffrey Hinton
S/S 2001 Ready-to-Wear
    11 October 2000; Carrousel
        du Louvre, Paris
    Hair: Eugene Souleiman
        for VS Sassoon
    Make-up: Stéphane Marais
    Accessories: Givenchy
    Casting: Maïda Gregori Boïna
    Lighting: François Austerlitz
    Production: La Mode en Images
    Video: Videopolis
    Music: Frédéric Sanchez
S/S 2001 Haute Couture
    21 January 2001; 3 avenue George V,
        Paris
    Hair: Eugene Souleiman for VS Sassoon
    Make-up: Stéphane Marais
    Silver corsets: Shaun Leane
    Shoes: Rossimoda
    Accessories: Givenchy
    Casting: Maïda Gregori Boïna
    Production: La Mode en Images;
        Gainsbury and Whiting
    Video: La Mode en Images
    Music: John Gosling
A/W 2001–2002 Ready-to-Wear
    16 March 2001; 3 avenue George V, Paris
    Hair: Guido Palau

Make-up: Linda Cantello
Furs: Saga Furs of Scandinavia;
    Nature & Fourrures
Shoes: Rossi Moda for Givenchy
Accessories: Givenchy
Casting: Maïda Gregori Boïna
Production: La Mode en Images;
    Gainsbury and Whiting
Video: La Mode en Images
Music: John Gosling

JULIEN MACDONALD
A/W 2001–2002 Haute Couture
    Avenue Foch, Paris
    Hair: Orlando Pita
    Make-up: Tom Pecheux
    Furs: La Fédération Nationale
        de la Fourrure and Saga Furs
        of Scandinavia
    Shoes and accessories: Givenchy
    Special accessories: Johnny Rocket
    Hosiery: Wolford
    Lighting: Philippe Martinaud
    Chandeliers: Baccarat
    Furniture: Galerie Domenico Casciello
    Illustration: François Berthoud
    Production: Bureau Betak
    Video: Videopolis
    Music: Frédéric Sanchez
S/S 2002 Ready-to-Wear
    10 October 2001; Stade Charlety,
        Salle Pierre Charpy, 17 avenue
        Pierre de Coubertin, Paris
    Hair: Eugene Souleiman for VS Sassoon
    Make-up: Tom Pecheux
    Shoes and accessories: Givenchy
    Lighting: Philippe Martinaud
    Production: Bureau Betak
    Music: Michel Gaubert
S/S 2002 Haute Couture
    Hair: Eugene Souleiman for VS Sassoon
    Make-up: Tom Pecheux
    Shoes and accessories: Givenchy
    Jewelry: Erik Halley
    Silk organza with paper application:
        Aviva Stanoff Textile Design Studio
    Concept, set and production:
        Bureau Betak
    Lighting: Philippe Martinaud
    Illustration: François Berthoud
    Music: Michel Gaubert
A/W 2002–2003 Ready-to-Wear
    Espace éphémère, bassin du Trocadéro,
        Paris
    Hair: Eugene Souleiman for VS Sassoon
    Make-up: Tom Pecheux
    Furs: Saga Furs of Scandinavia
    Shoes and accessories: Givenchy
    Jewelry: Givenchy
    Hosiery: Fogal, Wolford
    Production: La Mode en Images
    Music: Michel Gaubert
A/W 2002–2003 Haute Couture
    Palais Brongniart, Paris
    Headpieces: Scott Wilson
        with Atelier Givenchy
    Hair: Eugene Souleiman for VS Sassoon
    Make-up: Stéphane Marais
    Shoes and accessories: Givenchy
    Special accessories: Erik Hailey
    Acknowledgments: Nike; Saga Furs
        of Scandinavia; La Fédération
        Nationale de la Fourrure
    Production and video: La Mode
        en Images
    Music: Michel Gaubert
S/S 2003 Ready-to-Wear
    Carousel du Louvre, Paris
    Production: La Mode en Images
S/S 2003 Haute Couture
    Ambassade de Roumanie,
        5 rue de l'exposition, Paris
    Production: La Mode en Images

A/W 2003–2004 Ready-to-Wear
    Espace éphémère, bassin du Trocadéro,
        Paris
    Production and video: La Mode
        en Images
A/W 2003–2004 Haute Couture
    Grand Hôtel, Salon Opéra,
        2 rue Scribe, Paris
    Hair: Orlando Pita
    Make-up: Tom Pecheux
    Shoes and accessories: Givenchy
    Acknowledgments: Saga Furs of
        Scandinavia; Nada
    Production: La Mode en Images
    Music: Michel Gaubert
S/S 2004 Ready-to-Wear
    Hair: Orlando Pita
    Make-up: Tom Pecheux
    Shoes and accessories: Givenchy
    Jewelry: Givenchy
    Production: YO Events Designers
    Music: Michel Gaubert
S/S 2004 Haute Couture
    20 January 2004; Baccarat,
        11 Place des Etats-Unis, Paris
    Hair: Orlando Pita
    Make-up: Charlotte Tilbury
    Shoes and accessories: Givenchy
    Production: YO Events Designers
    Music: Michel Gaubert
A/W 2004–2005 Ready-to-Wear
    5 March 2004; Carrousel du Louvre,
        Salle Le Nôtre, 99 rue de Rivoli, Paris
    Hair: Orlando Pita
    Make-up: Nicolas Degennes,
        Charlotte Tilbury
    Furs: Saga Furs
    Shoes and accessories: Givenchy
    Jewelry: Givenchy
    Production: YO Events Designers
    Music: Michel Gaubert

RICCARDO TISCI
A/W 2005–2006 Haute Couture
    7 July 2005; 3 avenue George V, Paris
    Hair: Luigi Murenu
    Make-up: Peter Philips
    Production: OBO
    Music: Mode-F
S/S 2006 Ready-to-Wear
    5 October 2005; Tennis Club de Paris,
        84 avenue Georges Lafont, Paris
    Hair: Luigi Murenu
    Make-up: Val Garland
    Casting: Patrizia Pilotti
    Production: OBO
    Music: Mode-F
A/W 2006–2007 Ready-to-Wear
    1 March 2006; Carreau du Temple, Paris
    Hair: Luigi Murenu
    Make-up: Peter Philips
    Casting: Patrizia Pilotti
    Production: OBO
    Music: Mode-F
A/W 2006–2007 Haute Couture
    6 July 2006; Ateliers Berthier
    Hair: Luigi Murenu
    Make-up: Peter Philips
    Casting: Patrizia Pilotti
    Production and video: La Mode
        en Images
    Music: Funktrip
S/S 2007 Ready-to-Wear
    4 October 2006; Carreau du Temple,
        Paris
    Hair: Luigi Murenu
    Make-up: Peter Philips
    Casting: Patrizia Pilotti
    Production and video: La Mode
        en Images
    Music: Dan Lywood
S/S 2007 Haute Couture
    23 January 2007; Ateliers Berthier
    Hair: Luigi Murenu
    Make-up: Peter Philips

Casting: Patrizia Pilotti
Production and video: La Mode en Images
Music: Funktrip

A/W 2007–2008 Ready-to-Wear
28 February 2008; Palais omnisports de Paris-Bercy
Hair: Luigi Murenu
Make-up: Aaron de Mey
Casting: Patrizia Pilotti
Production and video: La Mode en Images

A/W 2007–2008 Haute Couture
3 July 2007; Couvent des Cordeliers, Paris
Hair: Luigi Murenu
Make-up: Aaron de Mey
Casting: Patrizia Pilotti
Production: La Mode en Images
Music: Frédéric Sanchez

S/S 2008 Ready-to-Wear
3 October 2007; Carreau du Temple, Paris
Hair: Luigi Murenu
Make-up: Aaron de Mey
Casting: Patrizia Pilotti
Production: La Mode en Images
Music: Frédéric Sanchez

S/S 2008 Haute Couture
22 January 2008; Couvent des Cordeliers, Paris
Hair: Luigi Murenu
Make-up: Stéphane Marais
Casting: Patrizia Pilotti
Production and video: La Mode en Images
Music: Frédéric Sanchez

A/W 2008–2009 Ready-to-Wear
27 February 2008; Carreau du Temple, Paris
Hair: Luigi Murenu
Make-up: Aaron de Mey
Casting: Patrizia Pilotti
Production and video: La Mode en Images
Music: Frédéric Sanchez

A/W 2008–2009 Haute Couture
1 July 2008; Couvent des Cordeliers, Paris
Hair: Luigi Murenu
Make-up: Tom Pecheux
Casting: Patrizia Pilotti
Production and video: La Mode en Images
Music: Frédéric Sanchez

S/S 2009 Ready-to-Wear
1 October 2008; Carreau du Temple, Paris
Hair: Luigi Murenu
Make-up: Tom Pecheux
Casting: Patrizia Pilotti
Production and video: La Mode en Images
Music: Frédéric Sanchez

S/S 2009 Haute Couture
27 January 2009; Couvent des Cordeliers, Paris
Hair: Luigi Murenu
Make-up: Tom Pecheux
Casting: Patrizia Pilotti
Production: La Mode en Images
Music: Frédéric Sanchez

A/W 2009–2010 Ready-to-Wear
8 March 2009, Carreau du Temple, Paris
Hair: Luigi Murenu
Make-up: Tom Pecheux
Casting: Patrizia Pilotti
Production and video: La Mode en Images
Music: Frédéric Sanchez

A/W 2009–2010 Haute Couture
7 July 2009; Halle aux Chevaux, Parc Georges-Brassens, Paris
Hair: Luigi Murenu
Make-up: Aaron de Mey

Casting: Patrizia Pilotti
Production: La Mode en Images
Music: Frédéric Sanchez

S/S 2010 Ready-to-Wear
4 October 2009; Lycée Carnot, 145 boulevard Malesherbes, Paris
Hair: Luigi Murenu
Make-up: Aaron de Mey
Casting: Patrizia Pilotti
Production and video: La Mode en Images
Music: Frédéric Sanchez

S/S 2010 Haute Couture
26 January 2010; Hotel Westin, Paris
Hair: Luigi Murenu
Make-up: Pat McGrath
Casting: Patrizia Pilotti
Production and video: La Mode en Images
Music: Frédéric Sanchez

A/W 2010–2011 Ready-to-Wear
7 March 2010; Lycée Carnot, Paris
Hair: Luigi Murenu
Make-up: Pat McGrath
Casting: Patrizia Pilotti
Production and video: La Mode en Images
Music: Frédéric Sanchez

A/W 2010–2011 Haute Couture
5, 6, 7 July 2010; Hôtel d'Évreux, Place Vendôme, Paris
Hair: Akki
Make-up: Frankie Boyd
Casting: Patrizia Pilotti
Production: Jean Hugues de Chatillon
Photographer: Willy Vanderperre (group shoot)
Music: Frédéric Sanchez

S/S 2011 Ready-to-Wear
3 October 2010; Lycée Carnot, Paris
Hair: Luigi Murenu
Make-up: Pat McGrath
Casting: Patrizia Pilotti
Production and video: La Mode en Images
Music: Frédéric Sanchez

S/S 2011 Haute Couture
24, 25, 26 January 2011; Hôtel d'Évreux, Place Vendôme, Paris
Hats: Philip Treacy
Hair: Akki
Make-up: Frankie Boyd
Scent: Francis Kurkdjian, vert d'amande
Casting: Patrizia Pilotti
Production: Jean Hugues de Chatillon
Photographer: Willy Vanderperre (group shoot)
Music: Frédéric Sanchez

A/W 2011–2012 Ready-to-Wear
6 March 2011; Palais de Tokyo, 13 avenue du Président Wilson, Paris
Hair: Luigi Murenu
Make-up: Pat McGrath
Scent: MAW, purple mood
Casting: Patrizia Pilotti
Production and video: La Mode en Images
Music: Frédéric Sanchez

A/W 2011–2012 Haute Couture
5, 6 July 2011; Hôtel d'Évreux, Place Vendôme, Paris
Hair: Rutger
Make-up: Sil Bruinsma
Scent: MAW, wild lily
Casting: Patrizia Pilotti
Production: Jean Hugues de Chatillon
Photographer: Willy Vanderperre (group shoot)
Music: Frédéric Sanchez

S/S 2012 Ready-to-Wear
2 October 2011; Lycée Carnot, Paris
Hair: Luigi Murenu
Make-up: Pat McGrath
Scent: MAW, sea breath
Casting: Patrizia Pilotti

Production and video: La Mode en Images
Music: Frédéric Sanchez

S/S 2012 Haute Couture
24 January 2012; Hôtel d'Évreux, Place Vendôme, Paris
Hair: Rutger
Make-up: Sil Bruinsma
Scent: MAW, wild lily
Casting: Patrizia Pilotti
Production: La Mode en Images
Photographer: Willy Vanderperre (group shoot)

A/W 2012–2013 Ready-to-Wear
4 March 2012; Lycée Carnot, Paris
Hair: Luigi Murenu
Make-up: Pat McGrath
Scent: MAW, patine de cuir
Casting: Patrizia Pilotti
Production and video: La Mode en Images
Music: Discodromo

A/W 2012–2013 Haute Couture
2, 3, 4 July 2012; Hôtel d'Évreux, Place Vendôme, Paris
Hair: Rutger
Make-up: Sil Bruinsma
Scent: MAW, cannabis rose
Casting: Patrizia Pilotti
Production: La Mode en Images
Photographer: Willy Vanderperre (group shoot)
Music: Discodromo

S/S 2013 Ready-to-Wear
30 September 2013; Lycée Carnot, Paris
Hair: Luigi Murenu
Make-up: Pat McGrath
Scent: MAW, encens
Casting: Patrizia Pilotti
Production and video: La Mode en Images
Music: Discodromo, Matthias Lecomte

A/W 2013–2014 Ready-to-Wear
3 March 2013; Halle Freyssinet, Paris
Hair: Luigi Murenu
Make-up: Pat McGrath
Scent: MAW, rosa canina
Casting: Patrizia Pilotti
Production and video: La Mode en Images
Music: Antony and the Johnsons with the Heritage Orchestra and Gael Rakotondrabe

S/S 2014 Ready-to-Wear
29 September 2013; Halle Freyssinet, Paris
Hair: Luigi Murenu
Make-up: Pat McGrath
Scent: MAW, rosa canina
Casting: Patrizia Pilotti
Production and video: La Mode en Images
Music: Discodromo

A/W 2014–2015 Ready-to-Wear
2 March 2014; Halle Freyssinet, Paris
Hair: Luigi Murenu
Make-up: Pat McGrath
Scent: MAW, velours de musc
Casting: Patrizia Pilotti
Production and video: La Mode en Images
Music: The Martinez Brothers

S/S 2015 Ready-to-Wear
28 September 2014; Lycée Carnot, Paris
Hair: Luigi Murenu
Make-up: Pat McGrath
Scent: MAW, figue
Casting: Patrizia Pilotti
Production and video: La Mode en Images
Music: The Martinez Brothers

A/W 2015–2016 Ready-to-Wear
    8 March 2015; Lycée Carnot, Paris
    Hair: Luigi Murenu
    Make-up: Pat McGrath
    Scent: MAW, encens IPH BG/4
    Casting: Patrizia Pilotti
    Production and video: La Mode
        en Images
    Music: The Martinez Brothers
S/S 2016 Ready-to-Wear
    11 September 2015; Pier 26,
        New York
    Hair: Luigi Murenu
    Make-up: Pat McGrath
    Casting: Patrizia Pilotti
    Production: La Mode en Images, KCD
    Video: Bader
    Music: Philippe Maillard
S/S 2016 Haute Couture
    22 January 2016; Entrepôt Eiffel, Paris
    Hair: Guido Palau
    Make-up: Pat McGrath
    Scent: MAW, rosa canina
    Casting: Patrizia Pilotti
    Production and video: La Mode
        en Images
    Music: Dixon
A/W 2016–2017 Ready-to-Wear
    6 March 2016; Carreau du Temple,
        Paris
    Hair: Guido Palau
    Make-up: Pat McGrath
    Scent: MAW, smoky cistus
    Casting: Patrizia Pilotti
    Production and video: La Mode
        en Images
    Music: Dixon
A/W 2016–2017 Haute Couture
    24 June 2016; Lycée Janson de Sailly,
        106 rue de la Pompe, Paris
    Hair: Guido Palau
    Make-up: Pat McGrath
    Scent: MAW, Encens 17493
    Casting: Patrizia Pilotti
    Production: La Mode en Images
    Music: Dixon
S/S 2017 Ready-to-Wear
    2 October 2016; Esplanade du Jardin
        des Plantes, Paris
    Hair: Guido Palau
    Make-up: Pat McGrath
    Casting: Patrizia Pilotti
    Production and video: La Mode
        en Images
    Music: Dixon
S/S 2017 Haute Couture
    Casting: Patrizia Pilotti

CLARE WAIGHT KELLER
S/S 2018 Ready-to-Wear
    1 October 2017; Palais de Justice,
        Paris
    Hair: Guido Palau
    Make-up: Pat McGrath
    Scent: Feu de bois
    Casting: Piergiorgio Del Moro
    Production: La Mode en Images
    Music: Steve Mackey
S/S 2018 Haute Couture
    23 January 2018; Archives Nationales,
        Paris
    Hair: Guido Palau
    Make-up: Pat McGrath
    Scent: Aoyama
    Casting: Piergiorgio Del Moro
        and Samuel Ellis Scheinman
    Production: Villa Eugénie
    Music: Steve Mackey
A/W 2018–2019 Ready-to-Wear
    4 March 2018; Palais de Justice, Paris
    Hair: Guido Palau
    Make-up: Pat McGrath
    Scent: Feu de bois 2

    Casting: Piergiorgio Del Moro
    Production: Villa Eugénie
    Music: Steve Mackey
A/W 2018–2019 Haute Couture
    1 July 2018; Archives Nationales,
        Paris
    Hair: Guido Palau
    Make-up: Pat McGrath
    Casting: Piergiorgio Del Moro
    Production: Villa Eugénie
    Music: Steve Mackey
S/S 2019 Ready-to-Wear
    30 September 2018; Palais de Justice,
        Paris
    Hair: Guido Palau
    Make-up: Pat McGrath
    Scent: Hemingway bar
    Casting: Piergiorgio Del Moro
    Production: Villa Eugénie
    Music: Steve Mackey
S/S 2019 Haute Couture
    22 January 2019; Musée d'Art
        Moderne de la Ville de Paris
    Hair: Guido Palau
    Make-up: Pat McGrath
    Scent: Cuir Blanc
    Manicure: Anatole Rainey
    Production: Villa Eugénie
    Music: Steve Mackey
A/W 2019–2020 Ready-to-Wear
    3 March 2019; Jardin des Plantes,
        Paris
    Hair: Guido Palau
    Make-up: Pat McGrath
    Scent: Cut grass
    Production: Villa Eugénie
    Music: Steve Mackey
A/W 2019–2020 Haute Couture
    2 July 2019; Musée des Arts
        Décoratifs, Paris
    Hair: Guido Palau
    Make-up: Pat McGrath
    Scent: Corkwood
    Production: Villa Eugénie
    Music: Steve Mackey
S/S 2020 Ready-to-Wear
    29 September 2019;
        Garde Républicaine, Paris
    Hair: Guido Palau
    Make-up: Pat McGrath
    Scent: Cedre Crayon
    Casting: Piergiorgio Del Moro
        and Samuel Ellis Scheinman
    Production: Villa Eugénie
    Music: Steve Mackey
S/S 2020 Haute Couture
    21 January 2020; Couvent des
        Cordeliers, Paris
    Hats: Noel Stewart
    Hair: Paul Hanlon
    Make-up: Pat McGrath
    Scent: Dandelion
    Casting: Piergiorgio Del Moro
    Production: Villa Eugénie
    Music: Thomas Roussel
A/W 2020–2021 Ready-to-Wear
    1 March 2020; Hippodrome Paris
        Longchamp, Paris
    Hair: Paul Hanlon
    Make-up: Pat McGrath
    Scent: Smoke
    Casting: Piergiorgio Del Moro
    Production: Villa Eugénie
    Music: Steve Mackey

MATTHEW M. WILLIAMS
S/S 2021 Ready-to-Wear
    4 October 2020; lookbook shot at
        Givenchy Showroom, 2 avenue
        Montaigne, Paris
    Make-up: Florence Teerlinck
    Scent: Accord Particulier
    Photographs: Heji Shin
    Music: Surkin

A/W 2021–2022 Ready-to-Wear
    7 March 2021; Paris La Défense Arena
        (virtual catwalk show)
    Hair: Duffy
    Make-up: Aaron de Mey
    Manicure: Anatole Rainey
    Director: Jasmine Loignon
    Casting: Piergiorgio Del Moro
        and Samuel Ellis Scheinman
    Production: Villa Eugénie
    Sound curator: Surkin
    Music: Robert Hood
S/S 2022 Ready-to-Wear
    3 October 2021; Paris La Défense
        Arena
    Hair: Duffy
    Make-up: Lucia Pieroni
    Manicure: Anatole Rainey
    Scent: Accord Particulier
    Casting: Piergiorgio Del Moro
        and Samuel Ellis Scheinman
    Production: Villa Eugénie
    Set design: Etienne Russo
    Sound curator: Surkin
    Music: Young Thug
    Artist: Josh Smith
A/W 2022–2023 Ready-to-Wear
    6 March 2022; Paris La Défense
        Arena
    Hair: Duffy
    Make-up: Lucia Pieroni
    Manicure: Anatole Rainey
    Scent: Accord Particulier
    Casting: Piergiorgio Del Moro
        and Samuel Ellis Scheinman
    Production: Villa Eugenie
    Sound curator: Surkin
    Music: Outtatown and StarBoy
S/S 2023 Ready-to-Wear
    2 October 2022; Jardin des Plantes,
        Paris
    Hair: Duffy
    Make-up: Lucia Pieroni
    Scent: Accord Particulier
    Production: Villa Eugénie
    Sound curator: Surkin
A/W 2023–2024 Ready-to-Wear
    2 March 2023; École Militaire, Paris
    Hair: Duffy
    Make-up: Lucia Pieroni
    Scent: Accord Particulier
    Production: La Mode en Images
    Sound curator: Surkin

Credits included reflect the information available at the time of publication. We would be pleased to insert an appropriate acknowledgment for missing credits in any subsequent reprint.

PICTURE CREDITS

ACKNOWLEDGMENTS

The authors and the publisher would like to thank the team at Givenchy for their expertise and support in the making of this book: Renaud de Lesquen, Valérie Leberichel, Laure Aillagon, Juliette Chaussat, Sophie Colombo, Thomas Nicol, Isabelle Tasset, Isabelle Franchet, Barbara Kuta and Armenouhie Ekmektchian.

A special thank you from the publisher to Olivier de Givenchy and James de Givenchy, Sean Hepburn Ferrer and Luca Dotti and also to Maria Kublin and to Victor Skrebneski (1929–2020).

The team at Givenchy would like to thank Véronique Benitah, Maxime Benoist, Romuald Leblond and Kaled Moghraoui at La Mode en Images.

Alexandre Samson would like to thank Louise Habert, Antoinette Alba, Emmanuelle Beuvin and Sylvie Roy for their help during his research for this book.

INDEX OF MODELS

Considerable efforts have been made
to identify the models featured in this
book, but in some cases we have been
unable to do so. We would be pleased to
insert an appropriate acknowledgment
in any subsequent reprint.

INDEX

See also the Index of Models.

Cover bellyband (from left to right):
S/S 1952 Haute Couture © Nat Farbman /
The LIFE Picture Collection / Shutterstock;
A/W 1960–1961 Haute Couture GIVENCHY
© All Rights Reserved; A/W 2008–2009 Haute
Couture © firstVIEW / Launchmetrics Spotlight;
A/W 2023–2024 Ready-to-Wear © firstVIEW /
Launchmetrics Spotlight

Frontispiece (p. 2): Robert Doisneau /
Gamma-Rapho / Getty Images

First published in the U.S. and Canada in 2023 by
Yale University Press
P.O. Box 209040
302 Temple Street
New Haven, CT 06520-9040
yalebooks.com

Published by arrangement with
Thames & Hudson Ltd, London

Givenchy Catwalk: The Complete Collections
© 2023 Thames & Hudson Ltd, London

Introduction, designer biographies
and collection texts 1952–2001
© 2023 Alexandre Samson

Designer biographies and collection
texts 2001–2023 © 2023 Anders Christian Madsen

Photographs © 2023 firstVIEW / Launchmetrics
Spotlight unless otherwise stated

All catwalk outfits represented © Givenchy

All official Givenchy collection titles are
presented in quotation marks.

Series concept by Adélia Sabatini
© 2023 Thames & Hudson Ltd, London

Design by Fraser Muggeridge studio

Library of Congress Control Number: 2023937912

ISBN 978-0-300-26407-4

MIX
Paper | Supporting
responsible forestry
FSC® C008047

Printed and bound in China
by C & C Offset Printing Co. Ltd